A CONCISE HISTORY OF ANCIENT ISRAEL

CRITICAL STUDIES IN THE HEBREW BIBLE

Editors

ANSELM C. HAGEDORN, *University of Osnabrück*
NATHAN MACDONALD, *University of Cambridge*
STUART WEEKS, *Durham University*

A Concise History
of Ancient Israel

From the Beginnings Through the Hellenistic Era

BERND U. SCHIPPER

Translated by Michael J. Lesley

EISENBRAUNS | University Park, Pennsylvania

Library of Congress Cataloging-in-Publication Data

Names: Schipper, Bernd U., 1968– author. | Lesley, Michael, translator.
Title: A concise history of ancient Israel : from the beginnings through the Hellenistic
    era / Bernd U. Schipper ; translated by Michael J. Lesley.
Other titles: Geschichte Israels in der Antike. English | Critical studies in the Hebrew
    Bible ; 11.
Description: University Park, Pennsylvania : Eisenbrauns, [2019] | Series: Critical
    studies in the Hebrew Bible ; 11 | "This is the extended English version of my book
    Geschichte Israels in der Antike (Beck Wissen 2887; Munich: C.H. Beck, 2018)"—
    Preface. | Includes bibliographical references and index.
Summary: "Presents a reconstruction of the history of Ancient Israel in biblical times,
    taking into account biblical and extra-biblical texts as well as archaeological mate-
    rial"—Provided by publisher.
Identifiers: LCCN 2019028822 | ISBN 9781575067322 (paperback)
Subjects: LCSH: Bible. Old Testament—History of Biblical events. | Jews—History—
    To 70 A.D. | Palestine—History—To 70 A.D.
Classification: LCC DS121.S3513 2019 | DDC 933—dc23
LC record available at https://lccn.loc.gov/2019028822

Eisenbrauns is an imprint of The Pennsylvania State University Press.

The Pennsylvania State University Press is a member of the Association of University
Presses.

It is the policy of The Pennsylvania State University Press to use acid-free paper. Publications on uncoated stock satisfy the minimum requirements of American National
Standard for Information Sciences—Permanence of Paper for Printed Library Material, ANSI Z39.48–1992.

CONTENTS

ILLUSTRATIONS

Figures

Maps

PREFACE

This is the extended English version of my book *Geschichte Israels in der Antike* (Beck Wissen 2887; Munich: C.H. Beck, 2018). Like the German original, this book is not intended to give a lengthy discussion of the subject but a brief outline of the history of ancient Israel. It should help students and other readers get an overview of the rather complex and nearly in all respects controversial subject. For all who are interested in a more detailed discussion, additional references can be found in the footnotes and the bibliography.

I am grateful to Michael J. Lesley for the translation and especially to Jonathan Böhm and Yannick Ehmer for their assistance in proofreading the translation, adjusting the bibliography for an Anglophone audience, and revising the footnotes. In addition, kind thanks goes to Maria Bruske for her excellent artwork and the drawings of the maps. Already when writing the German edition I received substantial feedback from a number of colleagues: Reinhard G. Kratz (Göttingen), Konrad Schmid (Zurich), Omer Sergi (Tel Aviv), Gunnar Lehmann (Beersheba), and Sebastian Grätz (Mainz). Finally, I would like to thank Anselm C. Hagedorn, Nathan MacDonald, and Stuart Weeks for accepting the manuscript for the distinguished series "Critical Studies in the Hebrew Bible" and Jim Eisenbraun and Matthew Williams for their kind help with making a book out of the manuscript.

Berlin, July 1, 2019
Bernd U. Schipper

ABBREVIATIONS

ADPV	Abhandlungen des Deutschen Palästina-Vereins
ANET	Pritchard, *Ancient Near Eastern Texts*
Ant.	Josephus, Jewish Antiquities
AOAT	Alter Orient und Altes Testament
BASOR	*Bulletin of the American Schools of Oriental Research*
BZAW	Beihefte zur Zeitschrift für die alttestamentliche Wissenschaft
CHANE	Culture and History of the Ancient Near East
FAT	Forschungen zum Alten Testament
COS	Hallo and Younger, *Context of Scripture*
DJE	Pearce and Wunsch, *Documents of Judean Exiles*
HeBAI	*Hebrew Bible and Ancient Israel*
Hist.	Herodotus, *Histories*
IEJ	*Israel Exploration Journal*
JHS	*Journal of Hellenic Studies*
JSJSup	Journal for the Study of Judaism Supplement Series
JSOTSup	Journal for the Study of the Old Testament Supplement Series
LHBOTS	The Library of Hebrew Bible/Old Testament Studies
LSTS	The Library of Second Temple Studies
OBO	Orbis Biblicus et Orientalis
OLA	Orientalia Lovaniensia Analecta
PEQ	*Palestine Exploration Quarterly*
RB	*Revue biblique*
TA	*Tel Aviv*
TAD	Porten and Yardeni, *Textbook of Aramaic Documents*
Transeu	*Transeuphratène*
TSAJ	Texte und Studien zum antiken Judentum
UF	*Ugarit-Forschungen*
VT	*Vetus Testamentum*

VTSup	Supplements to Vetus Testamentum
WO	*Die Welt des Orients*
WUNT	Wissenschaftliche Untersuchungen zum Neuen Testament
ZAW	*Zeitschrift für die alttestamentliche Wissenschaft*
ZDPV	*Zeitschrift des deutschen Palästina-Vereins*

CHRONOLOGY

The dates of the reigns of the kings of Israel and Judah are intended only to give the reader broad chronological bearings and should not be understood as reflecting historically precise dates.

Egypt	Palestine/Israel	Mesopotamia
		(Hittites)
Ramesses II 1279–1213	*1274 Battle of Kadesh*	Muwatalli II 1290–1272
Amenhotep IV 1353–1336	*1350 Amarna Letters*	
Merneptah 1213–1203	*1208 Merneptah Stela*	
(21st Dynasty 1076–944)	David 1004/1003–965/964	*(Neo-Assyrians)*
Siamun 978–959	Solomon 965/964–926/925	Ashur-dan II 935–912
(22nd Dynasty 943–ca. 746)		
Shoshenq I 943–923	Rehoboam 926–910	
	Omri 882–871	
	Battle of Qarqar (853)	Shalmaneser III 858–824
	Mesha Stela (after 850)	
	Tribute of Jehu (841)	
(24th Dynasty)		Tiglat-pileser III 745–727
Osorkon IV 730–715	Hoshea 732–723	Shalmaneser V 727–722
		Sargon II 722–705
	Conquest of Samaria 722/720	
(25th Dynasty 722–655)		
Shabaka ca. 722–707	Hezekiah 725–697	Sennacherib 705–681
Shebitku ca.702–690	Manasseh 696–642	Esarhaddon 681–669
Taharqa 690–664		Assurbanipal 669–630

Egypt	Palestine/Israel	Mesopotamia
(26th Dynasty 664–525)		*(Neo-Babylonians)*
Psammetichus I 664–610	Josiah 639–609	Nabopolassar 625–605
Necho II 610–595	Jehoiakim 608–598	Nebuchadnezzar II 605–562
Psammetichus II 595–589	Jehoiakin 598/597	
	1. Conquest of Jerusalem 598/597	
Apries 589–570	Zedekiah 598/597–587/586	
	2. Conquest of Jerusalem 587/586	
		(Persians)
		Cyrus II 559–530
(27th Dynasty. First Persian Period 525–404)		Cambyses II 530–522
519/518 Udjahorresnet		Darius I 522–486
464–454 Inaros rebellion		Artaxerxes I 465–424/423
	407 Elephantine petition	Darius II 424–404
(28th Dynasty 404–399)		Artaxerxes II 405/404–359
(29th Dynasty 399–380)		
(30th Dynasty 380–343)		
(Second Persian Period 343–332)		*(Greeks)*
		Alexander the Great 336–323
(Ptolemies 323–30)	*(274–168 Six Syrian wars)*	*(Seleucides 312–64)*
Ptolemy II Philadelphos 285/283–246		Antiochus I Soter 281–261
Ptolemy IV Philopator 221–204		Antiochus III Megas 222–187
Ptolemy VI Philometor 180–145		Antiochus IV Epiphanes 175–164
	(167–143/142 Maccabean revolt)	
	(135/134–37 Hasmonean kingdom)	
	(Romans in Palestine)	
	Herod the Great 37–4 BCE	
	Herod Antipas 4 BCE–39 CE	
	(66–70 CE Jewish War)	
	(70 CE Destruction of the Second Temple)	

CHAPTER 1

Introduction

In the study of the ancient Near East no field has changed as drastically over recent decades as the history of ancient Israel. While earlier scholars generally accepted the history found in the Bible as broadly accurate, subsequent scholarship has shown that the books of the Hebrew Bible offer only a partial view of the actual historical events—and often not even that. The history found in the Hebrew Bible is theological writing, and its authors were attempting to explain their present situation and offer a guide to the future in reference to the past.[1]

One of the ironies of the history of biblical scholarship is that most of these discoveries were made by scholars who had set out to demonstrate the truth of biblical history. From the earliest archaeological research of the nineteenth century up to the present, it was often scholars of faith conducting archaeological research with the Bible in tow who discovered that the archaeological evidence scarcely corresponded to the biblical account.[2] This situation continues today as scholars with spades and measuring lines try to determine the size of the kingdoms of David and Solomon—whether in the so-called "city of David" in Jerusalem or in Khirbet Qeiyafa in the hilly area between Jerusalem and Gath (Tell eş-Şafi).

This history of ancient Israel is not concerned with the faith of scholars, however, or with the political dimension of archaeology in Israel/Palestine. It is an attempt to find the most plausible history of ancient Israel that can be reconstructed through both extrabiblical and biblical sources. As such, this book will often only pose questions rather than give irrefutable answers. After all, there is much we do not yet know, since numerous archaeological sites remain unexcavated, many excavation findings have not yet been made public, and countless objects lie in museum storerooms waiting to be analyzed.

This book is intended as an introductory guide to help the reader navigate the dense thicket of archaeological research, texts, and objects with the help

---

1. See Gertz et al., *T & T Clark Handbook*, 3–4.
2. For a short overview on the history of research, see Mazar, *Archaeology*, 10–34, especially 30–33.

2 Chapter 1

of the most recent research on the history of ancient Israel. It is for this reason that reference is made to standard translations in the main text and to secondary literature in the footnotes.[3]

1.1 Ancient Israel and Biblical Israel

Every work on the "history of Israel" begins with a basic caveat: the history narrated in the Hebrew Bible does not correspond to the evidence found in archaeological and extrabiblical sources.[4] To anyone who has spent any amount of time with the literature of the ancient Near East more broadly, this will come as no surprise. Ancient Near Eastern royal inscriptions involve a political theology that presents "history" from a particular point of view.[5] The most well-known example of this comes from the famous battle of Kadesh, an area about 25 km southwest of present-day Homs, Syria, in 1274 BCE.[6] The Egyptian texts of the military conflict between Ramesses II and the Hittite king Muwatalli II—of which more than twenty texts and copies are preserved—are an account of a great victory in which the pharaoh personally beat the enemy into retreat (*COS* 2.5A, 5B).[7] The Hittite texts, meanwhile, offer an entirely different picture, one in which Muwatalli II was victorious, not Ramesses II.[8]

The grounds for such disparate accounts lie in the ancient Near Eastern worldview. The king was the guarantor of order (*Ma'at* in Egyptian), receiving regalia of power from the deity to preserve the order of the world. Were he not to do so, the world would descend into chaos.[9] The official account of a battle thus demanded a victorious pharaoh, as the enemies were the living embodiment of chaos. This religious dimension can be seen in the location of the texts themselves: accounts of the victorious pharaoh were affixed to the external wall of the temple; on the inside walls the pharaoh is represented as the high priest. Outside, the ruler's abilities to keep chaos at bay are portrayed; inside, his religious importance.

While the texts of the Hebrew Bible differ from other ancient Near Eastern literature in certain respects, they are fundamentally similar, as both are religious literature whose purpose transcends particular historical events. As such, the history of ancient Israel presented here will only rarely rely on texts from the

---

3. The following textbooks will be referred to: *Ancient Near Eastern Texts* (*ANET*, 3rd ed.), *Context of Scripture* (*COS* 1–4); Pearce and Wunsch, *Documents of Judean Exiles* (*DJE*) and *Textbook of Aramaic Documents from Ancient Egypt* (*TAD* 1–4).
4. See Grabbe, *Can a 'History of Israel'?*, and Bishop Moore, *Philosophy and Practice*, 181–83.
5. Assmann, *Mind of Egypt*, 197–203.
6. On Ramesses II, see Redford, *Egypt, Canaan, and Israel*, 183–86.
7. See Goedicke, *Perspectives*.
8. See Götze, "Zur Schlacht von Qades," 832–38.
9. See Assmann, *Mind of Egypt*, 143–47.

Hebrew Bible to ground its historical claims. One biblical source that will be used, however, is the so-called "royal annals" referred to in the books of Kings. From 1 Kgs 14:19 through 2 Kgs 24:5, frequent mention is made of "chronicles" of the kings of Israel and Judah, each offering the age of a particular king and the length of his reign.[10] Annals were indeed kept in royal courts and recorded important events. The Egyptian story of Wenamun from the late eleventh to the early tenth centuries recounts that the king of Byblos had at his disposal "daybooks of his forefathers," in which payments for merchandise were listed (*COS* 1.41, 2.08–09).[11] While this demonstrates that annals with archival intent existed, no ancient Near Eastern text has yet been found that lists the ages of kings at their ascension to the throne and the length of their rule.[12] While the Babylonian Chronicle from the seventh and sixth centuries notes the dates of the kings and some important events from their reigns, for example, these are not direct parallels to the annals found in the book of Kings.[13] Looking more closely at the entries in 1–2 Kings, however, it's hard to miss the rhetorical function they serve. They also betray a strongly Judean perspective, with a particular focus on Jerusalem—a position not dissimilar to the Deuteronomistic History. This bias can be clearly seen in the account of Shoshenq I's campaign of 926 BCE (1 Kgs 14:25–28, see below, 2.7), or the juxtaposition of the Judean kings and the kings of the Northern Kingdom (see, for example 1 Kgs 16:8–28; see below, 3.2).[14] In what follows, therefore, the basic information from the annals—the sequence of the kings of Judah and Israel—will be used without drawing further conclusions from it.

All of this is to say that the history contained in the Hebrew Bible offers little in the way of solid foundations upon which to reconstruct the history of ancient Israel, though in particular cases one might still look its theologically-influenced depiction of history in hope of finding a historical kernel.[15]

1.2 The Approach of This Work

Most histories of ancient Israel written in the last twenty years share one notable trait: while they read the biblical account of the early history of Israel

---

10. For the following, see Na'aman, "Temple Library," 129–52, and Knauf and Guillaume, *History of Biblical Israel*, 90–91.

11. See Schipper, *Die Erzählung des Wenamun*, 192–93.

12. See Na'aman, "Royal Dynasties," 61.

13. See Grayson, *Assyrian and Babylonian Chronicles*, and Kratz, *Composition of the Narrative Books*, 159–61.

14. For a recent discussion on the chronicles of the kings of Israel/Judah, see Leuchter, "Sociolinguistics and Rhetorical Implications," 119–34, and, for an opposing position, see Levin, "Synchronistic Excerpt," 183–93.

15. On the issue as a whole, see Frevel, *Geschichte Israels*, 17–22.

critically—including the era of the patriarchs, the exodus, and the conquest of the land, as well as a skeptical take on the period of David and Solomon—they then increasingly follow the ensuing history as presented in the Bible.[16] Beginning with the Babylonian exile and reconstruction of the Jerusalem temple in 515 BCE these scholars take the biblical account of events more or less at face value. They view the sequence of events in the book of Ezra and Nehemiah as essentially historical, for example, even though in the nineteenth century scholars had already asserted that the biblical account in Ezra and Nehemia was not simply to be linked with historical events from the Persian period.[17]

This book takes a different approach. For the entire era of ancient Israel, beginning with the first reference to a group called "Israel" on the Merneptah Stela from 1208 BCE to the Maccabean revolt in the second century BCE, I make a single, fundamental distinction: the *history of "biblical Israel"* is what is found in the Hebrew Bible, and it is the story of God's people living between promise and fulfillment. The *history of "ancient Israel,"* meanwhile, is what can be reconstructed from extrabiblical and archaeological evidence.[18] This means that even for the period after the Babylonian exile extrabiblical evidence will be given central significance. In particular, recent archaeological excavations from the Persian Era at a YHWH sanctuary on Mount Gerizim and YHWH communities in Babylonia and Elephantine offer fresh perspectives on this period and will be of central importance for this study.

The following work is divided into five sections, each of which concerns a period of two to three centuries: (1) origins and early history (1208–926/925), (2) the period of the Northern Kingdom of Israel until the conquest of Samaria (926/925–722/720), (3) the southern Kingdom of Judah until the conquest of Jerusalem (722/720–587/586), (4) the Persian period (550–333), and (5) the Hellenistic period (333–64/63). It goes without saying that the boundaries between these periods are fluid, and the dates given here serve only as broad guides. The conquest in 722/720 of Samaria, capital of the Kingdom of Israel, and the capture in 587/586 of Jerusalem, capital of Judah, marked sharp caesuras in the political histories of ancient Israel—though not in the cultural history. The material culture shows continuities that caution against seeing too sharp a break between eras. What is described in the biblical history as a change of eras was above all a change in political rule, with few economic consequences. Local elites were probably hardly affected by the change. Similarly, the scribal culture of ancient Israel did not end with the destruction of the Kingdoms of Israel and

16. See, for example, Miller and Hayes, *History of Ancient Israel and Judah*, 498–510.

17. See Torrey, *Composition and Historical Value*, 51–65.

18. For this differentiation, see Kratz, *Historical and Biblical Israel*, 2–3; Liverani, *Israel's History*, xvi–xvii; Davies, *In Search of 'Ancient Israel,'* the fourth chapter of the latter distinguishing between three Israels: "ancient Israel," "biblical Israel," and "historical Israel."

Judah. In fact, the evidence tells us that it was only then that the production of texts really began to flourish.[19]

1.3 Israel/Palestine and the Southern Levant

The history of ancient Israel occurred against the backdrop of very particular geographic conditions. The land of the Bible, "Israel/Palestine," is a region that begins, to the south, at the Red Sea, goes north, beyond the Dead Sea, and ends about forty-five kilometers above the Sea of Galilee (map 1).[20] This was not a large territory, but it was part of a greater, geopolitically significant region often referred to as Syria-Palestine or as the "Southern Levant."[21]

"Palestine" and "Palestinian" are not modern terms but are taken from ancient sources: Herodotus (*Hist.* 1.105) uses the term *Palestine* (from the Aramaic $p^e lištā'în$) to refer to the area of Philistine settlement. In 135 CE, Palestine is attested to in the name of the Roman province *syria palaestina*.[22]

The land of Israel/Palestine was not large. From Dan at the northern border to Jerusalem is around 160 kilometers, from Philistine Ashdod on the Mediterranean coast to Jerusalem around 60 km, and from the southern end of the Sea of Galilee to the Dead Sea, around 105 km. In 414 CE the theologian Jerome, who had grown up knowing the wide dimensions of the Roman empire, wrote to the prefect in Gaul, Dardanus: [23]

> I am almost ashamed to give the breadth of the Promised Land, in fear
> of inviting the pagans' mocking. From Jaffa to our spot of Bethlehem is
> 46 miles (ca. 70 km). Then immediately after is a great wilderness.

Given that a person in the biblical era could travel an average of around 30 km a day, the trip from Jaffa to Bethlehem would take a little more than two days. In other words, one could traverse the whole land remarkably quickly.

Israel/Palestine was a land of widely varied natural features: in the south was a desert, through which the most important trade route crossed, leading to Arabah. Central Palestine was characterized by a small-scale, densely forested hill country, in which each valley was a world of its own. In the north was the

---

19. On this, see Levin, *Old Testament*, 61, and Schmid, *Old Testament*, 107–11.

20. For this, see Aharoni, *Land of the Bible*, 21–42.

21. On the term "Syro-Palestinian land bridge," which is especially popular in German scholarship, see Donner, *Geschichte des Volkes Israel* I:52.

22. See Mazar, *Archaeology*, 1–9.

23. Hieronymus, *Epistles* 129, cited in Keel et al., *Orte und Landschaften* I:182. English translation by Michael Lesley.

enormous Jezreel Valley, and along the coast ran the Via Maris. This road, along with the King's Highway in Transjordan, and the trade road through the Judean desert, were the most important trade routes of ancient Israel.[24]

Judah (later referred to as Yehud or Judea), the heartland of the Bible, was cut off from the important trade routes and commercial regions and had no access to the sea: on its western side lay the Shephela foothills, which at the time were still heavily wooded, while on the east it was bounded by the Judean desert. To the north lay the Ephraimite and Samarian mountains, which in the Late Bronze Age was a separate political territory. Finally, there was the area that drew the most attention from the great powers of the ancient Near East: the coastal plain, with the Philistine cities in the south and the Phoenicians to the north, as well as Megiddo, the economically important center at the edge of the Jezreel Valley.

It is practically a truism in scholarship on the history of ancient Israel that the kings of Samaria and Jerusalem only began to draw the attention of the rulers of the ancient Near Eastern empires either when they moved into geopolitically important areas, such as the coastal plains, or when they took part in political coalitions against the prevailing hegemonic power. This can be seen as far back as the fourteenth century BCE, with the ruler of the Late Bronze Age city-state of Shechem (see below, 2.2), and continued to be the case into the second century. Otherwise, neither Egyptian pharaohs nor Neo-Assyrian or Babylonian kings nor the Persian, Ptolemaic, or Seleucid rulers had any interest in the heartland of Israel and Judah. The Samarian and Judean hill countries were of little importance. Ancient Near Eastern rulers were interested in securing and defending the key trade routes and the geopolitically important coastal plains, and they founded military bases in strategically significant places such as Gaza, Megiddo, and Beth Shean.

1.4 Story and History: Preliminary Methodological Remarks

Whether Samuel or Kings, Ezra-Nehemiah or Chronicles, the Hebrew Bible presents its own historiography. Following the historian Hayden White, one can speak of *narratives* that have significance for both the present and the future.[25] At the same time these narratives are not fully formed, as White has argued in his influential work. Rather, as historiographic scholarship has shown, the narratological categories of *plot* and *story* cannot simply be applied to historical writing. In contrast to fiction, historiography always functions within a frame of reference.[26]

---

24. For the system of trade routes, see Dorsey, *Roads and Highways*, 57, 147.
25. See White, *Tropics of Discourse*, 121–22.
26. For the criteria of referentiality, see Cohn, *Distinction of Fiction*, 112.

Every historical construction is subjective, insofar as it is generated by a particular interest. It is less concerned with saying something "true" or "historically accurate" about the past than it is with constructing meaning. As the historian Jörn Rüsen has put it, "Experiences of the past without normative intent for the future are historically blind; normative views on the future without experiences of the past are historically empty."[27] Therefore current scholarship stresses the significance of a historical perspective of the past for a construction of the future.[28]

The biblical texts offer not only historical texts, but historical narratives. As such, the boundaries between history and story are fluid. Both help create memory that shapes meaning and identity, and both are important to the sociopolitical discourse.[29] Historiography is a tool that helps make collective memory and engenders *master narratives*.[30]

In the Hebrew Bible one can find such a master narrative in the literary correlations between the books of Joshua, Judges, Samuel, and Kings. These books, generally referred to as the "Deuteronomistic History," present an outline of history that explicitly sees the past as something that explains the present and offers a guide for the future.[31] Through its connection with the book of Deuteronomy it lays the groundwork for a historical paradigm: Israel came from outside the land, and before entering they received the law—the Torah—from God, teaching them right behavior toward God and toward others. But the subsequent "history of Israel" was understood to be a history of decline. The perfect conditions that existed outside the land were gradually lost with the entrance into the land and the formation of the monarchy. This theological outline has been further uncovered through recent scholarship on the connections between the Deuteronomic composition of the books of Joshua, Judges, Samuel, and Kings, and the narrative of the exodus from Egypt and conquest of the land (the so-called Moses-Exodus-Conquest narrative).[32] The Deuteronomic image of the salvific origins of Israel through the destruction of Jerusalem is an explanation of why the people of Israel are in exile.[33]

This broad-brush explanation of the Deuteronomistic History shows that historiography is not simply a subjective interpretation, but a vehicle for the construction of collective identity. What makes this possible is that writing history

---

27. Rüsen, *Zeit und Sinn*, 229.

28. See Hagedorn, "Historiography," and Hölscher, *Die Entdeckung der Zukunft*.

29. See Clark, *History, Theory, Text*.

30. See Confino, "History and Memory," 36–51, and Knauf, "From History to Interpretation," 26.

31. See Römer, *So-Called Deuteronomistic History*, 3–11, 163–64, 177–78.

32. For the following, see Gertz et al., *T & T Clark Handbook*, 356–60, 376–78.

33. A possible literary historical model is offered by Römer, *So-Called Deuteronomistic History*, and Schmid, *Old Testament*, 72–80, 116–20.

always involves selectivity.[34] The historian chooses particular facts and connects them with one another in particular ways. Here the historiography of the Hebrew Bible converges with the work of modern historians: every reconstruction of history is finally a construction and a hypothesis of those who write it, and it is always necessary to note the position of the historian and their intention— i.e., the specific interests that led the writer to choose as they did.[35] Such an approach is important because "the historian's construction of the past is the result of a process of selection, cultural location, and ethnic identity."[36]

This fact about historical writing, whether ancient or modern, can be illustrated by another example from the Bible, one that helps illuminate the title of this book: the history of ancient "Israel." The "theological historiography" of the books of Chronicles, which stems from the Hellenistic period, focuses on the history of the "true Israel," the community around the Second Temple in Jerusalem.[37] The theological objectives of the Chronistic history entailed that, in contrast with the picture given in the Pentateuch, the real establishment of Israel was to be understood as beginning with the era of David and Solomon, and that the history of "this Israel" is connected with the subsequent kings of Jerusalem. The monarchs of the Kingdom of Israel in the north, with its capital in Samaria, are entirely absent from the picture.[38] In other words, in the period of the Hebrew Bible the term "Israel" could be understood in significantly different ways.[39]

Historically, the name "Israel" is first mentioned on the stela of the Egyptian pharaoh Merneptah (1208 BCE). While the stela refers to a group of people, the Neo-Assyrian royal inscriptions of the ninth and eighth centuries concern a kingdom with its seat in Samaria, and hence they denote a territorial-political entity. After this kingdom fell in 722/720, "Israel" was appropriated to the Southern Kingdom of Judah and its capital Jerusalem (Jer 17:13). When this kingdom ended with the conquest of Jerusalem, in 587/586, the term Israel became theologically weighted. In the Persian and Hellenistic periods "Israel" was the self-description of a group of worshippers of the god YHWH. In some texts this group was understood in relation to the community around the Second Temple in Jerusalem (Ezra-Nehemiah), in other texts with the YHWH community of the Samaritans on Mt. Gerizim (Delos Inscriptions).[40]

---

34. See Kistenfeger, *Historische Erkenntnis*, 205–7; Jenkins, *On 'What Is History?,'* 13; Jenkins, *Re-thinking History*, 82.
35. On this, see Banks, *Writing the History*, 232–34.
36. Hagedorn, "Historiography," forthcoming.
37. For this, see Gertz et al., *T & T Clark Handbook*, 690.
38. See Schmid, *Old Testament*, 194–97.
39. See Weingart, *Stämmevolk—Staatsvolk—Gottesvolk?*, 373–75.
40. For the Delos Inscriptions, see Bruneau, "Israelites de Délos," 466–504.

As this is a scholarly historical work, the "history of ancient Israel" refers neither to the people of God of that name nor to the Kingdom of Israel in the ninth and eighth centuries, but simply to a historical period that runs from the Merneptah Stela to the time of the Roman Empire.

The Origins of Israel and Its Early History (1208–926/925 BCE)

Israel's origins are shrouded in darkness. The biblical stories of the patriarchs (Gen 12–36) and the exodus from Egypt (Exod 1–15) offer no solid historical starting point. These accounts originated in the (late) monarchic period and developed over a long period of time afterward; they are thus unhelpful in reconstructing Israel's historical origins. This is also the case for attempts to connect the "Hebrews" of the Hebrew Bible with the Hapiru of the Amarna letters, or to equate the nomadic character of the stories of Abraham, Isaac, and Jacob to the seminomadic Shasu (*Šꜣśw*) referred to in Egyptian texts from the end of the second millenium.[1] No less speculative are identifications of a tribe of Abraham with the "Asians of *rhm*" referred to in the Beth Shean Stela of Sety I (1290–1279).[2] Each of these identifications has been used to support different theories of the origins of Israel and the conquest of the land by the Israelites. None of them, however, can withstand critical scrutiny.[3]

If one begins only with what can be historically corroborated, the first reliable piece of information is the Victory Stela of Pharaoh Merneptah, which attests to a group with the name "Israel" in the Southern Levant in the year 1208.[4] A second is the Palestine list of Pharaoh Shoshenq I from 926/925. With these two, Israel's earliest history is framed by two extrabiblical sources: one text confirms "Israel" as a group, the other offers the first evidence of the history of ancient Israel that overlaps with the biblical narrative, even if the accounts do not agree with one another: 1 Kgs 14:25–26 refers to the campaign of Shoshenq I attacking Jerusalem, though Jerusalem was not its ultimate goal. According to the Egyptian source Shoshenq was not interested in Jerusalem at all.[5]

---

1. For a classical view, see Bright, *History of Israel*, 93–96, and Noth, *History of Israel*, 33–34. For a critical perspective, see Dever, *Beyond the Texts*, 102–12.

2. As is argued, for instance, in Knauf, *Die Umwelt des Alten Testaments*, 103.

3. See the overview in Frevel, *Geschichte Israels*, 72–77.

4. The stela can be dated to the fifth regnal year of Merneptah (1208 BCE). Morenz, "Wortwitz—Ideologie—Geschichte," 12, however, dates the campaign to the second or third regnal year (1211 or 1210). See also Yurco, "Merenptah's Canaanite Campaign and Israel's Origin," 27–55.

5. See, for example, Mayes, "Palestinian Campaign," 63, and for a contrary position see note 112 below.

What we have here holds true for the whole history of ancient Israel: The biblical account, whether in Samuel, Kings, or Ezra-Nehemiah displays some historical knowledge, but presents it through the lens of a scribal elite for whom Judah and its capital Jerusalem were paramount.

2.1 Egypt and the Southern Levant (Fifteenth to Twelfth Cent.)

To understand the significance of the Merneptah Stela, some Egyptian history is necessary. During what is referred to as the "New Kingdom" (1539–1077) the pharaohs undertook several campaigns in the Southern Levant. This brought them into conflict with an equally powerful and expansive opponent, the Hittites. After the Hittite king Šuppiluliuma I (1370–1336) conquered the Mitanni Empire, he and his successors made a claim for Syria/Palestine. This led to military conflict with the Egyptians, including the Battle of Megiddo in 1468 (Thutmose III) and the aforementioned Battle of Kadesh in 1274 (Ramesses II).[6] Though some of these battles ended in defeat for the Egyptians, the pharaohs were ultimately able to bring the Southern Levant under their control and preserve it through military campaigns, marriage politics, and diplomatic contracts until around 1150/1140 (between the reigns of Ramesses III and Ramesses VI).

Alongside Egyptian rule over the strategically important Southern Levant, an administrative system was established, attested to by the more than 380 clay tablets from the period of Pharaoh Amenhotep IV, Akhenaten (1353–1336), known to scholars as the Amarna letters.[7] Among other things, these cuneiform letters contain correspondence between pharaoh and the kings of cities such as Megiddo, Jerusalem, and Byblos. These texts generally consist of short reports about enemies and threats, usually followed by requests to the pharaoh for military support and help for the loyal ruler. It is in this context that Hapiru are mentioned, though the text does not make clear what sort of group they are. Based on the textual information, it presumably refers to migrants of various origins who lived in the hills and presented a threat to the cities in the plains.[8]

The territory controlled by the Egyptians encompassed what would later become the Phoenician cities of the north, the Philistine cities of the south, and the area in which the Kingdoms of Israel and Judah were to arise (map 2). The Amarna letters also offer a window into contemporary political situation: there were several city-states in the Southern Levant, of which the two in the hill

---

6. See Morkot, *Short History*.

7. For the Amarna letters, see Rainey et al., *El-Amarna Correspondence*, 1–36.

8. For a possible identification with the biblical term "Hebrew" (*'ibrîm*: Gen 39:14, 17; 40:15; 41:12; 43:32; Exod 1:15, 19; 1 Sam 4:6, 9; 13:3, 19), see Grabbe, "Late Bronze Age Canaan," 25.

country, Jerusalem and Shechem, were territorially far larger than city-states on the trade routes but had the lowest population density.[9] The most important city-states were Hazor/*Tell Waqqāṣ* in the north and Gath/*Tell eṣ-Ṣafi*, which lay at the transition to the coastal planes, and which contained a monumental city complex as late as the tenth century.[10]

The different types of city-states and the density of settlements already exhibit a basic characteristic of Israelite history: ancient Near Eastern kingdoms, in this case Egypt, were not interested in the hill country of central Palestine but in controlling the coastal plains. This meant that the inhabitants of the city-states in the hinterlands were only noticed when they expanded into economically and strategically significant regions.

An example of this tendency can be seen in the case of *Lab'āya*, ruler of the city-state of Shechem.[11] According to the Amarna letters, he formed a pact with nearby city kingdoms—notably, not including Jerusalem—in order to take control of the trade routes in the coastal plain and the Jezreel Valley (EA 289, *COS* 3.92B).[12] The kings of Israel in the ninth and eighth centuries were often involved in such affairs as they attempted, through political alliances with their neighbors, to expand from the hilly regions of central Palestine outward into the economically and strategically crucial coastal plains (see below, 3.2).

There is reason to believe that the borders of the city-states remained in place after Egyptian control over the Southern Levant had ended. Even if the transition from the second to the first millenia saw the end of the urban culture of the Late Bronze Age—referred to as the "Canaanite city-states" in older scholarship—archaeological evidence shows that the structures erected by the Egyptian pharaohs survived through Iron Age I and into Iron Age IIA.[13]

One should presumably also understand what would later become the Kingdoms of "Israel" and "Judah" against the backdrop of the group of Late Bronze Age city-states, as the events in the history of Israel—its conquest of land, the growth of the state, and the Kingdoms of Israel and Judah—all took place in the area of the old city-states of Jerusalem and Shechem—especially the latter (see map 3).

Among the administrative structures built by the Egyptians in the thirteenth century were the garrison towns of Beth Shean and Gaza, both of which were situated in strategically important locations. Beth Shean was at the crossroads of

---

9. See Finkelstein, "Territorial-Political System," 236.

10. See Maeir, "Philistine Gath," 133–54.

11. Labaya's residence in Shechem has been determined through clay analysis of his letters; see Goren et al., *Inscribed in Clay*, 262–65.

12. See Finkelstein, *Forgotten Kingdom*, 17–21.

13. See, for example, Finkelstein and Na'aman, "Shechem of the Amarna Period," 172–93. On the dating of these periods see Archaeological Periods, 117.

the north-south route through the Jordan Valley and the east-west route through the Jezreel Valley. Gaza was an important stop on the Via Maris, the land route from Egypt through the Sinai to the Southern Levant, whose southern portion is referred to in Egyptian texts as the Way of Horus.

The archaeology of Beth Shean illustrates they way an Egyptian garrison town in the Southern Levant would have appeared: Egyptian temples, administrative buildings, and a layout like an Egyptian city (e.g., Tell el-Amarna and Deir el-Medina), as well as monumental stone stelas on which the politico-religious claims of the pharaohs were engraved.[14] Egyptian influence was so significant that the local workshops produced Egyptian ceramics and local inhabitants maintained their Egyptian heritage even after Egyptian authority in the area had ended.[15] In Stratum VB/S1 (tenth to ninth cent.) Egyptian monuments, including a seated statue of Ramesses III and the victory stelas of Sety I (*COS* 2.4B; 4D) and Ramesses II (*ANET* 255) continued to be in use.[16] The archaeology of Beth Shean is not only exemplary of what such a town would have looked like under Egyptian rule, but shows that this influence continued afterward, even long into the monarchic period of ancient Israel.

Another example can be found in Gaza. While the current political situation in Israel makes excavation of the city impossible,[17] texts and archaeological discoveries in the region offer some information on this important Egyptian administrative center in the Southern Levant. Gaza was founded by Thutmose III (1479–1425) and presumably survived until the end of the Ramesside period. An Egyptian papyrus from the time of Ramesses IV (1156–1150) refers to a temple for the main deity of the Egyptian New Kingdom, the god Amun-Re in Gaza (*ANET* 260–61). If three scarabs from Beth Shean and *Tell el-Farʿah* [South] are interpreted in connection with this papyrus, it would mean that Gaza was a significant administrative center for the southern coastal plains, one to which the local estates were required to pay their taxes.[18] The Egyptian influence is also attested to by Egyptian-inspired buildings found both at *Tell el-Farʿah* [South] and in an area in the hinterlands of Gaza (Qubur al-Walaydah). These "Egyptian residences" are also found in Tell es-Šerīʿa IV, Tell Ǧemme (Building JF), and Lachish VI.[19]

---

14. For the category "politico-religious," see Matthieu, "Mais qui est donc Osiris?," 77, and for the archaeology and the history of excavation on Tell Beth Shean, see the instructive overview by Mazar, "Egyptian Garrison Town," 171–73.

15. See, for example, Cohen-Weinberger, "Petrographic Analysis," 406–12, and Higginbotham, *Egyptianization and Elite Emulation*, 270–71, 286, 297–300.

16. See Mazar, "Egyptian Garrison Town," 171–73, including a discussion of differing arguments by Higginbotham in n40.

17. See Maeir, "Gaza," 451–53.

18. See Uehlinger, "Amun-Tempel Ramses' III," 5–9.

19. See Lehmann et al., "Excavations at Qubur al-Walaydah," 142, and Oren, "Governor's Residences," 37–56.

Gaza is also of interest for religious history in giving evidence for worship of multiple deities at once both Egyptian and non-Egyptian. While the city contained a temple for the worship of the Egyptian God Amun-Re, a letter from an Egyptian garrison scribe to his superior refers to a festival celebrating "'Anat of Gaza," a local version of the goddess 'Anat, daughter of El and sister of Baal, who is referred to as far back as Ugarit (ca. 2400 BCE).[20]

Add to these examples the important city of Megiddo in the western Jezreel Valley, which was renovated by Ramesses III and which may show traces of Egyptian influence as late as Ramesses VI,[21] and the following claim can be made: between the fifteenth and the twelfth centuries the Southern Levant was under Egyptian rule. Local vassal lords were required to pay tributes, which were collected in transregional centers, where Egyptian officials resided. Egyptian culture and religion influenced the region. Finally, both the organization and the cultural influence did not stop with the end of Egyptian control of the Southern Levant in the twelfth century but continued beyond the Ramesside perod—in the case of Beth Shean, into the tenth/ninth centuries and thus into the time of David and Solomon.

2.2 "Israel" in the Merneptah Stela and the "Conquest of the Land" (Thirteenth to Twelfth Cent.)

On a 3.10 m high victory stela from the fifth regnal year of Pharaoh Merneptah (1208 BCE) is a poem commemorating a military victory against the Libyans (*COS* 2.6; *ANEP* 342–43). After this follows a sixteen-line section that presumably dates from Merneptah's campaign in the Southern Levant in 1211/1210 BCE.[22] The wording of line 26, "The rulers were crushed and say shalom (*šɜ-r-m*)!" shows the text to be working with historical information: *Shalom* ("peace") is a Semitic word, not an Egyptian one.[23]

At the end of the text is a list of names, including Gaza (referred to in the text as "the Canaan" [*pɜ Kn'n*]), Ashkelon, Gezer, and Yanoam, after which comes the sentence "Israel is laid waste—it has no more seed." The hieroglyphics leave no doubt that "Israel" does not refer to a city or a region, but a group of people. The phrase "it has no more seed," meanwhile, can have more than one meaning. It could indicate that Israel, as a group of small farmers, no longer controlled any

---

20. On this, see the Hieratic Ostraca Michaelides 85, cited in Weippert, *Historisches Textbuch*, 174n199. See also Goedicke and Wente, *Ostraka Michaelides*, table xciii.

21. See Schipper, *Israel and Egypt*, ch. 2.1, and for the archaeological evidence see Finkelstein et al., "New Evidence," 261–80.

22. On the historical problem, see Morenz, "Wortwitz—Ideologie—Geschichte," 10n37.

23. On the variety of references in Egyptian texts, see Hoch, *Semitic Words*, 285–86 [no. 408].

seed, or that its descendants, its "seed," were killed (cf., e.g., Gen 12:7; 13:15–16), though the composition of the text and references to the various places and peoples seem to support for the former interpretation. The geographical ordering from the south (Gaza) along the coast (Ashkelon) and the lowlands (Gezer), to Yanoam/*Tell en-Nāʿam*[24] at the southwest of the Sea of Galilee, might mean that Israel refers to a group of people south of the Sea of Galilee. Since they are mentioned on an Egyptian monumental stela, they should be understood to have lived in a city or region of significance for Egypt—an Egyptian monumental stela would not mention an unimportant people.[25] The only city in the area that fulfills these criteria would be Beth Shean. Although the city lies around 25 km south of Yanoam/*Tell en-Nāʿam*, if one means to locate the group called "Israel" referred to on the stela, Beth Shean is the most likely candidate.[26]

Whatever the case, the Merneptah Stela indicates that in the Late Bronze Age Israel was a group that lived in the lowlands, practiced agriculture, and at some point behaved in such a way as to warrant Egyptian attention. Perhaps what precipitated this was that "Israel" had left the hinterlands of the city and moved to the highlands, leaving no one to tend to the agriculture of the urban center (see below, 2.3). If one were intent on finding a historical connection to the biblical idea of a "conquest of the land," this scenario has the strongest connection to the archaeological record.

Shortly before 1200 BCE the hill country began to be settled not only in the Galilee, near the sea, but also within the territory of the Late Bronze Age city-state of Shechem.[27] This would have been an ideal safe haven for a group of people intent on leaving the Egyptian urban culture on the lowlands and around Beth Shean: the highlands of the city-state of Shechem in the Samarian-Ephraimite hill country. In Iron Age I numerous, often very small, settlements were founded in the northern region of the Samarian hills, next to the Jezreel Valley (map 3). Of the nearly 150 settlements known to scholars, only around two dozen were continuations of earlier settlements from the Late or Middle Bronze Age. Alongside small homesteads abandoned early on—referred to as "one period sites"—larger settlements with an area of more than one hectare were founded, mostly around springs, which ordinarily survived longer.[28] Recent studies have led to a complex picture of the settlement history, with old

24. Yanoam is the same as Januamma in the Amarna letters, and it is already mentioned by Thutmose III. On its location in reference to *Tell en-Nāʿam*, see Hasel, *Domination & Resistance*, 146–50, and for a discussion of the evidence, see Naʾaman, "Yenoʿam," 168–77.

25. On this, see Faust, *Israel's Ethnogenesis*, 163.

26. For the problem of pinpointing the location of the Israel of the Merneptah Stela, see Dever, *Beyond the Texts*, 192–94.

27. For an overview, see Faust, *Israel's Ethnogenesis*, 111–34, and Finkelstein, *Archaeology*, 324–27.

28. See Zwingenberger, *Dorfkultur*, 138–204, and Finkelstein, *Forgotten Kingdom*, 22.

city-states in the lowlands, and clans and villages, including territorial chief-doms, in the highlands.[29]

Broadly speaking, the settlements of the hill country related to the development of urban culture in the Southern Levant in two ways: they were founded during a cultural upheaval in Late Bronze Age cities, and they disappeared when urban culture began to regain its strength in the tenth/ninth centuries. This offers a plausible connection between the "Canaan" of the Late Bronze Age, the Israel of the Merneptah stela, and the Kingdom of "Israel" of the ninth century, if one were looking for it. It might also offer a historical basis for the "Canaanite" legacy in the Hebrew Bible, as in the memory of the conversion of older, pre-Israelite holy sites (Bethel, see Gen 28) or in elements of the Syro-Palestinian religion, as in the divine name El Elyon (see Ps 83:19; 97:9).[30]

The small settlements in the highlands show archaeological characteristics generally referred to as "Israelite."[31] These include (1) a new type of ceramic, the "collared rim jar" (an approximately one-meter-high storage jar with a folded rim and short neck), (2) a particular kind of building, the so-called "four-room house," and (3) the terracing of land in some areas. None of these three elements suffice to serve as ethnic markers for an Israelite culture, however. Methodologically speaking, the same objection made in discussions of Philistine culture of the coastal region can be made here: it is difficult to connect archaeological evidence with one particular *ethnos* to the exclusion of other *ethnoi*.[32] Rather, distinctions between Early Iron Age village culture and urban culture should be understood as stemming from differences in economies and by regionally distinct locations. Villages in the hill regions did not take part in cross-regional trade but produced goods as they needed them (subsistence economics). At the same time there are archaeological commonalities between the highlands and other regions of the Southern Levant: the so-called "four room house"—a large room (living area/stall) and a courtyard in the center, with pillars dividing the house into covered and open sections—is found outside the hill country as well. Furthermore, the architecture of these houses varies greatly (see for example *Ḥirbet el-Mšāš/Tel Masos* in the Negev, or Tel Hazor V–VI).[33] The situation with collared rim storage jars is also similarly complex. They are found neither uniquely in the hill country nor only in Iron Age I: the oldest, from Aphek, dates to the Late Bronze Age, while the latest comes from the eighth century.[34]

---

29. See Lehmann, "Northern Coast Plain," forthcoming.

30. On the Syro-Palestinian religion, see Dietrich et al., *Die keilalphabetischen Texte aus Ugarit* 1.16.3.8.

31. See the discussion in Faust, *Israel's Ethnogenesis*, 11–19.

32. See Finkelstein, "Pots and People Revisited," 216–37.

33. See Zwingenberger, *Dorfkultur*, 257, fig. 44.

34. See Kamlah, "Das Ostjordanland," 118–33, and the map in Faust, *Israel's Ethnogenesis*, 192, fig. 19.2.

Another purported ethnic marker that has recently received attention is pig bones. Few pig bones have been found in the highlands. Rather, according to paleobotanical research, between 40 and 80 percent of the bones found in the region were from sheep or goats. Even though some scholars want to take this as evidence for "Israelites" whom they believe were already not consuming pig meat, recent analysis has shown that the consumption of pig cannot serve as ethnic marker, either.[35]

Looking at the settlements in general, some were laid out as farmsteads, either with adjacent buildings, or in a ring. None of the buildings served uniquely administrative functions, however. A potsherd with a five-line inscription was found in ʿIzbet Ṣarṭah, on the edge of the highlands near the city of Aphek, which indicates the beginning of literacy.[36]

Thus while the archaeology offers little in the way of information about the form of society of the groups living in these settlements, at least one thing can be securely determined: the inhabitants of these hill country settlements of the Early Iron Age did not constitute a single group of nomads who might have settled there after a long migration, but were an amalgamation of a variety of people.[37] This "mixed multitude" included lowlanders and highlanders, rural population from Late Bronze Age city states, displaced peasants and mobile pastoralists, and other groups such as the Hapiru and Shasu of the Amarna correspondence.[38] These different forms of social existence were not disconnected from a new urban landscape that emerged alongside an expansion of rural settlements.[39]

Israel's "conquest of the land" could thus be understood as the move, in the Early Iron Age, from urban to village culture, and in the opposition of "lowlanders" and "highlanders." In the areas of the earlier Late Bronze Age city-states, a regional division occurred in the settlements. Because of its previously meager settlement, the hill region of the city-state of Shechem offered the best opportunity for expansion. In this sense the origins of Israel are to be found in the land itself. The group, which around 1200 BCE was already called "Israel," had not entered from outside the land—as nomads traveling through the ancient Near East for example—but were a product of the urban landscape of the Late Bronze Age. "Israel," first referred to as a group in the Merneptah Stela, stopped in the

---

35. For a discussion of the evidence, see Faust, *Israel's Ethogenesis*, 34–40, and Sapir-Hen et al., "Pig Husbandry," 1–20.

36. See Demsky, "ʿIzbet Sartah Ostracon," 186–97.

37. For a critique of the classical theory of the nomadic origins of ancient Israel, see Rosen and Lehmann, "Hat das biblische Israel?," 160–82.

38. See Killebrew, *Biblical Peoples*, 149 (and for the term "mixed multitude," 184). For further details, see Faust, "Emergence of Iron Age Israel," 469–71.

39. See Gadot, "Iron I in the Samaria Highlands," 103–14.

plains, and apparently acted in a manner that brought the Egyptians to view them as an enemy worthy of mention on a royal stela. Whether, in a situation in which Egyptian control of the Southern Levant was waning, the departure of a group of small farmers who had earlier worked around what had been an important city for Egypt (e.g., Beth Shean) was somehow worth mentioning is a matter of speculation. What is beyond doubt, however, is that Israel emerged out of "Canaan" and did not come from outside the land.

All of this paints a picture at odds with the biblical texts. The history of "biblical Israel" found in Joshua, Judges, Samuel, and Kings makes much of Israel's origins outside the land, not from within Canaan. For the biblical authors this is theologically significant, above all, in the contrast between "Israel" and "Canaan": the authors wanted to make clear that the people of YHWH, the God of the Hebrew Bible, had no connection with the gods and the religion of Canaan.[40] From a historical perspective, however, the opposite is true. As can be seen on map 3, the new settlements of the thirteenth and twelfth centuries show that the "conquest of the land" occurred primarily in the area of the Late Bronze Age city-state of Shechem, far less in the Jerusalem area. This makes clear that the north was more significant than the south, and that Israel's origins are more likely to be found there, rather than in Judah or Jerusalem. This also concurs with recent findings in the history of the YHWH religion, according to which YHWH, the God of Israel, has its origins in the northern region, and not the southern regions, such as the Sinai.[41] What, then, does all this mean for the biblical tradition of the exodus from Egypt?

2.3 Israel in Egypt? The Exodus

The profession that God brought his people Israel out of Egypt is among the central tenets of biblical Israel (see Exod 20:2; Deut 5:6). The extent to which this belief is based on historical events is hard to say in light of currently available evidence. At the very least, the thesis that the Israelites helped build the cities of Pithom and Rameses and were oppressed by Pharaoh Ramesses II cannot be supported in its traditional form.[42]

The classical scholarly model builds upon a brief reference in Exod 1:11 about how the Israelites worked as forced labor in the building of "supply cities, Pithom and Rameses." This was understood as a reference to the "City of

---

40. See Schmid, *Old Testament*, 79–84.
41. See Pfeiffer, "Origins of YHWH," 115–44.
42. On this, see Schipper, "Raamses, Pithom, and the Exodus," 265–88, and the overview in Davies, "Was there an Exodus?," 23–40.

Rameses," the new capital city that Ramesses II (1279–1213) had founded, but which it was believed had fallen out of memory at end of the Ramesside period (i.e., after 1077).[43] Since the Ramessides were also forgotten, the mention of the name Rameses in Exod 1:11 must be an authentic memory. Otherwise it would be impossible to explain how the term had made its way into the beginning of Exodus, a book composed in a much later period.

Hebrew Bible scholarship has stood by this theory over the years, even if it rests on shaky footing. In fact, the memory of the Ramessides did not disappear, nor did that of the place called "Rameses," which is mentioned in Egyptian texts as the "City of Ramesses" (*pr Rʿ-ms-sw*), and not simply as a personal name, as it is in Exod 1:11. Instead, the use of both the name Rameses and the city name "Pithom," (Egyptian *pr Jtm*, "House of [the god] Atum") should be understood as originating out of a seventh-century context. Since the idea of "forced labor" for Egypt can just as plausibly be connected to this later period, one should be very cautious in drawing historical conclusions from Exod 1:11. The literary character of the passage at the beginning of the Exodus narrative gives no evidence that it can be reliably mined for information about the second millenium BCE, either.[44]

What, then, *can* be said about "Israel in Egypt," and what might historical information on the exodus from Egypt even look like? Even if there is no choice but to speculate, as there are no unquestionably reliable sources, the following scenario is possible.

Egyptian sources from the Middle Kingdom refer to "Asians" (Egy. *ꜥm.w*, *ANET* 228), who are also pictorially depicted in graves (Beni Hassan, Twelfth Dynasty, ca. 1900 BCE).[45] At the same time, texts from the New Kingdom, refer to *Shasu*-nomads (*COS* 2.4), among them a famous report from a border officer, from the time of Merneptah, that refers to a group of *Shasu* who had come to Egypt to graze their livestock (*COS* 3.5). There is therefore no doubt that in the second millenium groups from the Southern Levant came to Egypt. These texts do not state that these people were Israelites, though. For a reference to "Israelites," we turn back to the Merneptah Stela. Insofar as the stela is the product of a military campaign, it is possible that at least some of the group referred to as "Israel" might have been taken to Egypt as prisoners of war.[46] The story of the deliverance from Exodus might then be understood as these prisoners of war achieving freedom, under circumstances that can no longer be reconstructed, and returning to the Southern Levant.

---

43. See Donner, *Geschichte des Volkes Israel* I:105, and Bright, *History of Israel*, 120–24.
44. Schmid, *Genesis and the Moses Story*, 63–65.
45. See Yurco, "Merentpah's Canaanite Campaign and Israel's Origin," 33.
46. Most recently Knauf and Guillaume, *History of Biblical Israel*, 35.

The Merneptah Stela does make another scenario at least possible, though not as plausible as the previous one, which should be mentioned briefly, for the sake of thoroughness.

The Israeli historian Nadav Na'aman has pointed out that the core of the Exodus tradition can be explained in relation to the situation "in the land."[47] Insofar as a group of small farmers called "Israel" labored for the Egyptians in the area of an Egyptian city, it is possible the Exodus tradition is referring to a disengagement—a "redemption," so to speak—from Egypt, but one which took place in the Southern Levant. The exodus would be understood as part of the process of transformation of the Late Bronze Egyptian province of Canaan, possibly in line with a scenario suggested by the aforementioned Amarna letter. In the letter of the king of the city of Megiddo, Biridiya, to the pharaoh (EA 365), the king refers to corvée workers coming from Jaffa (near modern Tel Aviv) and the Jezreel Valley who were required to engage in agricultural work. Insofar as this occurred at the same period as Merneptah it is possible to explain the liberation from Egyptian bondage as the group "Israel" mentioned in the Merneptah Stela having freed themselves from corvée labor and settling in the hill country. In this scenario, "Exodus" and "conquest of the land" would have been one and the same process.

Whatever the case, and whether one looks for the nucleus of the Exodus tradition in Egypt or in Israel/Palestine or not, the biblical reference to a man called "Moses" does point to an ancient connection between Israel and Egypt. "Moses" is the short form of the name "Ramesses," which is itself a conjunction of the name of the god, "Re," and the verb *msj* ("give birth to": "he whom [the god] Re bore"). Considering that in the Hebrew Bible the names "Ramesses" and "Moses" are based on the same Egyptian verb (*msj*), its orthography is noteworthy. In the Hebrew text of Exod 1:11 Moses is spelled with a different letter than Ramesses: the former with a *shin* (שׁ), the latter with a *samech* (ס). This points to different periods of composition. "Moshe" suggests a late second millenium usage, while "Ramesses" is a first millenium derivation. The spelling of "Moses" could thus refer to an older, presumably historical tradition, while the orthography of "Ramesses" is to be dated to a later period (seventh cent.).[48] This holds not only for Exod 1:11, in which the name Ramesses is mentioned, but to the possibility of there being a historical core to the Exodus story at all. After all, the name "Moses" is a fundamental part of the "Israel and Egypt" tradition. If the goal is to find the historical core to the biblical tradition of the "exodus from Egypt," the name Moses and the significant connection between Israel and

---

47. See Na'aman, "Out of Egypt?," 527–33, and "Exodus Story," 39–69.
48. See Schipper, "Raamses, Pithom, and the Exodus," 272–76, and Knauf and Guillaume, *History of Biblical Israel*, 34.

Egypt would seem to be a genuine lead. If one assumes that the name Moses could not have originated in the Southern Levant, but only in Egypt, one might imagine the following scenario to be true: a group came to Egypt (as prisoners of war?) in the period of the Ramesside rulers (nineteenth–twentieth dynasty), and went from there to the Southern Levant under circumstances that can no longer be reconstructed. This group assimilated with the "Israelites," who had by then settled among other groups in the region of the Late Bronze city-state of Shechem. Perhaps the combination of these two historical situations form the core of the two biblical traditions of "Israel's origins": (1) the narrative of the exodus from Egypt and entrance into the land (exodus/eisodus narrative) and (2) the narrative of the patriarchs, which begins in the land itself.[49]

2.4 Philistines, "Canaanites," Arameans, and the Early Monarchy in Israel (Eleventh to Tenth Cent.)

The biblical books of Judges and Samuel give an account of the rule of the judges in Israel and the establishment of a monarchy. Earlier scholarship generally dated this period to around the year 1000 BCE. This time period is at least as difficult to reconstruct historically as the preceding era. Some scholars follow a trimmed-down version of the biblical story, based on the book of Judges and the Song of Deborah in Judges 5, to suggest that there were various tribes living near one another who increasingly organized and formed coalitions with one another, ultimately leading to a demand for a monarch to rule over them.[50] After this first king, Saul, came David, a young ruler who fought the Philistines, according to 2 Sam 5, and who, after ascending the throne, made Jerusalem the capital of his kingdom.

To whatever extent there was a kingdom under Saul and David, it can only be understood against the background of the geopolitical situation in the Southern Levant of the period. Any proper reconstruction of the history of this area in the eleventh and tenth centuries must therefore begin with a consideration of the three ethnic groups referred to in the title of this section: Philistines, "Canaanites," and Arameans.

Around 1150/1140 Egypt suffered a significant loss of power, while in the Levant the influence of a number of other groups, the so-called Sea Peoples rose.[51] The term "Sea Peoples" refers to the various groups from the Aegean,

---

49. On this, see Schmid, "Genesis and the Exodus," 187–208.
50. See Miller and Hayes, *History of Ancient Israel and Judah*, 159–60, and the overview in Frevel, *Geschichte Israels*, 89, with reference to the positions of Walter Groß und Ernst A. Knauf.
51. For this, see Killebrew and Lehmann, *Philistines and Other "Sea People."*

Balkans, Asia Minor, and the Near East who entered the Southern Levant beginning in the twelfth century.[52] Egyptian temple reliefs from the time of Ramesses III offer dramatic depictions of military conflicts between the Egyptians and the Sea Peoples in 1175 (reliefs in the mortuary temple of Medinet Habu on the west bank of Luxor, *ANET* 262–63).[53] Following the Egyptian perspective, previous scholarship has reconstructed a scenario in which a group of Sea People pillaging and marauding through the Southern Levant and putting an end to its Late Bronze Age urban culture. What this scholarship overlooked, however, was that military reliefs from an Egyptian temple do not necessarily offer historical information but communicate the politico-religious claims of the pharaoh. At the command of the God Amun-Re the pharaoh beat the enemy into retreat, guaranteeing continuity of order (*Ma'at*, see 1.1). Scholars have also learned that the decline of Late Bronze Age urban culture occurred for a number of reasons and over a longer period of time.[54]

Two Egyptian texts appear to offer more reliable historical information, though. The eleventh to tenth-century "Onomasticon of Amenemope" includes, among a list of place and group names from Southern Palestine, the cities of Ashkelon, Ashdod, and Gaza, as well as three groups of Sea Peoples, *Šardana* (Sardinians), *Ṯkr/Tjekker* (Sikil?) and the *Prst/Palaštu* (Philistines).[55] These references are expanded upon in the "Story of Wenamun," which recounts the travels of a temple official, Wenamun, across Syria-Palestine, with stops in Dor and Byblos (*COS* 1.41). According to the text, the *Ṯkr/Tjekker* lived in Dor and controlled part of the economic region of the Palestinian coast.[56] Both sources show that the Sea Peoples settled in the Southern Levant along the coastal strip—whether on the orders of Ramesses III or by their own initiative is not clear—and played an important role in the Early Iron Age economy.[57]

This is what we find in the archaeological record as well, which shows a move from Egyptian imports to a two-color (bichrome) pottery. These resemble Mycenean ceramics (Mycenean IIIC 1b) and which, because of their local production, are referred to as "submycenean" or, less correctly, "Philistine" pottery.[58] Early Philistine culture is marked by a diversity of cultural influences that

52. For the Aegean migration, see Yasur-Landau, *Philistines and Aegean Migration*, 335–45.

53. See Ben-Dor Evian, "Battle between Ramesses III and the 'Sea Peoples,'" 151–68, and Redford, *Medinet Habu Records*.

54. See Dever, *Beyond the Texts*, 107–12.

55. See Gardiner, *Ancient Egyptian Onomastica* 3:190*–205*, and Alt, "Syrien und Palästia," 231–45.

56. On both, see Schipper, *Die Erzählung des Wenamun*, 140–41, and Gilboa, "Dor and Egypt," 247–74.

57. See Gilboa et al., "Dor, the Carmel Coast," 85–109.

58. On this, see Dothan and Ben-Shlomo, "Mycenaean IIIC:1 Pottery," 29–35.

includes Anatolian, Mycenean, and Cypriot elements.[59] Whatever their origins, the rise of urban culture on the southern coastal plain in the Early Iron Age is also connected with the Philistines.[60] With Gaza they controlled a former Egyptian center, alongside which they had the cities of Ekron, Ashdod, and Gath/ *Tell eṣ-Ṣafi*, the latter the most significant city in Southern Palestine, at 45–50 hectares (map 1).[61]

Near Gath was a city whose identity has recently been hotly debated: *Khirbet Qeiyafa*. The archaeologist of the site wanted to attribute the city, which was only settled a short time (ca. 1025–975),[62] to King David, as the biblical *Shaarayim* (literally, "two gates"; see Josh 15:36; 1 Chr 4:31).[63] The archaeological evidence does show that *Khirbet Qeiyafa* was a fortified city, with a casemate wall and two gates. Archaeologists also found two ostraca, one of which, in proto-Canaanite script, includes the name Ishbaal (see 1 Chr 8:33; 9:39). A variety of cultic objects such as massebahs, figurine fragments, cult stands, and two model shrines were also found.

The material culture of the site shows clear differences from both the Philistine coastal plain settlements and neighboring Gath/*Tell eṣ-Ṣafi*, while exhibiting similarities with Early Iron Age Judean sites, which might point to a connection to the Kingdom of Judah.[64] At the same time, it is possible that, as a result of Philistine settlement on the coastal plain, the previous inhabitants of the shoreline moved inland and settled in *Khirbet Qeiyafa* before disappearing entirely into the new culture of the Early Iron Age.[65] One argument for this is the fact that the city was abandoned after one generation. This militates against drawing conclusions from *Khirbet Qeiyafa* about the size and significance of the Davidic monarchy.[66] Instead, the archaeological evidence seems to point to various peoples and groups living side-by-side.

The same situation is found in the north of the Southern Levant: groups of Sea Peoples living alongside local inhabitants who had remained from the Late Bronze Age city-state period. At the Sea of Galilee this can be seen in the material culture from the ancient city of Kinneret/*Tell el-ʿOrēme* where, in the middle of the eleventh century, a city of around six hectares existed that included a

59. For a recent perspective on the Philistines, see Maeir et al., "Philistine Names," 321–40.
60. In addition to ibid., see Middleton, "Telling Stories," 45–65.
61. See Maeir, "Philistine Gath," 139–42.
62. Finkelstein and Fantalkin, "Khirbeit Qeiyafa," 38–62, have dated it to between 1050 and 915 BCE.
63. For the following, see Schroer and Münger, *Khirbet Qeiyafa*, and in particular the contributions of Yosef Garfinkel and Aren M. Maeir.
64. This is the conclusion of Maeir, "Khirbet Qeiyafa," 67–68. For a critical evaluation, see Niemann, "Comments and Questions," 245–62.
65. See Naʾaman, "Khirbet Qeiyafa," 516–17.
66. Though this is argued by Garfinkel, "Khirbet Qeiyafa." See note 63 above.

palace complex, cultic institutions, fortifications, and economic facilities, including a mill, a bakery, and a site for producing olive oil. The pottery shows contact with the Phoenicians, the Transjordan, and the Syrian region.[67] Similar evidence was found in Tel Hadar (Stratum IV) at the northeastern bank of the sea, leading to the conclusion that Kinneret V and Tel Hadar IV formed a single sociopolitical unit.[68] The importance of control over trade routes to Damascus and the sourthern orientation of the Arameans led, in the tenth century, to contact between Aram-Damascus and the cities at the Sea of Galilee. This latter might be related to the Kingdom of Geshur attested to in the Bible (2 Sam 3:3; 13:37; 15:8).[69]

Add to this the Phoenician cities on the coast, as found in the Story of Wenamun and the archaeological record (Dor),[70] and there is evidence of reurbanization in the period beginning in the south, along the coastal plain, and northward to the Sea of Galilee. Such a development could not have been without significance for the central Palestinian hill country. If one were looking for an explanation as to why a kingdom developed under Saul, it might be this: it was a response to the cultural development that occurred in the eleventh to tenth century, when foreign trade injected new life into urban centers on the coastal plains and at the same time introduced new political calculi with the Arameans in the north and the Philistines in the south. This might have lead the people in smaller settlements in the central Palestinian highlands to form regional coalitions, arrange marriages outside their villages (exogamy) to build alliances, and set up a leadership ("chiefdom") among these communities.[71] Such a development might have been encouraged by the fact that, after its destruction in the Late Bronze Age (thirteenth to twelfth century) the old center of the Late Bronze Age city-state Shechem, *Tell Balaṭah*, was weak (Stratum XII/XI),[72] while the urban centers of the coast evidently had not expanded into the hill country. This accords again with the Hebrew Bible texts that place Saul's rule south of Shechem, in the region of the tribe of Benjamin (see 1 Sam 9:1–2).[73]

In the eleventh and tenth centuries, therefore, "Israel" is still to be situated primarily in the highlands, on what had previously been the Late Bronze age city-states of Shechem and Jerusalem, above all the former. Only about twenty

---

67. See the overview in Sergi and Kleiman, "Kingdom of Geshur," 3.

68. For more details, see Münger, "Early Iron Age Kinneret," 149–82.

69. Sergi and Kleiman, "Kingdom of Geshur," 7.

70. See above note 57 and below, ch. 3, note 23.

71. On this, see Yoffe, *Myths of the Archaic State*, 22–31, and for an archeological perspective, see Lehmann, "Reconstructing the Social Landscape," 141–75.

72. For a revised chronology of Shechem, see Finkelstein, "Shechem in the Late Bronze and Iron I," 349–56.

73. For a detailed discussion of the archaeological and biblical evidence, see Sergi, "Rethinking Israel," 371–88.

of the settlements that might have been ascribed to "Israel" lay south of Jerusalem, while the others—more than one hundred—were to its north (map 3). What, then, does all of this imply for the Davidic monarchy, which, in the Hebrew Bible, was concentrated in the south?

2.5 The Davidic Monarchy and Jerusalem (Tenth Cent.)

Notwithstanding the difficulties in historically reconstructing the kingdom of David, it is nearly certain that there was a real "King David." An Aramaic inscription from biblical Dan (*Tell el-Qadi*) mentions that the Aramean king Hazael (ca. 843–803) defeated a king from Israel and a ruler from *bytdwd* (*COS* 2.39). Even if the fragment does not mention who this king is (see below, 3.4), the meaning of *bytdwd*, "House of David" (*Beth David*) is clear.[74] The reference to a "House of David" should be understood analogously to "the House of Omri" on the Black Obelisk of Shalmaneser III of 841 (*COS* 2.113F). The particular king referred to is indicated as member of a dynasty that leads back to the founder of the dynasty: Omri in one case, David in the other (see below, 3.3).

However much reliable historical information is to be found in the biblical texts on "King David," their historical focus is narrow.[75] This is as true for the geographical information as it is for the narrative of the conquest of Jerusalem. While Philistine Gath, mentioned in 1 Sam 17; 21:27; 2 Sam 15, is attested to in the tenth century, Hebron (at *Ḡebel er-Rumēde*)—where 2 Sam 2:1–4 states David was anointed king (see also 2 Sam 2:11; 5:5; 1 Kings 2:11)—had no notable settlement in Iron Age I or early Iron Age IIA.[76]

When searching for any historical kernel in the King David tradition, the places to look would be in the conflict with the Philistines and in the historical focus on Jerusalem. Since Shechem now lay in ruins, Jerusalem became central as the only remaining Late Bronze Age city in the hill country.[77]

Jerusalem had a long history before Israel, having been settled since the Chalcolithic period (ca. 4500).[78] By Middle Bronze Age II (from ca. 1700) at the latest, Jerusalem had been fortified with a city wall and controlled a spring

---

74. This is not the case for the reading of *bt[. D]wd* suggested by André Lemaire on the Mesha Stela. On this, see Na'aman, "King Mesha," 83–92, and, more broadly, Weippert, *Historisches Textbuch*, 248.

75. See Pioske, "Memory and Its Materiality," 78–95.

76. On this, see Chadwick, "Discovering Hebron," 24–33, 70–71.

77. For the discussion of the occupational gap between Shechem Strata XI and X, see Finkelstein, "Shechem in the Late Bronze," 353, with an overview on the dating of Drew-McCormick (1150/1125–975) and Finkelstein himself (late tenth cent.).

78. For the following, see Bieberstein, *Brief History of Jerusalem*, 20–22, 24–36.

protected by stone fortifications.[79] Egyptian sources from the nineteenth to eighteenth century (the so-called Execration Texts) refer to Jerusalem (*COS* 1.32),[80] while the Amarna letters from the fourteenth century mention a city king called *Abdi-Ḫepa* (EA 286+289; *COS* 3.92A+3.92B).

It is unclear how Jerusalem came under Israelite control. A military conquest by David (2 Sam 5:6–8) seems improbable. Some archaeologists suspect Jerusalem of the tenth century to have been a small, sleepy place, while others imagine it to have been a great administrative center. The difference in these interpretations comes from divergent analyses of the archaeological evidence, which turns on two questions: (1) the date of the massive so-called "Stepped Stone Structure" and its various architectural components on the southeast hill, and (2) the area where tenth century Jerusalem began: whether at the so-called city of David (see 2 Sam 5:7, 9) or on the Temple Mount (see map 4). Since excavation up to the present in what is referred to as the "Givati Parking Lot" has turned up hardly any Late Bronze Age pottery on the southeastern hill, some archaeologists take this to mean that the Late Bronze Age and Early Iron Age city is not to be found on the site of the Middle Bronze Age fortress, but rather on the Temple Mount.[81] Yet since no excavations have actually occurred on the Temple Mount, this thesis cannot be confirmed or rejected. It should be noted, however, that a settlement on the Temple Mount would not have had any connection to a water supply from the Gihon Spring. For the time being, therefore, the classical theory is preferable: tenth-century Jerusalem is to be connected with the southeast hill (the city of David) and the settlement there, either on the hill, or on its slope.[82] At some point in its subsequent development the massive "Stepped Stone Structure" was built. The presumed core of the structure, the "stone terraces" (Area G of the Shiloh excavation), date to the pre-Davidic period and evolved over a long span of time.[83] It most likely reached its present form in the ninth century, consisting of Early Iron Age terraces surrounded by a mantle wall built of semi-worked stones (see below, 3.4).[84]

Given that in the eleventh century Jerusalem had already been the seat of a local elite that controlled small nearby settlements (*Har-Nōf, Tell el-Fūl, Ḫirbet*

---

79. New data from excavations near the Gihon Spring indicate that the monumental towers, often dated in the Middle Bronze Age, were renovated (or even built?) in the ninth or probably early eight centuries; see Uziel and Szanton, "New Evidence," 429–39, and ch. 3.4 below.

80. See Rainey, "World of Sinuhe," 395–408.

81. See Finkelstein et al., "Mound on the Mount," 2–24.

82. On this, see the discussion in Frevel, *Geschichte Israels*, 114–16, and Bieberstein, *Brief History of Jerusalem*, 58.

83. On this, see the overview in Bieberstein, *Brief History of Jerusalem*, 42–46, and Mazar, "Jerusalem in the 10th Century," 255–72.

84. See the helpful overview in Sergi, "Emergence of Judah," 3–5.

Bīr el-Ḥammām),[85] it may be concluded that in the tenth century Jerusalem was still a local seat of power of around one hectare, now with a maximum of two thousand inhabitants.[86] It is likely that the area controlled by David did not extend beyond the borders of the Late Bronze Age city-state of Jerusalem but was simply more densely settled (see map 3).[87] In the Amarna letters the king of the city of Jerusalem *Abdi-Ḫepa* writes that he could control his dominion with fifty soldiers (EA 289, *COS* 3,92B). This gives a sense of size and balance of power in his period, and it was probably much the same under David.

2.6 The Reign of Solomon and the Ancient Near East (Tenth Cent.)

Like David, Solomon is said to have reigned for forty years (1 Kgs 11:42; cf. 2:11). In other words: the biblical scribes did not know the actual length of their reigns. While scholarship of the 1960s took it for granted that the monumental structures in Megiddo, Hazor, and Gezer were part of a "Solomonic empire" (six-chamber gates), there is now no longer any doubt that Solomon's kingdom did not extend beyond the borders of David's territory (see map 3).[88]

Contemporaneous with the Solomonic period was the rise of other new rulers in Mesopotamia and Egypt. After the collapse of the Middle Assyrian Kingdom in the eleventh century, Asshur-dan II (934–912) was beginning to build the Neo-Assyrian Kingdom, which would later expand into the Southern Levant under Shalmaneser III, beginning in the ninth century.[89] In Egypt, meanwhile, consolidation began somewhat earlier: after the collapse of Ramesside rule in 1077 Shoshenq I (943–923) finally succeeded in reunifying the land. The Twenty-second Dynasty he founded proceeded from the twenty-first dynasty, which had been established in 1077 by Libyan rulers. At that time there were two religio-political centers, Tanis in the north and Thebes in the south, that kept Egypt in internal political tension. This perhaps explains why there is no record of an active foreign policy from the pharaohs in the eleventh and tenth centuries.[90]

As concerns Solomon's period, the question is whether this situation was ongoing during the reign of Siamun (978–959), the penultimate pharaoh of

---

85. Ibid., 7–8 with fig. 3.
86. See Geva, "Jerusalem's Population," 138, with an overview on the various positions.
87. For the Late Bronze period Finkelstein estimates the amount of territory controlled by Jerusalem to have been 2400 sq. meters but only eight settlements. See the overview by Niemann, "Juda und Jerusalem," 150–51.
88. See Ofer, "'All the Hill Country,'" 121.
89. See Miller and Hayes, *History of Ancient Israel and Judah*, 234–38.
90. See Schipper, *Israel and Egypt*, ch. 3.1.1.

the Twenty-first Dynasty. Some scholars take there to have been direct contact between Solomon and Siamun. According to 1 Kings Solomon married the "daughter of a pharaoh" (1 Kgs 3:1; 7:8; 9:24; 11:1) and was given the city of Gezer by the Egyptian king (1 Kgs 9:16) as a wedding gift.[91] The texts do not offer any precise information, however, as they mention neither the name of the pharaoh nor that of the daughter.[92] References to the pharaoh's daughter are given in the context of other passages in the Solomon story in 1 Kgs 3–11 intended to portray Solomon as a king of a stature equal to other ancient Near Eastern rulers. This includes references to international trade on the Mediterranean as far as Spanish Tartessos, from the Red Sea to the land of Ophir and, by land, with horses and carriages, between the area of earlier Hittite rule and Egypt.[93] While analysis of the relevant passages of 1 Kgs 9–10 shows that the image of Solomon as a powerful king with extensive international contacts does presuppose historical relations consistent with the Assyrian period (seventh cent.),[94] it is unclear to what extent Solomon's trade relationships and his contact with the Egyptians— his marriage to the pharaoh's daughter in particular—has any historical basis. As explained above (in 2.4) international trade began again in the early Iron Age, and "long-distance trade" was possible even before the western expansion of the Neo-Assyrian kings in the ninth to eighth century.[95] The best example of this is the copper trade, for which we have evidence that older copper mines from Feinan in the Arabah (present-day Jordan) and Timna to its south were in production already in the eleventh century (map 1). The copper was transported by land to the Phoenician coastal cities, where it then traveled as far as Greece. Metallurgic studies of Greek tripods from 950 to 750 BCE have shown that the copper they used did not come from Cyprus, but from Feinan. Similarly, in the Phoenician city of Sidon, though a great deal of Cyprian pottery was found, the copper found there had been imported from mines in the Sinai. If it is true that the Sinai copper mines were run by seminomadic tribal groups in contact with comparable groups in the Negev (e.g., in Ḥirbet el-Mšāš/Tel Masos),[96] it is possible to construct a trade route from the Arabah, along the trade roads of the Negev, to the Philistine and Phoenician coastal cities, and from there across the Mediterranean to the Aegean world. According to archaeological findings, however, the kingdom of Solomon played no part in this trade network, and international trade was conducted beyond the borders of the Solomonic realm.

---

91. See, for example, Lemaire, "Solomon et la fille," 699–710, and Kitchen, *Third Intermediate Period*, 279–83.

92. See Schipper, *Israel and Egypt*, ch. 3.3.1.

93. On the literary character of 1 Kgs 3–11, see Na'aman, "Sources and Composition," 57–80.

94. Schipper, *Israel and Egypt*, chs. 3.2.4; 3.3.1, and Gertz, "Konstruierte Erinnerung," 3–29.

95. On this, Kiderlen et al., "Tripod Cauldrons," 303–13.

96. See Martin and Finkelstein, "Iron IIA Pottery," 38–39.

But what contact existed with Egypt at this time? Previous scholarship took for granted a connection between Solomon and Siamun, the penultimate pharaoh of the Twenty-first Dynasty, as objects had been found in the Southern Levant inscribed with the name Siamun—including a terracotta bifacial rectangular plate from Gezer, the city given to Solomon by his father-in-law as a wedding present at Solomon's marriage to his daughter, according to 1 Kgs 9:16.[97] More careful study of the material, however, shows that only one of the four pieces can reliably be connected with Siamun. This piece, however, a scarab from *Tell el-Farʿah* [South] that contains Siamun's Horus name, comes from an undated find.[98] The only dated piece, a scarab from Dor, has an inscription that cannot be read as Siamun.[99] As such, there is no way to prove official contact between Siamun and Solomon from this piece. Rather, the Egyptian objects in Southern Palestine are to be explained by trade contacts which included the pharaohs from the end of the Twenty-first Dynasty.[100] The founder of the Twenty-second Dynasty, Shoshenq I, extended these connections, and in his era mining production in the Wadi Feinan copper mines intensified as a result of advances in mining technology. As such, it is not surprising to find a scarab with the name Shoshenq I in the Feinan area.[101]

Contact between Egypt and the Southern Levant, especially the Philistine region, is also attested to by Egyptian pottery and a group of seal amulets. Referred to as "post-Ramesside mass-produced scarabs" based on their iconography and wide distribution, this group is found in Egypt, the Southern Levant, and as far as Cyprus.[102] The iconography of the often very coarsely worked seals is both Egyptian and Philistine: there are classical Egyptian motifs such as the divine name Amon or the falcon-headed Horus, alongside motifs such as Baal, Reshef, the lord of animals, as well as geometric patterns.[103] The former might be connected with production in the Temple of Tanis, while the latter may have been produced outside Egypt, perhaps in the area of the former Temple of Gaza.[104]

The broad distribution of seal amulets is to be understood in the context of the international trade routes from the period.[105] A Late Bronze Age shipwreck

---

97. The object from Gezer was treated as early as Macalister, "Sixteenth Quarterly Report," 20, fig. 3.

98. See the recent overview by Münger, "References to the Pharaoh," 41.

99. See Keel, *Corpus der Stempelsiegelamulette*, 472 (21), and for a discussion of the material Schipper, *Israel and Egypt*, ch. 3.1.2.

100. See Ben-Dor Evian, "Egypt and the Levant," 112–13.

101. See the scarab of Sheshonq I found in the Fenan area; Münger and Levy, "Iron Age Egyptian Amulet Assemblage," 748–49 (catalog no. 6, fig. 11.6) and Frevel, *Geschichte Israels*, 144–45.

102. See Münger, "References to the Pharaoh," 42–44.

103. On this, see the overview in Münger, "Stamp-Seal Amulets," 384–93.

104. See Ben-Tor, "Scarab of the Mass-Production Groups," 319–22.

105. See Ben-Dor Evian, "Egypt and the Levant," 112–13.

from Uluburun/Kaş on the southwest coast of contemporary Turkey shows that small objects such as scarabs or amulets were included in long-distance trade. Alongside three hundred bars of copper, thirty tin, and thirty glass found in the fourteenth-century shipwreck, luxury goods were also discovered, including a gold scarab of Nefertiti.[106] As such, the seal amulets—with or without the names of pharaohs—more likely point to trade, not to political and cultural exchange, nor, as in the case of the "post-Ramesside mass-produced scarabs," to any special relationship between Egypt and Israel. In sum, even though there was an international trade network with Egypt, the Mediterranean, and the Phoenician and Philistine cities, the evidence so far does not indicate that Jerusalem and Solomon's kingdom played any part in it.

2.7 The Palestine Campaign of Shoshenq I (926/925) and Solomon's Architectural Politics

The consolidation of ancient Near Eastern kingdoms in the tenth century led to changes in Egypt as well. With the beginning of the Twenty-second Dynasty, an active foreign policy became possible for the first time since the end of Ramesside rule. Having unified the land internally,[107] Pharaoh Shoshenq I (943–923) moved into the Southern Levant near the end of his reign.[108] Some scholars have suggested that Shoshenq I hoped to restore Ramesside power in the region.[109] The path of the pharaonic army, however, shows him instead to have been concerned with trade routes. Beyond those that ran through the Negev, he was also interested in the coastal trade route (Via Maris). In Megiddo, meanwhile, archaeologists discovered a large stone fragment (36 × 33 × 51 cm) with the royal cartouche and the name Shoshenq I. Whether or not the fragment was part of a royal stela or a building, it suggests that Shoshenq I had made Megiddo the center of political power, and not the older Egyptian garrison town of Beth Shean.[110] If so, it would have been a result of the significance of the coastal plain in the tenth century as the meeting place of Philistine land trade and Phoenician sea trade.

The main information about Shoshenq I's campaign comes from a relief on the Bubastide portal of the Temple of Karnak, which contains what is referred

---

106. See Pulak, "Uluburun Shipwreck," 188–224, and Zangani, "Amarna and Uluburun," 230–44.

107. For the following, see Jansen-Winkeln, "Zur historischen Authentizität," 165–76, and Schipper, *Israel and Egypt*, ch. 4.1.2.

108. On the problem of dating the campaign, see Gaß, "Schoschenq und Jerusalem," 117–22.

109. See, for example, Knauf and Guillaume, *History of Biblical Israel*, 80–82.

110. For a discussion of the object, see Schipper, *Israel and Egypt*, ch. 4.1.2, and most recently Ben-Dor Evian, "Egypt and the Levant."

to as the Palestine list (*COS* 4.3). The order of names on the list suggests that smaller military units moved inland from Megiddo in 926/925 and should not be understood as referring to a variety of military undertakings from different times as some scholars belief.[111] It is also notable that important places in the history of the Northern Kingdom of Israel are mentioned in this list: Adamah (No. 56), Penuel (No. 53), Succoth (No. 55), Mahanaim (No. 22) and Tirzah (No. 59). Jerusalem is not mentioned, though, and the pharaonic army seems to have had little interest in the Judean hill country.[112] This suggests that, shortly after the death of Solomon—1 Kgs 14:25 dates the campaign to the fifth year of the reign of Solomon's successor Rehoboam—the Judean monarchy was only a regional power, lacking any notable influence and not controlling any areas that would have drawn the attention of the Egyptian pharaoh.

What can be said about Solomon if he had neither significant trade partners nor direct contact with Egypt? The biblical text connects Solomon with the construction of the temple in Jerusalem, a three-part, long room temple built in the Syrian style, possibly on top of a building from an earlier period. The dimensions given in 1 Kgs 6–7 for the temple are obviously exaggerated: were one to take them seriously, it would have been the largest temple in the Levant, significantly larger than the Iron Age temples in Atarot, Pella/*Ṭabaqāt Faḥil*, *Tell ʿĀfis* and *Tell Taʿyīnāt*.[113] Such an enormous structure would have far exceeded the economic capacity of the Jerusalem city-state under Solomon. Moreover, its nearest parallels, the temples of *Tell Taʿyīnāt* and *ʿĒn Dārā*, were built in the late ninth and early eighth centuries, respectively. This suggests that caution is in order when researching the Solomonic temple and the details of its construction, as it is quite possible that the description of the temple found in 1 Kgs 6–7 is from a later period, not from the tenth century.

If one were to look for historically plausible information on the construction of a temple under Solomon, 1 Kgs 5:15–26 and 9:10–14 offer some hints. Both texts, which reached their final forms in the late monarchic period,[114] mention that Solomon purchased cedar wood from Hiram, king of the city of Tyre, which he paid for with food (wheat and oil). This is consistent with the Egyptian Story of Wenamun, which mentions that the cedar trade was controlled by the

---

111. On this, see the overview of the various interpretative approaches in Gaß, "Schoschenq and Jerusalem," 131–37. For a contrary position, see ibid., 147–49.

112. Ibid., 146, however, following 1 Kgs 14:25–26, believes the military attacked Jerusalem as well in 929 or 927 BCE.

113. See Kamlah, "Temples of the Levant," 507–34.

114. These texts should be ascribed to the presumably pre-Deuteronomistic "Book of the Acts" of Solomon, which based simply its name is not to be identified with the "annals" of the kings of Israel and Judah. On this, see Naʾaman, "Sources and Composition," 57–58.

Phoenicians, and that wood for a temple was purchased from them (*COS* 1.41).[115] The information in 1 Kgs 5 and 9 may well contain a kernel of historical fact, but it is highly doubtful, for example, that Solomon gave Hiram twenty cities in the Galilee (1 Kgs 9:11–13), as there is no evidence that Solomon ruled the Galilean territory at all.[116]

The Solomonic period is thus exemplary of the history of ancient Israel as a whole: the biblical version and the history that can be reconstructed from extrabiblical sources diverge significantly. In the historically supported picture, Solomon was the king of a city which, if one moved outward from the hill fortress of Jerusalem, included a region that did not extend beyond the borders of the Late Bronze Age city-state of Jerusalem (map 3). Construction of the temple lying to the west of the city of David (the southeast hill) required contact with Phoenicians, since the wood and other materials referred to in the account of the construction of the temple in 1 Kgs 6–7 could only have been acquired through trade.

Perhaps contact with the Phoenicians and the construction of a small temple formed the historical core of what was later to become the portrait of Solomon. Either way, after *Abdi-Ḫepa*, from the Amarna letters, Solomon was the first king of Jerusalem to reestablish contact with the wider international world (e.g., with the Phoenicians) and, with the construction of the temple, to found a sanctuary whose fate would play a central role in the history of ancient Israel.

2.8 Summary

Every reconstruction of the early history of Israel involves significant difficulties. From the stela of Merneptah (1208) to the Palestinian campaign of Shoshenq I (926/925), "Israel" is ephemeral. It refers to a group of people living in the lowlands (perhaps in the outskirts of a larger Egyptian city). With the collapse of the Late Bronze Age urban culture, it settled in the highlands, freeing itself of Egyptian control. Over time it built alliances between smaller settlements, leading ultimately to a (tribal) kingdom under Saul. David, according to the biblical text, was active in the south, and he set his sights on the only remaining Late Bronze Age city in the hill country: Jerusalem. Already in the Late Bronze Age Jerusalem was the bureaucratic center of a large region, though one with no broader political significance (map 3).

---

115. See Schipper, *Die Erzählung des Wenamun*, 209–11. See also Lipiński, "Hiram of Tyre," 251–72.

116. This is already the view of Donner, *Geschichte des Volkes Israels* 1:246.

While David is credited for making Jerusalem into an Israelite city, it was Solomon who turned the former fortress into a religious center. In order to construct what at that time was only a very small temple, trade contacts with the Phoenicians were needed, as they controlled the vital cedar wood. This does not mean Solomon had the significant trading connections suggested by the biblical story, however. Rather, the available archaeological evidence suggests that the trade routes were controlled by the Phoenicians (by sea) and the Philistines (by land), the latter having contacts with the Egyptians and as far as the mining areas of the Arabah. The kingdom of Solomon was a long way away from these routes and lived in the shadows of the great powers of the time.

CHAPTER 3

Israel and Judah from 926/925 to the Conquest of Samaria in 722/720 BCE

According to the biblical depiction of Israel's history, after David and Solomon a "schism" occurred that led to the "divided monarchy."[1] The single kingdom split into two kingdoms, Israel and Judah. Historically, such a division is highly improbable, since neither David and Solomon controlled the North to begin with. Instead, the situation at the end of the tenth century was most likely the same as it had been at the beginning. There were two territorial units: in the north, the area of the Late Bronze Age city-state of Shechem, whose capital city Shechem/ *Tell Balaṭah* was occupied in the late tenth century, in the south, the territory of the Late Bronze Age city-state of Jerusalem (map 3). As for development in the north, all that can be said with any certainty is that it underwent a reurbanization in the tenth century, paving the way for the Omride Kingdom in the ninth century. In Shechem, this can be seen in a small settlement from Iron Age IIA (ninth cent.), which was founded several decades after the destruction of the city and which was then replaced a short while later by a well-planned city.[2] The political-economic center of the Samarian hills, however, shifted to the city of Samaria, where a lavish palace was built on what had previously been an agricultural estate.[3]

The Hebrew Bible gives no account of this development in the North. The biblical historiography was interested above all in Jerusalem and Judah, to such an extent that the book of Chronicles, which dates from the fourth to third century does not mention the Northern Kingdom at all.[4] Historically speaking, however, the case was exactly the opposite: beginning in the ninth century a powerful monarchy emerged in the Northern Kingdom of Israel, while the Southern Kingdom of Judah began to blossom when the Northern Kingdom had ceased to exist, after 722/720.

---

1. See Bright, *History of Israel*, 230–32, and Noth, *History of Israel*, 224–26.

2. For an overview, see Bornstein, "Shechem," 348–56, and for a detailed analysis, Finkelstein, "Shechem in the Late Bronze," 351–54.

3. For the stratigraphy and archaeology of Samaria, see the overview in Sergi and Gadot, "Omride Palatial Architecture," 105–6.

4. See Schmid, *Old Testament*, 196.

3.1 The Ancient Near East and the Western Expansion of the Neo-Assyrians

The history of the Northern Kingdom of Israel can be extrapolated from wider political events of the ancient Near East. While the history of Late Bronze Age Southern Levant was dominated by Egypt, the era of the kingdoms of Israel and Judah was shaped by the Neo-Assyrians. As a result of Neo-Assyrian western expansion, city-states and local kingdoms of the Southern Levant that had previously been independent now had to form political coalitions with one another. From the ninth century until the middle of the seventh century, Neo-Assyrian kings were confronted with anti-Assyrian alliances whose members changed frequently. These alliances never managed to prevent the Assyrians advance, however. Only when the Neo-Assyrians moved against Egypt in the seventh century—a situation the Neo-Babylonians exploited in order to advance on the Assyrian heartland—did the Neo-Assyrian ruler withdraw from the Southern Levant (see below, 4.4).

The expansion by the Neo-Assyrian kings began with Tiglath-pileser I (1117–1077). His goal was to take up the legacy of the Hittites, and he advanced as far as the Mediterranean, receiving tribute payments from the coastal cities of Sidon, Byblos, and Arwad (map 1). This expansion was short-lived, however, and many of the subsequent Neo-Assyrian rulers were weak. It was not until the turn of the tenth to ninth century, under Adad-nirari II (912–891) that western expansion began anew.[5] Adad-nirari II undertook campaigns against the Babylonians and the Arameans and placed the conquered territories under state control. His successors built on his policies, the most significant of which being the administrative system. Tukulti-ninurta II (891–884) and Assurnasirpal (884–859) later conquered large parts of northern Syria and Cilicia.[6] Their successor, Shalmaneser III (859–824) extended the empire further to the east and south and, between 853 and 838, undertook six campaigns to southern Syria, which are extensively recounted in Neo-Assyrian royal inscriptions (*COS* 2.113).[7] A period of Assyrian weakness followed, beginning in the second half of the ninth century, that was promptly exploited by Aramean city-states, especially Damascus. Neo-Assyrian expansion reached its pinnacle under Tiglath-pileser III (745–727), who took over nearly the whole of Asia Minor and organized it through a strict system of vassalage grounded in a political theology of the universal claims of the national God Assur. Vassals were required to pay

---

5. See Frahm, "Neo-Assyrian Period," 165–67, and Lamprichs, *Westexpansion des neuassyrischen Reiches,* 61–80.

6. See Mayer, *Politik und Kriegskunst,* 267–74.

7. For details, see Elat, "Campaigns of Shalmaneser III," 25–35.

tribute and, should they fail to fulfill their duties or rebel against the hegemon, they would be punished with deportations, replacement of rulers, or having their region turned into an Assyrian province.[8]

This uncompromising policy was connected to an administrative system with clear economic goals. Combined, they served as a catalyst for cultural development in these areas, as the Neo-Assyrians encouraged the development of cities in the Southern Levant and a further internationalization of the trade routes. At the high point of Neo-Assyrian expansion in the eighth century, for example, the Phoenicians widened their trade connections on the Mediterranean as far as Southern Spain.[9] At the same time, wholesale merchants appointed by the Neo-Assyrians (*tamkarru*) served as cross-regional trading agents in the Northern and Southern Levant. A brief mention in the Solomon story of 1 Kgs 10:28–29 seems to weave this into the narrative, referring to wholesale merchants attached to Solomon who traded between Egypt, the Southern Levant, and Northern Syria. As with the references to Solomon's international trade on the Mediterranean and the Red Sea in 1 Kgs 9:26–28 and 10:11–12, 21–22, these stories reflect conditions from the Assyrian period introduced backward in time by later authors into the Solomonic history (map 1).[10]

Put succinctly, the cultural development of Israel in the North—and, almost thirty years later, of Judah in the South—can be understood in relation to the connections to the outside world brought about by international trade. This occurred with the Omrides, who established ties with the Phoenicians (perhaps through marriage; see 1 Kgs 16:31), and with the subsequent kings of Israel and Judah—though, in contrast to the Omrides, the latter were not independent, but vassals of the Neo-Assyrians (see below).

Egypt played hardly any role in this. After Shoshenq I, Egyptian pharaohs had to deal with internal instability: under Osorkon II (874–835/830) parallel and opposing local rulers kept Egypt in tension until Cushite rulers regained power in the last quarter of the eighth century The second part of the Twenty-second Dynasty (874–716/713) was a period of weakness in which Egypt broke into rival regional power centers.[11] While Egypt was able to preserve official trade connections with the Phoenicians at the beginning of this period (as attested to in the statues of Osorkon I, Shoshenq II, and Osorkon II in Byblos, map 1)[12]—

8. See Donner, *Geschichte des Volkes Israel* 2:328.
9. See Sagona, "Phoenicians in Spain," 240–66, and "Phoenician Settlement," 351–72.
10. See Schipper, *Israel and Egypt*, ch. 3.2.4.
11. Under Osorkon II a dynasty with rival kings was founded in Thebes, which is counted as the Twenty-Third Dynasty and which existed from 838/833 until near the end of the Twenty-Second or Twenty-Third Dynasty (732/727); Kitchen, *Third Intermediate Period*, 313.
12. On this, see Schipper, *Die Erzählung des Wenamun*, 185–86; Lemaire, "Levantine Literacy," 12–14; Ritner, *Libyan Anarchy*, 219–20, 233–34, 288.

as well, presumably, as the overland trade with the Philistine region[13]—Egypt ultimately turned inward. After Shoshenq I's campaign in 926/925 there were no direct Egyptian incursions into the Southern Levant for nearly 200 years.[14]

This is not to say that Shoshenq I's campaign was without consequences, however. Locally produced scarabs with the name Shoshenq or double-cartouches attest to the effect of this campaign on the material culture of Israel/ Palestine, and can be read alongside the biblical evidence.[15] From the note in 1 Kgs 14:25–27 (which presumably comes from a later era), to a reference in the narratives of Jeroboam from Israel (1 Kgs 11:40), to the books of Chronicles from the fourth to third century (2 Chr 12:2, 5, 7, 9), the name Shoshenq is mentioned six times the biblical history, more than any other Egyptian pharaoh. Given both its place in the material culture and in the Hebrew Bible, Shoshenq I's campaign seems not to have been as an unimportant episode as is often suggested.[16]

The third factor that must be taken into account in the history of Israel and Judah from the period of Shoshenq I's campaign (926/925) to the conquest of Samaria in 722/720 is the place of the Arameans. In the tenth and ninth centuries local Aramean kingdoms and small states emerged, from the Euphrates to Southern Syria, the most important of which for ancient Israelite history was Aram-Damascus.[17] In contrast with the Phoenician cities on the north and central coasts and the Philistine associations of cities in the south, neither of which were interested in expansion, the Arameans attempted to exploit the ever-changing political constellations for their own expansionist purposes. In the ninth century an increasingly powerful Aram-Damascus subjugated the small kingdoms of Geshur on the Sea of Galilee, as well as Beth Rehob and Abel-bet-maachah, among others.[18] This is significant for the history of Israel insofar as it rules out the possibility that Jeroboam I controlled the area Bethel to Dan in the tenth and ninth centuries, as asserted in the Bible. Biblical Dan/*Tell el-Qāḍī*—which according to 1 Kgs 12:29 was the spot of a national sanctuary (alongside Bethel)—only became Israelite in the eighth century (see below, 3.5), after a period of Aramean control (map 1).[19]

---

13. See Ben-Dor Evian, "Egypt and the Levant," 94–119.

14. On this, see Schipper, *Israel and Egypt*, chs. 4.1.3–4.1.5.

15. See Keel, *Orte und Landschaften* 4/1:343–44, including. figs. 240–42, and on the material, Münger, "References to the Pharaoh," 46–47.

16. Ernst A. Knauf's thesis (most recently Knauf and Guillaume, *History of Biblical Israel*, 82) that Egypt under Sheshonq I obtained supremacy in Palestine that the Egyptians remained until 850, still requires more examination. See Frevel, *Geschichte Israels*, 170–71, and for a critical evaluation of the evidence Schipper, *Israel and Egypt*, ch. 4.1.2.

17. On this, see the overview in Younger, *Political History*, 109–220.

18. On this, see Lipiński, *Arameans*, 336–38, and the overview in Frevel, *Geschichte Israels*, 188–91.

19. See Finkelstein, *Forgotten Kingdom*, 127–28, and for a critical evaluation of the archaeological evidence, see Thareani, "Enemy at the Gates?," 169–97.

3.2 The Israelite Monarchy in the Ninth Century and the Omrides

The history of the Kingdom of Israel in the ninth century can be reconstructed out of four ancient Near Eastern sources: (1) the inscription of King Mesha of Moab; (2) the annals of Shalmaneser III; (3) the "Black Obelisk" from the year 841; and (4) the Tel Dan inscription, which was discovered in 1993. Connected with contemporary ancient Near Eastern history more broadly and with the archaeological record, a picture emerges of the events beginning with the territorial expansion of the Omrides of Israel, around 880, the Neo-Assyrians rise to power thirty or so years later, and the Aramean King Hazael who exploited a weak period among the Assyrians, around 830, to attack Israel and the (dependent?) king of the "house of David" in Jerusalem.

These events are exemplary of the changing configurations of power in the period: After fighting side-by-side with the Israelites in 853 against the army of Shalmaneser III at the Battle of Qarqar, the Arameans took advantage of Assyrian weakness shortly afterward to attack the king of Israel. These political alliances were alliances of convenience and were easily broken.

The Mesha Stela from Transjordanian Dibon/*Ḍībān* (*COS* 2.23) offers some information about the expansion by Israelite kings. Taking advantage of the situation in which the Arameans were attempting to resist the western expansion of the Neo-Assyrian king Assurnasirpal II (884–858), the Omride kings of Israel undertook an expansion of their own.[20] The inscription of the sanctuary of the Moabite national god Kemosh (see Judg 11:24; 1 Kgs 11:7, 33; 2 Kgs 23:13) includes a series of places apparently taken by Mesha after having freed himself from Omri and "his son/his sons."[21] Evidently King Omri succeeded in extending his own sphere of control as far as Moab in Transjordan. The place, called "Jahaz" in the text (line 19), is presumably *Ḥirbet el-Mudēyine* in northern Moab, which was expanded into a fortress, with a casemate wall and a six-chamber gate.

These latter archaeological features are generally attributed to the Omride period.[22] For the first time in the history of the kingdom of Israel, there was an enormous growth of areas with fortifications and palace complexes, which included the construction of casemate walls and six-chamber gates. Such functional structures were found not only in Megiddo, Hazor, and Gezer, but in Shechem, Bethel, *Tell el-Mālāt*, Tirza/*Tell el-Farʿah* [North] and *Tell Qasile* (map 1). This does not imply that all of these places were controlled by the

---

20. For context, see Frevel, *Geschichte Israels*, 194–96, and Routledge, *Moab in the Iron Age*, 133–47.

21. It is unclear whether the word *bnh* is to be understood here as singular or plural; see Weippert, *Historisches Textbuch*, 245n16. More broadly, Gaß, *Moabiter*, 21–22.

22. See Finkelstein and Lipschits, "Omride Architecture," 29–42.

Omrides, though. While the architecture of Dor displays characteristics typical for the Omride period, for example, the archaeological evidence as a whole suggests that Dor was still controlled by the Phoenicians in Iron Age IIA and did not became Israelite until at least the second half of the ninth century.[23] One should therefore be cautious in identifying any monumental architecture of the period as specifically Omride. This is perhaps the same mistake made in older scholarship in connection with Solomon, which understood the six-chamber gates of Hazor, Megiddo, and Gezer as archaeological evidence of a Solomonic empire.[24]

Omri's marriage to the princess of Sidon referred to in 1 Kgs 16:31 might point to historical contact with the Phoenicians. If the note is historically factual, Omri might have been attempting to form a direct connection with the Phoenician coastal plain through marriage.

Connections with the Phoenician region are also reflected in the archaeology of Samaria. The city was made the capital of the Northern Kingdom under Omri (1 Kgs 16:24), as it lay at an advantageous point for traffic, on an east-west connection of the coastal road (Via Maris) and with access to the north-south axis connecting Jerusalem and the eastern part of the Jezreel Valley (Beth Shean). While Samaria was hardly settled in Iron Age I, for Iron Age IIA three stratigraphic phases can be distinguished. The first phase is an agricultural estate, the second (Building period 1) is characterizsed by a monumental building, while in the third phase (Building period 2) a huge casemate wall was constructed around the summit.[25]

At the same time the city retained its pre-Omride importance as a center of agriculture. Samaria was the heartland of wine and olive cultivation for the Southern Samarian hill country. The palace district encompassed only 2.4 hectares and was thus not significantly larger than in other cities ruled by the Omrides such as Shechem, Tirzah, Penuel, Megiddo, or Jezreel (Map 1). This might be explained either by the Omride monarchy having been mobile, moving among various locations,[26] or that the development of the agricultural center Samaria into a seat of royal power had not originally been connected with the territorial expansion of the city.

It was under the Omrides that the monarchy of the Northern Kingdom of Israel was increasingly connected with Samaria and developed into an important player on the political stage of the ancient Near East. This occurred in

---

23. A fundamental change to the city came with this. See Gilboa et al., "Capital of Solomon's Fourth District?," 209–44, and Na'aman, "Tel Dor," 1–5.

24. For Hazor X–XI, see the discussion in Sergi and Kleiman, "Kingdom of Geshur," 4n9.

25. See Finkelstein, "Observations on the Layout," 194–207, and Sergi and Gadot, "Omride Palatial Architecture," 105.

26. See Niemann, "Observations on the Layout," 325–34.

international trade as well. Precious Phoenician ivory works found in Samaria attest to their engagement in long-distance trade and to the influence of Syro-Phoenician traditions in the visual arts.[27] If these undated ivory works are identified with the "ivory house" belonging to Ahab (871–852), referred to in 1 Kgs 22:39, they would be dated to the Omride period. It is also possible, however, that they could be connected to the administrative structures founded by Jeroboam II (787–747), which included extensive foreign trade contacts (see below, 3.5). Whatever the case, it is with the Omrides that the Kingdom of Israel became a full member of the ancient Near Eastern world for the first time. Given the extent of their territory, it is also the first time they became the "geopolitical player" the Hebrew Bible associates with Solomon. Later scribes effected this transposition in the biblical account because the Omrides, as rulers of the Northern Kingdom, did not fit the historical-political agenda of the Judean scribes. The Omride dynasty only received a brief mention in the book of Kings, and it is described as an unstable period, with a rival claimant to the throne (1 Kgs 16:21–22).

3.3 Neo-Assyrians, Arameans, and Israelites in the Ninth Century

The reduction of Omride-controlled territory in the Transjordan mentioned in the Mesha Stela was a result of Neo-Assyrian expansion to the west. The Neo-Assyrian king Shalmaneser III (858–824) penetrated forcefully and deeply into southwestern territory (map 2).[28] Taking up his father Assurnasirpal II's politics of expansion, in the first year of his reign he had already advanced as far as the Mediterranean. In the course of his various campaigns, Shalmaneser III contended with a number of anti-Assyrian coalitions, detailed accounts of which are found in Neo-Assyrian royal inscriptions (*COS* 2.113).[29] In the Battle of Qarqar of 853 Shalmaneser III fought a coalition army under the leadership of the Aramean king Hadadezer of Damascus. The third king in the list of kings participating in the coalition is "Ahab of Israel," with "2000 chariots and 10,000 footsoldiers" (*COS* 2.113A [p. 263]). Even if the figures can hardly be historically factual, it is notable that Ahab is listed as having contributed the largest contingent of chariots of all the participating kings, pointing to the significance of the Omrides in this period.[30]

27. See Frevel, *Geschichte Israels*, 200, figs. 31 a–d, and Suter, "Images, Tradition and Meaning," 219–41.
28. On this, see Frahm, "Neo-Assyrian Period," 170–73, and Lamprichs, *Westexpansion des neuassyrischen Reiches*, 81–96.
29. See Gershon, "Shalmaneser and the West," 40–56, and Younger, "Shalmaneser III and Israel," 227–46.
30. It is possible that the lack of reference to Judah is a result of the Kingdom of Jerusalem's dependence on the Northern Kingdom. See Grabbe, "Kingdom of Israel," 81.

FIGURE 1. Jehu of Israel before Shalmaneser III (Black Obelisk). Drawing by Maria Bruske, after Frevel, *Geschichte Israels*, 179 (no. 26).

In contrast to what is found in the Neo-Assyrian royal inscription, the Battle of Qarqar did not mark the victorious end of Shalmaneser III's campaign. Rather, he continued to fight for over fifteen years against the anti-Assyrian coalition, which in early inscriptions is referred simply as the "twelve kings from the sea."[31] Reports of the events of 841 make clear that Samarian kings were also involved. In an account of a campaign of Shalmaneser III against Damascus, the list of rulers he subjugated includes "the tribute of the Tyrians, the Sidonians," and "that of Jehu of *Bīt Ḫūmrī*" (*COS* 2.113D [p. 268]).[32] This is consistent with what is found on the bas-relief of the "Black Obelisk" of Shalmaneser III from the same year, which in the second register depicts King Jehu and states "Tribute of Jehu of *Bīt Ḫūmrī*" (*COS* 2.113F [Epigraph 2, RIMA #88 [p. 270], fig. 1).

The relationship between Jehu and the "House of Omri" (*Bīt Ḫūmrī*) needs some clarification, however, since, according to the Hebrew Bible, Jehu (845–818) was not of the Omride dynasty. Indeed, he is said to have killed the last Omride ruler, Joram (851–845), in a coup (2 Kgs 9:24). The biblical account found in 2 Kgs 9–10 shows clear signs of religious propaganda, however, depicting Jehu as a warrior against the worship of Baal that was flourishing under Omri and, in a dramatic flourish, has him defenestrate Jezebel, the king's wicked wife.[33]

The actual history might be as simple as what is found in the account of Shalmaneser III's 841 campaign. There was a connection between Jehu and the Arameans with King Hazael of Damascus. Jehu's rise to power is therefore to be understood in the context of the Aramean expansion, and it is even possible that

---

31. On this, see Elat, "Campaigns of Shalmaneser III," 25.
32. Younger, "Shalmaneser III and Israel," 246–49.
33. On this, see Robker, *Jehu Revolution*, 37–69.

Jehu came to found his own dynasty as a vassal installed by Hazael. The dynasty was referred to as "Nimshide," based on his father's name (1 Kgs 19:16; 2 Kgs 9:20), and is attested to in inscriptions as well (Samaria Ostraca, Tel Rehov inscription).[34] Shalmaneser III's reference to Jehu as coming from the "House of Omri," meanwhile, can be explained in at least two ways: the Assyrian king might have believed he was fighting the same opponents as in 853, or perhaps the Omrides were still the only political power recognized outside Israel.

Connections between the Arameans and Israel are also to be found in the fourth ancient Near Eastern text significant in the study of ancient Israel in the ninth century, the Tel Dan inscription. This text can probably be connected with the Aramean king Hazael (ca. 843–803), who is referred to in the inscription of Shalmaneser III as "son of a nobody" (*COS* 2.113G)—perhaps a sign that Hazael was not of royal lineage, having come to the throne as a usurper (see 2 Kgs 8:7–15).

With Hazael's ascension to the throne the Arameans began expanding, ultimately pushing as far as the Southern Levant.[35] Naturally, this had implications for the kings of Israel and Judah. The Tel Dan Stela refers to a "King of Israel" and "[Kin]g of Beth-David" (*COS* 2.39), and the fragmentary text suggests that the first is "[Jeho]ram, son of [Ahab]" and the second "[Ahaz]iah" (l.7'–8').[36]

Thus in the second half of the ninth century, three political changes occurred at once that affected the whole kingdom founded by Omri. The area of the Transjordan broke away (Mesha Stela); the Neo-Assyrians, under Shalmaneser III, subjugated the Southern Syrian region (tribute of Jehu); and the Arameans, in particular Hazael of Damascus, expanded southward. This led to the conflict between the Arameans and the Kingdoms of Israel and Judah, which might have influenced the biblical narratives of the prophets Elijah and Elisha (1 Kgs 19:15; 20; 22; 2 Kgs 5–8).[37]

3.4 The Kingdom of Judah in the Ninth and Eighth Centuries

The territorial expansion of the Omrides as far as the Transjordan leads to the question of the relationship between the kings of the Northern and Southern Kingdoms. It is doubtful the Omrides could have expanded far into the west and the south without it affecting Jerusalem and Judah (map 1).

---

34. The name Nimshi is found on the Samaria Ostraca, on two Judean seals, and on two inscriptions from Tel Rehov. Frevel, *Geschichte Israels*, 215, and Mazar, "Culture, Identity and Politics," 108 with fig. 7.

35. On the course of historical events, see Lipiński, "Arameans in the West," 134–38.

36. See the overview on the possible readings in Younger, *Political History*, 607, and the summary of the various positions in Frevel, *Geschichte Israels*, 216–17.

37. See Gertz et al., *T & T Clark Handbook*, 374–76.

The biblical texts attest to various connections between the Omrides and the rulers of Jerusalem. Princess Athaliah, an Omride (2 Kgs 8:18: Ahab's daughter; 2 Kgs 8:26: Omri's daughter), was married to Jehoram, king of Jerusalem. Jehoram of Jerusalem reigned at almost the same time as a king with the same name in Samaria, just as North and South were later ruled at the same time by kings named Ahaziah and again later by kings Jehoash. Are these coincidences to be understood to mean that it was one and the same king ruling in Israel and Judah, and that Judah was a "subordinated kingdom" of Israel?[38] Even though the connections between the kings of Samaria and Jerusalem are unclear, more proof is needed to support the assumption that kings Jehoram, Ahaziah, and Jehoash in the South were in fact the same as the homonymous rulers in the North.[39] Yet one thing seems to be clear: beginning with Jehoshaphat (868–847) and for at least a century afterward (Jotham, 756–741) the Southern Kingdom was dependent on the North—presumably in a kind of a patron-client relation.[40] As such, the connection between Israel and Judah was closer or more distant depending on the political situation and particular ruler—in the case of Jehoash, it might indeed have been one and the same king for both Samaria and Jerusalem.

Since the Tel-Dan Stela mentions a "king of Israel" for the year 830 in the North, but only "king of the House of David" and not a "king of Judah" for the South, one might conclude that Israel and Judah were not equals: while in the ninth century Israel had an influential kingdom, Jerusalem presumably still only had a city-king.

Such an assumption would be consistent with the archaeological evidence, which shows Jerusalem and Judah thirty to fifty years behind the North, culturally speaking.[41] In Jerusalem this can be seen in its monumental architecture. The old "stepped stone structure" in the city of David from the Early Iron Age was surrounded by a mantle wall built of semiworked stones, which extended south and southeastward through two additional architectural components (a structure built of massive stones in Square AXXXIII, and an additional stepped structure unearthed in Trench I).[42] Recent excavations in the vicinity of the Gihon spring indicate not only new settlement along the eastern slopes of the city of David but also a new dating of the monumental spring towers. According to radiocarbon

---

38. See Frevel, *Geschichte Israels*, 203–8, and in approach already Miller and Hayes, *History of Ancient Israel and Judah*, 320–23.

39. For an overview of previous research, see Barrick, "Another Shaking," 12–15.

40. Donner, *Geschichte Israels* 2:279 speaks of "a vassal relationship of Judah to Israel that is covered up in the Bible" ["einem durch die biblischen Texte verschleierten Vasallenverhältnis Judas gegenüber Israels"]. See also Miller and Hayes, *History of Ancient Israel and Judah*, 320–22.

41. On this, see Bieberstein, *Brief History of Jerusalem*, 53–57.

42. See Sergi, "Emergence of Judah," 3–4.

analysis the so-called Middle Bronze towers (or probably parts of its architecture) should be dated to the late ninth, if not in the eighth century.[43]

The cities of Judah expanded to the west and the south in the ninth century as well,[44] while, in the Shephelah, Beth Shemesh and Lachish (Stratum IV) were fortified, as was Arad in the south (Stratum IX). These, alongside the casemate wall in *Tel Burna* and the complex on *Tell el-Ḥesī*, show an expansive fortification of the western and southern borders (map 1).[45]

In short, connections between the rulers of Jerusalem and the Omrides led to a remarkable cultural development in the south, including the extension of Jerusalem and the border regions—though not yet expansion into the Philistine regions. This occurred only after Hazael's campaign, after he had destroyed the Philistine capital of Gath/*Tell eṣ-Ṣafi* and other places on the coastal plain (e.g. *Tell el-Farʿah* [South] and *Tel Seraʿ*),[46] opening the way for the Jerusalemite kings to expand through the Shephela and further west.[47] All of this was about control of trade routes, whether Gaza to Lachish, which was secured with *Tell el-Ḥesī*, or the trade routes through the Negev. While the copper trade in the Arabah had ended in the middle of the ninth century, the trade routes in the south continued to be valuable.

An important archaeological discovery has shown that Judah's expansion into the trade regions cannot be understood independently of the interests of the Kingdom of Israel. On the ancient trade road to Eilat on the Red Sea, around fifty kilometers south of Kadesh-Barnea, archaeologists unearthed a fortified trading post.[48] At the site, *Kuntilet ʿAğrūd*, excavators discovered pithoi with inscriptions significant for the religious history of ancient Israel. In two of the inscriptions the Israelite god YHWH is mentioned in explicit connection with the goddess Asherah, an important deity in Syro-Palestinian religion. This is clearly in tension with the polemic in the Hebrew Bible against Asherah, especially in the book of Kings (cf. 1 Kgs 14:15; 15:13; 2 Kgs 17:10; 18:4, etc.).[49]

The paleography of the inscriptions, typology of the ceramic, and radiocarbon dating situate the site to somewhere in the late ninth century. The wall painting and the markings on the pithoi show Phoenician influence, while the name "YHWH of Samaria" points to the north. The trade station persisted until

43. See Uziel and Szanton, "New Evidence," 432 and note 71 below.
44. See Na'aman, "Kingdom of Judah in the 9th Century BCE," 247–76, and Sergi, "Judah's Expansion," 226–46.
45. Tell en-Naṣbeh (Mizpah) presents a case of its own. Since the "great wall" could be dated to late Iron Age IIA, the fortification of Mizpah probably predates the expansion of Judah in the west and the south. See Finkelstein, "Great Wall," 14–28, and Sergi "Emergence of Judah," 9–10.
46. On this, see Maeir, "Philistia and the Judean Shephelah," 241–62.
47. On this, see Lehmann and Niemann, "When Did the Shephela Become Judahite?," 77–94.
48. For the following, see Frevel, *Geschichte Israels*, 211–13.
49. See Day, *Yahweh and the Gods and Goddesses of Canaan*, 42–67.

the first quarter of the eighth century and might have been connected with Red Sea trade, perhaps constructed with Phoenician help (Ezion Geber/*Ğezīret Farᶜūn*).[50] It is notable, however, that the site shows no connection with Judah or Judean influence of any kind. Judah appears to have been excluded from this important trade operation. This might be related to a note in 1 Kings, though there the events were reversed: according to 1 Kgs 22:49–50 King Jehoshaphat turned down an Omride offer to cooperate in foreign trade.[51]

When the historical reconstruction of the Kingdom of Judah in the ninth century given above is read in connection with the historical reconstruction of the period of David and Solomon, it becomes clear that elements of an "official state" in Judah were found only when the rulers of Jerusalem were closely affiliated with the kings of Samaria. The policies of the Omrides served as a catalyst for cultural development in the Southern Kingdom of Judah and received additional stimulus with the Aramean expansion under Hazael in the second half of the ninth century. These help explain the new monumental architecture in Jerusalem and the growth of the city. While there is further research still to be done on the archaeology of Jerusalem, it appears the city had already undergone a first "monumental" period in the late ninth century, not in the eighth century.[52] Notwithstanding the expansion of fortifications in the west and the south of Judah, however, this did not mean that the influence of the kings of Jerusalem extended as far as controlling trade routes on their own, as the example of *Kuntilet ʿAğrūd* shows. Rather, they were dependent on the kings of the Kingdom of Israel, while at the end of the ninth century both were subservient to the Arameans (see the tribute payment of the Judean king Jehoash [849–801] to Hazael in 2 Kgs 12:18–19).[53] It was not until a century later that Judah became a kingdom whose rulers were no longer referred to by other ancient Near Eastern rulers simply as "king of the House of David," as on the Tel Dan Stela: in 729 a "king of Judah" is attested to for the first time in an ancient Near Eastern inscription (see below, 3.6).

3.5 Israel in the Eighth Century and the Consolidation of the State

With the death of Shalmaneser III in 824, the Neo-Assyrian expansion ended. It only began again with Adad-nirari III (811–783), who expanded into the

---

50. See Pratico, *Nelson Glueck's 1938–1940 Excavations*, 71–73.

51. On this reference, see Schipper, *Israel and Egypt*, ch. 4.2.4.

52. See Gadot and Uziel, "Monumentality," 123–40, with a plan of the area on page 126. In contrast, David Ussishkin dates the monumental architecture in the eighth cent.: Ussishkin, "Was Jerusalem a Fortified Stronghold?," 135–51.

53. See Younger, *Political History*, 627.

Southern Levant. He began by attacking the Arameans, who by then had taken over large swathes of the Southern Levant,[54] including the Kingdoms of Israel and Judah (cf. 2 Kgs 13:22–25). Between 805 and 802 he also defeated the kings of the Syrian region, who had stopped paying their yearly tributes, and who had unilaterally ended a vassalage that had existed since Shalmaneser III.

In 796 Adad-nirari III began a campaign against Aram and Damascus (map 2). In the Calah Orthostat Slab, he praises himself for conquering the cities and kingdoms from the Euphrates as far as "the land of Edom, the land of Philistia" and having received tribute from the king of Aram (Benhadad) after the siege of Damascus (*COS* 2.114G). In a further stela inscription Adad-nirari III refers to "the tribute of Joash (*Iu'asu*) the Samarian" (*COS* 2.114F).[55] Some scholars understand the addition "Samarian" to mean that the Northern Kingdom had lost significant territory and that "Israel" might have been reduced to no more than a city-state surrounding the capital Samaria.[56] An objection to this thesis is that, alongside Tyrus and Sidon, the Nimrud Slab also refers to an "Omri," which is equated with "the land of Israel" (*COS* 2.114G).[57]

By paying his tribute, Jehoash (802–787) returned Samaria to its vassalage to Assyria, but in the process freed it from Aramean control. According to the biblical account (2 Kgs 13:25), Jehoash won back the Israelite cities from the Arameans. At least in the north this was an attempt to roll back Aramean control of Israelite and Judean territory since, in Hazael's period, Israel and Judah had shrunk to encompass territory broadly consistent with the Late Bronze Age city-states of Shechem and Jerusalem (map 3).

The Neo-Assyrian victory against Benhadad of Damascus allowed the small kingdoms of the Southern Levant to expand once again, and under the rule of King Shalmaneser IV (Adad-nirari III's successor, 782–773) the king of Aram was forced to pay a significant tribute to the Neo-Assyrians (*COS* 2.116). Jehoash of Samaria took advantage of this situation, expanding into the north around the Sea of Galilee by taking over the kingdom of Geshur, which had been founded in the ninth century[58] In his reign, or in that of his successor Jeroboam II (787–747), the biblical Dan/*Tell el-Qāḏī* came under Israelite rule, having previously been controlled by the Arameans.[59] If there were a genuine historical setting for the narrative of the "Golden Bulls" in Bethel and Dan referred to in 1 Kgs

---

54. For the following, see Siddal, *Reign of Adad-nīrārī III*, 61–80, 171–87.
55. See Shea, "Adad-Nirari III," 101–13.
56. See Miller and Hayes, *History of Ancient Israel and Judah*, 345–47.
57. See Weippert, *Historisches Textbuch*, 274n27.
58. Sergi and Kleiman, "Kingdom of Geshur," 7.
59. On this, see Arie, "Reconstructing the Iron Age II Strata," 38.

12:26–33 it would be here, and with Jeroboam II, not Jeroboam I (927/6–907), as in the biblical account.[60]

Disengagement from the Arameans and formal submission to the Neo-Assyrians allowed for unprecedented military and economic gains. Under Jeroboam II strategically important areas became fortified cities: Kinneret/*Tell el-'Orēme* (Stratum II) on the Sea of Galilee, and to its north Hazor (Stratum VI/VA), Jokneam, and Jibleam, all three of which had previously been controlled by the Arameans, while the important trade center Megiddo (Stratum IVA/IVB) was significantly enlarged through administrative and military structures (map 1). With the development of these economically important regions in the west, the ground was laid for significant economic growth.[61]

In the palace district of Samaria, the so-called "Samaria Ostraca" attest to close connections between local elites and the palace in the time of Jeroboam II (*COS* 4.18).[62] Presumably this economic system forms the background of the social critique of the prophets at the end of the eighth century. Amos's criticism that the people of the land were being exploited by a rich elite occurred in the context of an economic development in which the older model of subsistence economics was being replaced by version of rent capitalism.[63] While society had previously followed the "one man, one house, one field" principle, farmers now had to lease the land. This meant that poor yields could result in debt slavery (see Amos 4–5).

What made this economic prosperity possible was the end of Aramean control over the Southern Levant, while the Neo-Assyrians under Shalmaneser IV and his successors were in no position to control the former Aramean territory directly. All of this would change with Tiglath-pileser III (745–728). Before this, however, there was a power vacuum on the coastal plain that both Israel and Judah were able to use to their advantage.

3.6 Judah and Its Capital Jerusalem in the Eighth Century

The decrease in Assyrian power after the death of Shalmaneser IV (782–773) and the weakness of the Arameans led to a phase of economic prosperity in the Kingdom of Judah as well. The implications of this can be seen, for example,

---

60. See Knauf and Guillaume, *History of Biblical Israel*, 83, and Römer, "How Jeroboam II Became Jeroboam I," 376.

61. See Dever, *Beyond the Texts*, 414–16.

62. For the recent discussion, see Nam, "Power Relations," 155–63.

63. For a critical evaluation of the historical and textual evidence, see Houston, "Was There a Social Crisis?," 130–49, and Kessler, *Social History of Ancient Israel*, 96–97.

in Lachish (*Tell ed-Duwēr*), in the Shephelah. In the eighth century this city, the second most significant in Judah after Jerusalem (Stratum IV–III), was developed into a military base and local administrative center, as Megiddo had been in the North.[64] Comparable fortifications are also found in *Tell Bēt Mirsim*. Further fortresses were built in Arad (Stratum X/IX) and *Tell es-Sebaʿ* (Stratum III-II), the former with a small temple to YHWH, including a sacrificial altar in the courtyard and a cultic niche.[65] In the Philistine region, meanwhile, the city of Ashdod profited from the decline of Gath, growing to a size of 30 hectares. In addition, new fortresses were built in the southern Negev (Kadesh-Barnea/ *Tell el-Qedērat*) and on the Red Sea (Ezion-Geber/*Ĝezīret Farʿūn* and Eilat/*Tell el-Hulēfe*).[66]

Overall the period witnessed the systematic growth of cities and fortresses along the trade roads making foreign trade possible both to the coastal plain or, through the Negev, to the Edomite-Arab region.[67] For the first time in its history, the Kingdom of Judah had a fully-developed state and a capital worthy of that title, Jerusalem.

In the eighth century Jerusalem was further expanded, including the development of an administrative apparatus.[68] While monumental architecture first appeared at end of the ninth century (see above, 3.4) the eighth century marked the growth of literacy. A hoard found near the Gihon Spring, presumed to be from the eighth century, included clay bullae with seals on them, some of which date to the ninth century.[69] The last quarter of the eighth century, meanwhile, shows an increase in ancient Hebrew ostraca (see below, 4.1).

The growth of administration came alongside the territorial expansion of the city (map 4). In the eighth century the area of settlement in Jerusalem expanded westward, while small settlements were developed on the hillside of the older city of David, as were buildings near the "stepped stone structure" (the so-called "Burned House").[70] As yet there was no city wall, however, and the southeastern hill near the acropolis was entirely unfortified.

Alongside this urban development came a change to the water supply as well. Until this period the city had continued to use the system from Middle Bronze Age II (ca. 2000–1550): water from the Gihon Spring led through a tunnel system into a 15 × 10 m storage basin protected by a "pool tower." In the second half

64. See Dever, *Beyond the Texts*, 421–24.
65. Herzog, "Fortress Mound," 52–58.
66. Summary in Frevel, *Geschichte Israels*, 238.
67. See Tebes, *Unearthing the Wilderness*, 14–19.
68. On this, see Niemann, "Juda und Jerusalem," 172.
69. On this, see Reich et al., "Recent Discoveries," 156–57.
70. Bieberstein, *Brief History of Jerusalem*, 53–69, and De Groot and Bernick-Greenberg, *Excavations*, 154–57.

of the eighth century this system was abandoned, and the large basin was filled in and built over. A more direct path to the spring appears to have been made at that time, though this was not sufficient either, and in the seventh century a 533-meter long tunnel was dug, the so-called Siloam Tunnel (see below, 4.3).[71]

Judah's new status becomes evident in a Neo-Assyrian inscription of 729: for the first time in ancient Israelite history there is reference to a king of "Judah." This king, given in the text as "Jehoahaz of Judah" (*COS* 2.117D), is Ahaz from the biblical narrative, who reigned from 736 to 725. This inscription makes something else clear as well: whatever the particulars of the relationship between kings of Samaria and Jerusalem in the ninth and eighth centuries, the period of Judah's subordination to the rulers of the Kingdom of Israel ended with Ahaz, if not with his predecessor Jotham (756–741).[72]

3.7 Israel and Judah from Tiglath-pileser III to the Conquest of Samaria (722/720)

The period of decline that followed Shalmaneser IV (782–773) finally made way for a return to western expansion, under the leadership of Tiglath-pileser III (745–727).[73] This expansion included the annexation of the Kingdom of Israel in 722/720 and continued until the conquest of Egypt and the capture of Thebes in 664. At the same time Egypt was also growing stronger under the new rulers of the 25th Dynasty, the so-called "Cushite" Dynasty. With them and with the successors of Tiglath-pileser III against them, the geopolitical balance in the Southern Levant was determined for the next century: the Egyptians in the southwest and the Assyrians in the northeast (map 2).

After Tiglath-pileser III came to power—presumably through a coup d'état[74]—and then consolidated his rule at home, he turned his attention westward beginning in 738 and quickly returned the area to Assyrian control. He conquered Middle Syria and Cilicia and moved into the Southern Levant, giving the small states no option other than to pay tribute to the Neo-Assyrians. In a royal stela of 738 (*COS* 2.117B) "Menachem of Samaria" is listed alongside Rezin of Damascus.[75] This agrees with 2 Kgs 15:19–20, which alludes to Menahem's

---

71. For a discussion of the archaeological and epigraphical evidence, see Reich and Shukron, "Date of the Siloam Tunnel," 147–57, and, for a contrary position, see Guil, "New Perspective," 155. Whereas the formers date the Siloam tunnel in the later ninth or early eighth cent., the latter argued for a Hasmonean date of Tunnel VIII.

72. See Miller and Hayes, *History of Ancient Israel and Judah*, 352.

73. See Bagg, *Die Assyrer und das Westland*, 212–13.

74. See Weippert, *Historisches Textbuch*, 284, and Frahm, "Neo-Assyrian Period," 177.

75. See Tadmor, *Inscriptions of Tiglath-pileser III*, Ann. 13*: 10, Ann. 27:2 and St. III A:5.

tribute to Tiglath-pileser III, referring to the Assyrian king by his Babylonian throne name, *Pul*. This is just one of several spots in the biblical text in which Neo-Assyrian kings are referred to by name:

Tiglath-pileser III (745–727)	2 Kgs 15:29; 16:7, 10; 1 Chr 5:6 (as "Pul" in 2 Kgs 15:19)
Shalmaneser V (727–722)	2 Kgs 17:3; 18:9
Sargon II (722–705)	Isa 20:1
Sennacherib (705–681)	2 Kgs 18:13; 19:20, 26; Isa 36:1; 37:21, 37
Esarhaddon (681–669)	2 Kgs 19:37; Isa 37:38

This list, in chronological order from Tiglath-pileser III to Esarhaddon, includes precisely those rulers who engaged in western expansion in the eighth and seventh centuries. It seems that, with the independence of the Kingdom of Judah in the eighth century scribal culture had begun in earnest, and the historical information on this period found in the book of Kings is more reliable—notwithstanding the book's having been composed much later, and keeping in mind its decidedly Judean-Jerusalemite perspective.

After Tiglath-pileser III took control of the Phoenician coastal cities and the Kingdom of Israel, he moved into the Philistine region. It appears he wanted to make a base in *Naḥal Muṣur* on the Egyptian border, in order to control the incense and spice trade in the Arabah.[76] According to the 729 inscription, tributes were given not only by Ahaz of Judah (see 2 Kgs 16:8) and by the city of Ashkelon, but also by the rulers of Ammon, Moab, and Edom (*COS* 2.117D).[77] Tiglath-pileser III had thus taken de facto control of the whole Levant, including the Transjordanian states. This had less to do with an interest in political rule than in establishing an economic area that encompassed all land trade of the period.

The enormity of the territory ruled by the Neo-Assyrians had the effect of bringing the smaller vassal states and city kingdoms into closer cooperation with one another. Thus after Tiglath-pileser III had left the the region, kings Rezin of Damascus, Hiram II of Tyre, and Pekach, the high-ranking officer who ruled Samaria (735–733/2)—who had come to power through a revolt (2 Kgs 15:23, 25)—tried to fend off the Assyrians.[78] According to the biblical narrative King Ahaz of Judah declined to join the anti-Assyrian coalition and asked for Tiglath-pileser's help when coalition partners Rezin and Pekach attempted to depose him by force (2 Kgs 16:7–8). The attack by the Kingdom of Israel

---

76. For the Arabian trade routes, see Knauf and Guillaume, *History of Biblical Israel*, 116–17 with fig. 28.

77. For a discussion of the tribute of Ahas, see Keel, *Orte und Landschaften* 4/1:379–80.

78. See Becking, *Fall of Samaria*, 5–8.

against the Judean kingdom was referred to by previous scholarship as the "Syro-Ephraimite War."[79] Whether this conflict between North and South was as extensive as it is portrayed in the biblical history (2 Kgs 16:5–6; Isa 10:27–32, Hos 5:5–14) is questionable. The various collaborations and conflicts between the kings of Damascus, Samaria, and Jerusalem would be better understood as related to the way the various leaders positioned themselves in relation to the Assyrian ruler. Ahaz clearly believed he would benefit from cooperation, while Rezin and Pekach believed they would be better served by opposing Assyria. Ahaz's choice was ultimately the right one, despite the strong opposition of the prophet Isaiah found in the biblical account (Isa 7:1–9).[80]

In response, Tiglath-pileser III began a punitive expedition, in 733, in which he conquered Damascus, significantly reduced the size of Israel's territory, and created new provinces for the Neo-Assyrian Empire: beyond Aram-Damascus and the formerly Phoenician coastal region, including Dor, he added the provinces of Megiddo and Gilead, which had previously been Israelite territory (map 1). A portion of the Samarian elite were deported to Assyria (2 Kgs 15:29), and after the death of Pekach (perhaps by pro-Assyrian forces; see 2 Kgs 15:30) a new king, Hoshea (731–723) was appointed in Samaria. According to Neo-Assyrian inscriptions, in 731 Hoshea paid tribute to Tiglath-pileser III in the Babylonian city of *Sarrabānu*.[81]

With the change in rulers from Tiglath-pileser III to Shalmaneser V (727–722) the situation altered again. Though the turnover in Assyrian rule went smoothly, Hoshea of Israel apparently saw an opportunity to stop paying tribute and to make diplomatic overtures to Egypt (2 Kgs 17:4).[82] Why he did so is unclear, however, given that in this period Egypt was not a strong ally. King Hoshea reached out to Osorkon IV, ruler of the Eastern Delta, a region which inclined toward the Southern Levant (map 2). But Osorkon was only one of four rulers in power in Egypt at the time.[83] Osorkon IV had neither the capability to intervene, nor the will to do so. Once the Philistine region—the territory immediately neighboring his—was directly affected, however, he proceeded quite differently.

The inscriptions of Tiglath-pileser III offer an account of a conflict with the Philistines in 734 in which Chanunu, the king of the city of Gaza, fled to Egypt (*COS* 2.117E). A short while later Chanunu fled again, "like a bird," from Egypt,

79. See Begrich, "Der syrisch-ephraimitische Krieg," 99–131. Generally, Siddall, "Tiglath-pileser III's Aid," 93–116.

80. On this, see the overview by Keel, *Orte und Landschaften* 4/1:385–400, and Høgenhaven, "Prophet Isaiah," 351–54.

81. See Tadmor, *Inscriptions of Tiglath-pileser III*, Summ. 4:17 and Summ. 9:r.10.

82. See Schipper, "Wer war 'So,'" 71–84.

83. On this, see Kitchen, *Third Intermediate Period*, 362–76.

and was reinstalled as king of Gaza by Tiglath-pileser III.[84] The precise details are unclear, but the outlines show that neither the Neo-Assyrian kings nor the Egyptian pharaoh (insofar as he was involved with Chanunu) had any interest in further complications. This was confirmed a few years later, in 720, when Osorkon IV responded to massive Assyrian presence in the Southern Philistine region with a gift to the Neo-Assyrian King Sargon II (*COS* 2.118E+F). Egypt had no interest in conflict with the Neo-Assyrians, at least as long as it did not see itself as militarily powerful. This changed only with the rise of the Cushite rulers of the 25th Dynasty, who decided to intervene on the Southern Levant at the turn of the eighth to seventh centuries.

Hoshea's request to Egypt for help in 727 went unanswered, and the Neo-Assyrians attacked. Shalmaneser V defeated Samaria and took Hoshea prisoner. In Neo-Assyrian texts both Shalmeneser V and Sargon II take credit for having conquered Samaria—the former once, the latter five times (*COS* 2.118). This can perhaps be connected to the account in 2 Kgs 17:3; 18:9–10, according to which Samaria was under siege for three years. If so, the siege of Samaria might have begun under Shalmaneser V, temporarily halted with his death in 722, and finally ended with the conquest by Sargon II in 720.[85]

According to Neo-Assyrian texts, the Assyrians deported the elite, including artisans and soldiers, and brought the cultic inventory of the Temple of Samaria, including the images of the gods, to Assur (*COS* 2.118A). Israel was integrated into the Neo-Assyrian Empire as the province *Samerīna* and given a governor. Sargon II's annals give an account of a resettlement policy in which other populations were brought into Samaria to settle.[86] In contrast with the biblical version (2 Kgs 17), however, this does not mean that some form of multiethnic state emerged on the territory of the former Northern Kingdom.[87]

In the wake of the events of 722/720 the Northern Kingdom lost its political independence. There is reason to believe that in this period a group of scribes fled from Samaria to Jerusalem, perhaps to avoid deportation to Assur or to continue living in the vicinity of a temple of YHWH. The situation in the Kingdom of Judah after 722/720 and the growth of Jerusalem under Hezekiah and Manasseh suggest that the effect of the flight from the North to the South and the accompanying "brain drain" should not be underestimated.[88] At the material

---

84. On the historical process, see Frahm, "Neo-Assyrian," 177, and Schipper, *Israel and Egypt*, ch. 5.3.4.

85. See Na'aman, "Historical Background," 206–55, and, for a different account, Tetley, "Date of Samaria's Fall," 59–77.

86. See Oded, *Mass Deportations*, 28, 48.

87. See Knoppers, *Jews and Samarians*, 42–49, and Knauf and Guillaume, *History of Biblical Israel*, 110–12.

88. Critically, Guillaume, "Jerusalem 720–705," 195–211, and Na'aman, "Dismissing the Myth," 1–14.

level, the conquest of the Kingdom of Israel had hardly any repercussions in the North. The Assyrians were still interested in foreign trade and in securing the trade routes. Samaria, Dor, and Dan were made into administrative centers, while in the seventh century palace complexes in the Assyrian style were built in Megiddo, Kinneret/*Tell el-Oreme* and Hazor (map 1).[89] Numerous Assyrian administrative texts attest to Assyrian influence in the provinces, extending as far as the use of Assyrian law.[90] For small farmers who had to pay taxes on their farmland the situation changed as little as for those with large land holdings. The only change was that these taxes no longer went to a royal registration located in Samaria, but went directly to Neo-Assyrian administrative centers.

3.8 Summary

The history of the kingdoms of Israel and Judah differs significantly from the biblical narrative. In the biblical account the Northern Kingdom of Israel is described in negative terms, with Judah and Jerusalem always the key player and center of attention.[91] The archaeological and extrabiblical sources (Mesha Stela, Neo-Assyrian royal inscriptions and the Aramaic Tel-Dan Stela), however, tell a diametrically opposite story. Judah was neither powerful nor influential; Israel was. It was not the kings of Jerusalem who were on a par with other ancient Near Eastern rulers, but the kings of Samaria. Until the Hasmoneans in the first century, the Omrides were the only kings in the history of ancient Israel who managed to form an empire extending from Megiddo in the northwest to the Transjordan. The rulers in Jerusalem, meanwhile, were dependent on the kings of Israel in the North. It appears that only beginning with Ahaz (741–735) the kings in Jerusalem became truly independent, no longer referred to simply as kings from "the House of David" (Tel Dan Stela), but as "kings of Judah" (Inscription of Tiglath-pileser III, 729).

Events of the ninth century show that Israel and Judah only began to achieve regional significance when the Arameans lost it. The destruction caused in 830 by Hazael on the coastal plain, the Shephelah, and in the south, as well as the subsequent political power vacuum, made possible an economic upturn in the North—and, with some delay, in Judah. This allowed for an independent Judean state for the first time in ancient Israelite history, with a "capital" in Jerusalem worthy of this title. Its independence from the Northern Kingdom

89. On this, see Schoors, *Kingdoms of Israel and Judah*, 76.

90. See, for example, the two sale contracts from Gezer in Becking, "Two Neo-Assyrian Documents," 76–89.

91. On this, see Fleming, *Legacy of Israel*.

and the policies of King Ahaz meant that the events leading to the conquest of the Kingdom of Israel in 722/720 did not extend into Judah.

Hoshea of Israel had chosen another path, however. His suspension of tribute payments and his turn to Egypt constituted a challenge to the Assyrians, one they answered with the conquest of Samaria. The defeat of the city in 722/720 marked the end of the Kingdom of Israel. This does not mean that the legacy of the YHWH religion or the local traditions disappeared, however. There were continuities in the north that became visible again in the Persian period, when a YHWH sanctuary on Mount Gerizim was founded (see below, 5.5). It is even possible the YHWH cult continued after 722/720 in Samaria itself, though to a more limited extent.

CHAPTER 4

The Judean Monarchy from 722/720 to the Conquest of Jerusalem in 587/586 BCE

There is a remarkable quantity of extrabiblical evidence related to the history of Judah from the conquest of Samaria to the capture of Jerusalem in 587/586. Alongside Neo-Assyrian royal inscriptions, there are Egyptian inscriptions, the Babylonian Chronicle, and a vast amount of archaeological material.[1] This abundance of material is above all a result of the continually changing political circumstances in the Southern Levant of this period. Neo-Assyrian expansion, which extended as far as Egypt, made it vulnerable to a Neo-Babylonian attack on the Assyrian heartland. This, in turn, led to an attack on the Southern Levant by the pharaohs of the Twenty-sixth dynasty. After the Neo-Babylonian ruler Nabopolassar conquered Assur (614) and Nineveh (612), his successor Nebuchadnezzar took over the region the Egyptians had taken from the Neo-Assyrians only a short while before, bringing about yet another change in rule in Syria-Palestine.

For the most part, the Kingdom of Judah could only stand by and watch as the balance of power swung back and forth. Of all the Judean rulers in this period, only Hezekiah had the opportunity to play a significant role in foreign affairs, while all others—including King Josiah, who is so highly praised in the Bible—stood on the sidelines in the battle over the Southern Levant.

4.1 Hezekiah and the Growth of Judah in the Eighth/Seventh Centuries

In the Hebrew Bible, Hezekiah (725–697) is remembered in connection with religious reforms, construction projects in Jerusalem, and a leading role in the anti-Assyrian coalition of 713 (2 Kgs 18–20). This image of Hezekiah as an important Near-Eastern king, which has been taken for granted in Hebrew Bible

1. See the overview in Miller and Hayes, *History of Ancient Israel and Judah*, 441–44, and, for the Babylonian Chronicle, see Grayson, *Assyrian and Babylonian Chronicles*, 104–11.

scholarship,[2] is only partly supported by archaeology.[3] Seal stamps and clay bullae attest to a leap forward in written culture as well as the existence of significant economic organization. While 170 clay bullae were discovered from the ninth to eighth century near the Gihon Spring (see above, 3.4), the remains from the same site from the eighth to seventh century include numerous ancient Hebrew inscriptions and administrative seals. The imprints of the seals, found on transportation and supply jars, consist of the inscription *lmlk* ("belonging to the king"), and can be divided into a two-winged and a four-winged type. In total more than 1200 seal imprints have been found in over fifty locations. Analysis of the clay shows that the four-handled storage jars were produced in the region around Lachish/*Tell ed-Duwēr*. In the late eighth century the area had been built into a military and administrative center (Stratum III).[4] The locations indicated on the seal imprints reflect an area that extended south of Jerusalem as far as Hebron (Hebron, Sokho, Ziph, *mmšt* [Mamshit, Memshelet = Ramat Raḥel?]).[5]

The growth of Judean government is best understood against the background of Assyrian policies of the period, since Judah was at that point a vassal of Assur and part of a territory controlled by Neo-Assyrian kings. Both the military development of certain cities and the growth of written culture and well-organized administrative system in Judah—attested to by the ancient Hebrew inscriptions, for example, and the numerous stamp seals, respectively—would have been impossible without the Neo-Assyrians, whose economic and administrative policies served a catalyst for cultural development in the Judean kingdom.

The settlement of Ramat Raḥel (*Ḥirbet Ṣāliḥ*) warrants special consideration (map 1). Located only around 4.5 km south of Jerusalem—halfway to Bethlehem—the settlement grew significantly in this period and began to have administrative buildings.[6] Sitting at the highest elevation in the region south of Jerusalem, Ramat Raḥel was visible for miles around at a strategically advantageous point along the two important roads connecting Jerusalem and the surrounding area. Ramat Raḥel was an important transportation hub for agricultural products and was also the most significant administrative center in the Judean heartland. The Assyrian-designed palace complex[7]—and the numerous seals, including the 224 *lmlk* stamp seals—all attest to the significance of this

---

2. See Bright, *History of Israel*, 278–80, and Young, *Hezekiah*, 285–93.

3. See also the discussion on bullae and seal imprints from Ahaz and Hezekiah in antiquities trade Weippert, *Historisches Textbuch*, 375–76, and the overview in Grabbe, *Ancient Israel*, 223–25.

4. On this, see Dever, *Beyond the Texts*, 424.

5. As suggested by Barkay in "Royal Palace," 34–44. On the location of the place names, see Frevel, *Geschichte Israels*, 250–51, and Lipschits, "Archaeological Facts," 1–15.

6. On this, see Lipschits et al., *What Are the Stones Whispering?*, 36–94.

7. On issues of architectural fragments, including the proto-Aeolian capitals and the stone window balustrades, see ibid., 51–56.

Neo-Assyrian administrative center on Judean soil.[8] Ramat Raḥel continued to be important even beyond the Persian period. As such, it is during Hezekiah's reign that the political geography that would determine the next 350 years began to take shape, with Jerusalem as epicenter of YHWH worship, with its scribal school at the temple, and Ramat Raḥel, an administrative center controlled first by the Assyrians, then by the Babylonians, and then the Persians.

Perhaps it was just this division of labor that led Jerusalem to become such a significant religious center under Hezekiah. Even if the summary about the cultic reforms in 2 Kgs 18:4 is not historically dependable,[9] three extrabiblical finds attest the growth of Jerusalem as a place for YHWH worship (see 2 Kgs 18:22). In the Arad fortress in the Negev, around 56 km southwest of Jerusalem, a small YHWH temple with a sacrificial altar and cultic niche was covered with a layer of dirt, making it unusable (Stratum VIII).[10] The same occurred at *Tel Moẓa*, 7 km northwest of Jerusalem, where a temple erected in the ninth century in the style of Syrian temples, including an altar on which animals had been sacrificed, was abandoned in the eighth century and the remains of the altar and the cultic objects were covered with a thick layer of earth.[11]

The centrality of Jerusalem for the YHWH religion is on display in a funerary inscription from an area near Lachish (*Ḥirbet Bēt Lay*): "YHWH, is the God of the whole land, the mountains of Judah belong to the God of Jerusalem."[12] The formulation shows YHWH to be the city deity of Jerusalem. The correspondence of the "mountains of Judah" and the "whole land" might be a reference to the situation after 701, when Judah had lost a significant amount of territory.

4.2 The Anti-Assyrian Coalition from 713 and Sennacherib's Siege of Jerusalem (701)

The loss of Judean territory was the result of Hezekiah's foreign policy. At the outset, at least, Hezekiah was a loyal Assyrian vassal, as his father Ahaz had been; he did not take part in the 720 revolt of Chanunu of Gaza (*COS* 2.118A+E), for example. His politics changed a few years later, however. When the Assyrians found themselves involved in a war with the Urartu kingdom in the north, the small city-states and kingdoms of the Southern Levant began to organize. Yamani, prince of the city of Ashdod, formed an anti-Syrian coalition in 713, after deposing Achmiti, the pro-Assyrian ruler, with the help of the city's aristocracy

---

8. See Na'aman, "Assyrian Residence?," 260–81.
9. See Schipper, "Die 'eherne Schlange,'" 369–87.
10. See Herzog, "Fortress Mound," 65–66.
11. On this, see Kisilevitz, "Iron IIA Judahite Temple," 147–64.
12. See Gogel, *Grammar*, 411, and Lemaire, "Prières en temps de crise," 559.

(*COS* 2.118F). Alongside the Transjordanian states of Moab and Edom, the coalition included Philistia, Judah and, for the first time, Egypt (map 2). Egypt's period of division into local kingdoms had been overcome and, under the Cushite pharaohs of the Twenty-fifth Dynasty, had again become a major power.[13] More importantly, beginning in the eighth century, Egypt had become more involved in land trade,[14] for which the Philistine region was key, and it was therefore willing to play an active role in the Southern Levant.[15] Finally, the Philistine region served as a buffer for them against Assyrian expansion.

The anti-Assyrian revolt of 713 led to an Assyrian punitive expedition (*COS* 2.118H). In 711 Sargon II conquered Ashdod and Gath, and he made the Philistine region into an Assyrian province.[16] After Sennacherib's ascension to the throne (705–681), a new and significantly larger anti-Assyrian coalition was briefly formed, which included nearly the entire region of the Southern Levant, from the Phoenician cities in the north (Byblos, Sidon, Tyre), across Judah in central Palestine and Philistia in the south, to the Transjordanian states of Ammon, Moab, and Edom. If Hezekiah was, in fact, the force behind the coalition,[17] it would have been the second time, after Omri, that an Israelite ruler acted as an equal alongside the other kings of the ancient Near East.

Whatever the case, the coalition did not last long. When Sennacherib (705–681) confronted the coalition it quickly dissolved, and Hezekiah found himself alone. In the Neo-Assyrian royal inscriptions Sennacherib boasts of having confined Hezekiah "like a bird in a cage" in Jerusalem (*COS* 2.119B). Before doing so, however, the Neo-Assyrians took military action against the cities of Judah: "As for Hezekiah, the Judean, I besieged forty-six of his fortified walled cities and surrounding smaller towns, which were without number." (*COS* 2.119B). Palace reliefs from Nineveh, now residing in the British Museum in London, depict the siege of Lachish as well as the punishment of soldiers and the deportation of the population.[18] Alongside Lachish, Timna'/*Tel Batash*, *Tell Beit Mirsim*, Beth-Shemesh, Arad, *Tell ʿĒṭūn*, *Tel Burna*/Libna, Mispah/*Tell en-Naṣbeh*, and Tell es-Seba were destroyed. As a result the amount of territory

13. For a brief history of the Cushite Twenty-Fifth Dynasty, see Török, *Kingdom of Kush*, 153–70.

14. On this, see Schipper, *Israel and Egypt*, ch. 5.2.2, and Kletter, *Economic Keystones*, 121–25, 142, 147.

15. For that, see the events with Jamani of Ashdod and the Tang-I-Var inscription: *COS* 2.118J and Frame, "Inscription of Sargon II," 31–57, plates i–xviii.

16. See Elayi, *Sargon II*, 81–83.

17. See Donner, *Geschichte des Volkes Israel* 2:354, and Miller and Hayes, *History of Ancient Israel and Judah*, 415–16.

18. See Uehlinger, "Clio in a World of Pictures," 221–305. See also Ussishkin, "Sennacherib's Campaign in Judah," 719–58, and Frevel, *Geschichte Israels*, 254–58 with fig. 40.

in the Shephelah that continued to be inhabited decreased by one third.[19] Sennacherib had attacked Jerusalem because Hezekiah was holding captive Padi, prince of the city of Ekron, who had been deposed by anti-Assyrian forces and delivered to Hezekiah.[20] As a result of the actions taken against Jerusalem—it is not clear whether it was an actual siege[21]—Hezekiah delivered Padi to Sennacherib, who reinstalled Padi as king of Ekron. The Neo-Assyrian king was thus fulfilling his part of the vassal contract: Neo-Assyrian military protection in exchange for the vassal fulfilling his contractual duties. As Padi had held up his end of the bargain, Sennacherib held up his as well until Padi was returned his office and rank. This means Sennacherib stopped his activities against Jerusalem when Padi was freed. According to Neo-Assyrian annals, Hezekiah payed a high tribute, which should be understood to mean that he subjected himself to Sennacherib. Thus Hezekiah again became what he had been at the beginning of his reign: an Assyrian vassal, obliged to pay his dues and stay as far from politics as possible.

Unsurprisingly, perhaps, the Hebrew Bible portrays the end of Sennacherib's "siege" of Jerusalem rather differently. The Assyrians departure from the city without destroying it was portrayed as a miraculous rescue, a story that underwent significantly literary embellishment (2 Kgs 18:17–19:37; Isa 36:2–37:38). It is possible the historical background for Zion theology and the image of the "impregnable city" is a result of this event.[22]

4.3 The Kingdom of Manasseh and the Neo-Assyrian Conquest of Egypt (Seventh Cent.)

In contrast to Hezekiah's confrontational foreign policy, Manasseh (696–642), his successor, cooperated with the Assyrians. Perhaps not coincidentally, Manasseh was not only the longest-reigning king in the history of Israel and Judah—fifty-five years—but was also one of its most successful.[23] This success, however, is not hinted at in the Bible. The narrative in 2 Kgs 21:1–23 is primarily interested in portraying Manasseh as the antithesis of King Josiah (see 2 Kgs 23:26; 24:3–4). According to the text, Manasseh undid religio-political developments, and it took Josiah to achieve the Deuteronomic goal: a pure and unified national religion in Jerusalem for the god YHWH.

---

19. On this, see Ussishkin, "Sennacherib's Campaign to Judah," 99–101.
20. See Frahm, "Revolts in the Neo-Assyrian Empire," 80–81.
21. See Mayer, "Sennacherib's Campaign," 179–81.
22. See Amit, "When Did Jerusalem Become a Subject of Polemic?," 367.
23. See Knauf, "Glorious Days of Manasseh," 164–88.

If the extrabiblical sources are to be trusted, much of the archaeological evidence that has been ascribed to Hezekiah by previous scholarship more likely comes from Manasseh's long reign.[24] This includes the fortification of Jerusalem with the so-called "broad wall," the demographic growth of the city, and the development of a new water supply. While the latter might have been initiated under Hezekiah (2 Kgs 20:20; Isa 22:9),[25] the other two appear to date to no earlier than the middle of the seventh century.[26]

Only a small part of the broad wall has been excavated, so the path the 6.4- to 7.2-meter thick wall took is not clear. The area between the southeastern hill— where the city of David was located—and the Temple Mount, the so-called Ophel, was built up and fortified with a 2 m thick wall (see 2 Chr 33:14). Alongside this construction there was presumably a further expansion of Jerusalem to the west, until the city increasingly covered the area of the modern Old City of Jerusalem (map 4). Based on assumptions about the size and settlement density, Jerusalem likely had between 8,000 and 25,000 residents.[27]

As mentioned above, in the course of this construction the water supply was changed. The Bronze Age pool had already been filled over and a house built on top of it in the eighth century (see above, 3.6). A 533-meter long tunnel was then dug, which ran from the Gihon spring to a pool on the southwest end of the city and left an inscription on it (the so-called Shiloh inscription). In the same period, numerous small farmsteads and villages sprung up in the hinterland of Jerusalem as well.[28] In the Neo-Assyrian administrative center of Ramat Raḥel in the seventh century, a monumental palace complex of 120 × 90 m with a large garden was constructed, which remained through the Persian period.[29]

During Manasseh's long reign the Assyrians conquered Egypt. The pharaohs of the Twenty-fifth Dynasty had acted much as Hezekiah had, having been active in a region the Assyrians wanted to control. A contingent of Egyptian troops are attested to in the region as early as the battle of Eltheke in 701.[30] While the Cushite kings Shabaka and Shebitku avoided open conflict, the situation changed under Pharaoh Taharqa (690–664). Taharqa increased his contact

24. For a discussion of the evidence, see Faust, "On Jerusalem's Expansion," 256–85.

25. Reich and Shukron, "Date of the Siloam Tunnel," 147–57, argued for dating the Siloam tunnel in the time before Hezekiah.

26. See also Finkelstein, who argued that the stamp seals with concentric circles should be attributed rather to Manasseh than to Hezekiah, "Comments on the Date," 203–11.

27. The former number is suggested by Geva, "Jerusalem's Population," 141, the latter by Lipschits, "Demographic Changes," 364.

28. On this, see Moyal and Faust, "Jerusalem's Hinterland," 283–98.

29. On the history of the construction of the palace, see Lipschits et al., *What Are the Stones Whispering?*, 60–64, 89–94 (with a reconstruction of the palace), and on the Persian period, 98–105.

30. On the question of whether Shabaka or Shebitku participated, see Schipper, *Israel and Egypt*, ch. 5.1.2, and Kahn, "Inscription of Sargon II," 1–18.

with the Philistine regions and the Phoenician coastal cities, and he apparently formed alliances with individual cities. In his annals, Sennacherib's successor, Esarhaddon (681–669) writes that Baal, King of Tyre, "had put his trust in his friend Tirhakah, king of Jubia, and (therefore) had thrown off the yoke of Ashur, my lord, answering (my admonitions with) isolence" (*ANET* 292).[31]

As with Hezekiah, what followed was a punitive expedition by the Assyrians. After conquering Tyre and returning order to the coastal plain, Esarhaddon attacked Egypt. Between 674/673 and 664/663 he and his successor, Assurbanipal (669–630) undertook five campaigns, which ultimately resulted in the conquest of Thebes (see *COS* 4.39–41, map 2).[32]

While the Hebrew Bible offers no mention of these Assyrian campaigns against Egypt, reverberations of the conquest of Thebes in 664 can be found in the book of Nahum: Nineveh is threatened with the same fate as Thebes (in the text as "the city of Amun" [*No-Amon*])—that it will be conquered and its population forced into exile (Nah 3:8–10).[33]

In an inscription by Assurbanipal from 667, twenty-two rulers are mentioned as having brought troops to aid in the campaign against Egypt, the second of whom is "Manasseh of Judah" (*COS* 4.39). This is an interesting bit of information for a number of reasons. First, in contrast to Baal of Tyre, Mitini of Ashdod, or Sil-Bel of Gaza, Manasseh is not referred to as the king of the city (e.g., "Manasseh of Jerusalem"), but as the ruler of a kingdom. He is thus in the company of rulers like the kings of Moab and Edom, who are referred to immediately after him. Second, a list from Esarhaddon's era referring to twenty-two rulers who delivered wood for the construction of a palace in Nineveh includes "Manasseh of Judah," again in the second position, which points to trade contact between the two. Third, it should be presumed that the kings and princes of the cities of Syria-Palestine had to swear a loyalty oath (*adê*) to the Assyrian king (*COS* 4.35). This is explicitly mentioned for Baal of Tyre, and it was demanded of all vassals of the Neo-Assyrian kings, Manasseh being no exception. In other words, Manasseh's prosperous fifty-five-year reign was only possible in the context of Assyrian politics, in which Manasseh fulfilled his duties and served as a faithful vassal.

The economic upsurge in Judah in the seventh century and the aforementioned growth in construction in Jerusalem were both made possible through the close connections with the Assyrians and the geopolitical situation they brought about. As a result of Sennacherib's destruction in the Shephelah and assignment

31. On this, see Na'aman, "Esarhaddon's Treaty," 3–8, and Klengel, *Syria*, 228–29.

32. On this, see Onasch, *Die Assyrischen Eroberungen Ägyptens* 1:147–69, and Kahn, "Assyrian Invasions," 251–67.

33. See Schipper, *Israel and Egypt*, ch. 5.1.4.

of parts of the region to the kings of Ashdod, Ekron, and Gaza, Judah lost a large part of the Shephelah. What followed was growth in the settlement of the Judean hills and the development of Gibeon and Mispah.[34] Judah concentrated its attention to the south and the east, which can be seen in the construction of a line of fortresses, including Arad, *Ḥorvat ʿUza*, *Ḥorvat Radum*, *Tel ʿIra* and ʿEin-Gedi. Outlying areas on the west banks of the Dead Sea and the Beersheba Valley were also cultivated, and Judah became an important grain supplier in the Neo-Assyrian economic region.[35] This concentration on a single product was related to Assyrian economic planning and was reflected in the Philistine region as well, with Ekron specializing in the production of olive oil and Ashkelon in viticulture (map 1).[36]

With Judah's integration into the Neo-Assyrian economic order came Neo-Assyrian cultural influence as well,[37] which is reflected in an increase in Aramaic-Assyrian symbols and cultic elements in Judean visual art.[38] The moon-god of Haran, the queen of heaven, and astral symbols such as heaven and stars all found their way into the symbolic language of Judah, perhaps even influencing the official cult in Jerusalem.[39]

4.4 Josiah, the Egyptian Intermezzo, and the "Cultic Reform"

According to the book of Kings, Josiah (639–609) was the most important king of Judah, and he was said to have introduced a religious reform throughout the land (see 2 Kgs 22–23). Josiah reigned in a period in which circumstances in Syria-Palestine were in flux. The massive expansion of Neo-Assyrian power as far as Egypt left them vulnerable to attack in their Assyrian heartland, which the Neo-Babylonians exploited. At the same time the Neo-Assyrian kings were in conflict with Elam in the south and with the Scythians in the north, all of which marked the beginning of a situation that resulted in the conquest of the cities of Assur (614) and Nineveh (612) by the Neo-Babylonian ruler Nabopolassar (625–605) and, under his successor Nebuchadnezzar II (605–562), to the conquest of Syria-Palestine and the capture of Jerusalem (598/597 and 587/586).

34. See Lehmann, "Survival and Reconstruction," 297, 305.
35. See Faust and Weiss, "Judah, Philistia, and the Mediterranean World," 71–92.
36. See Gitin, "Tel Miqne-Ekron," 219–42.
37. Whether Judah reached its highest point under Manasseh or Josiah remains an open question. Lipschits et al. have argued for the latter in "Judahite Stamped and Incised Jar Handles," 5–41.
38. On the move from Egyptian symbols to Aramaic-Assyrian, see Keel, *Orte und Landschaften* 4/1:476.
39. See Knauf and Guillaume, *History of Biblical Israel*, 128–31 with figs. 31–35.

In the course of this back-and-forth the Egyptian pharaohs were able to retake control of southern Syria-Palestine for about twenty-five years.[40] In the same year that Thebes was conquered by Assurbanipal (664), the ruler of the city of Sais in the Eastern Delta, Psammetichus I (664–610), founded a new dynasty— the Twenty-sixth, according to Egyptian counting. With help of Greek mercenaries (Herodotus, *Hist.* 2.152) who had come to the country through trading partners, Psammetichus was able to assert himself against the other contemporary rulers of Egypt.[41]

Over the following years Psammetichus extended his rule across all of Egypt and expanded into the Southern Levant (map 2). Archaeological material, ancient Hebrew inscriptions, and Egyptian texts show that Judah had become a dependent of Egypt—most likely under Josiah, and not his successor Jehoiakim.[42] Evidence from Ashkelon and Ekron indicates that the Egyptians appropriated the Assyrian administrative system but installed their own officials, who acted as emissaries between Egypt and southern Syria-Palestine (statue of Pediese).[43] On the coastal plains the Egyptians erected a fortress, Meẓad Ḥashavyahu, where Greek mercenaries were stationed and where Judeans had to work the nearby farms (*COS* 3.41).[44]

The archaeological evidence shows that Psammetichus I took control of the Philistine region with the help of Greek mercenaries. Imported Greek goods found in Ashkelon, Ekron, Timnaʿ, Tel Kabri, Meẓad Ḥashavyahu, and in Phoenician Dor, including cooking pots for daily use, attest to Greek influence in the area.[45] At the same time, a note in the Arad Ostraca suggests that at the end of the seventh century the fortresses in the Negev might have been headed by Greek soldiers working for the Egyptians, as the commander of Arad is instructed to deliver food to the *Kittim*, meaning Greeks (*COS* 3.43A-F).[46]

Like the Assyrians, the Egyptians were interested in controlling the trade routes, and the strength of their influence in trade is attested to in the use of Hieratic Egyptian symbols and in the range of Egyptian objects found (e.g., New Year's bottles and seal amulets).[47] A papyrus from 604 gives a sense of Egyp-

40. See the discussion in Vanderhooft, *Neo-Babylonian Empire*, 69–75 and note 47 below.

41. See Spalinger, "Psammetichus," 133–47.

42. See Schipper, "Egypt and the Kingdom of Judah," 200–226.

43. See Steindorff, "Statuette of an Egyptian Commissioner," 30–33, and for a historical interpretation, Schipper, *Israel and Egypt*, ch. 5.3.1.

44. See Fantalkin, "Mezad Ḥashavyahu," 3–165, and Takahashi, "Reconsidering Meẓad Ḥashavyahu," 5–19.

45. For a critical discussion of the evidence and its possible intepretations, see Fantalkin, "Was There a 'Greek Renaissance'?," 83–99.

46. On this, see Naʾaman, "Kingdom of Judah Under Josia," 47–48.

47. See Schipper, "Egypt and the Kingdom of Judah," 204–12, and for a discussion of the evidence, Gitin, "Neo-Assyrian and Egyptian Hegemony," 55*–61*.

tian political organization in the region: in a letter by Adon, the king of the city of Ekron requesting the pharaoh's help, the king depicts himself as a loyal "servant," and pleads with the pharaoh to send an army against the advancing Babylonians (*COS* 3.54). In other words, the Egyptians apparently not only adopted the Assyrian administrative system, but also the practice of vassal treaties.[48] Such treaties regulated the kinds of occurrences reflected in the events around Padi of Ekron and the Neo-Assyrian King Sennacherib at the end of the eighth century, in which the vassal paid the lord in return for military protection.

The political events between 625 and 601 show that the Kingdom of Judah under Josiah played no part in the conflicts of the period. According to a brief reference in 2 Kgs 23:29–30, Josiah was killed in 609 by Necho II at Megiddo. This, along with 2 Chr 35:20–25, has lead scholars to imagine a clash between Judah and Egypt that culminated in a great battle on the Jezreel Valley.[49] Presumably what actually occurred was that Josiah, as vassal, went to pay his respects and perhaps swear an oath of loyalty to the new pharaoh—Necho had come to power in 610—and simply died while there.[50]

How, then, should Josiah's reign be depicted? In contrast to the biblical account and previous scholarship, Josiah appears to have been a local ruler without significant influence.[51] At most, it is possible that there was a minor expansion northward under his reign, to bring the formerly northern sanctuary of Bethel under Judean control.[52] If this expansion included Jericho as well, Josiah would have ruled a territory approximately equivalent to what would be the province of Yehud in the later Persian period (see maps 1 and 5).[53]

This raises the question of whatever kernel of historical fact there might be to "Josiah's reform." If the focus on Jerusalem as the cultic center of Judah had already occured at the end of the eighth century, accompanied by the abandonment of other YHWH sanctuaries (Arad, *Tel Moẓa*; see above, 3.5), the vast cultic reform depicted in 2 Kgs 22–23 was probably limited to activities in Jerusalem alone. Evidently the reform involved a cultic cleansing of the temple of YHWH, in which elements of the Aramean-Assyrian astral religion, such as horses and sun chariots, were abolished and practices of divination from the Shamash cult eliminated.[54] As such Josiah was only making explicit domesti-

48. See Fitzmyer, "Aramaic Letter of King Adon," 231–41.

49. See Malamat, "Kingdom of Judah between Egypt and Babylonia," 322–37.

50. For a different position, see Kahn, "Why Did Necho II Kill Josiah?," 511–28, who is thinking of Josiah's rebellion (520).

51. See Donner, *Geschichte Israels* 2:374, 380.

52. For a new evaluation of the archaeological evidence, see Lipschits, "Bethel Revisited," 233–46.

53. On this, see Koch and Lipschits, "Rosette Stamped Jar Handle System," 55–78, and Kletter, "Pots and Polities," 34–37.

54. See Uchlinger, "Was There a Cult Reform?," 279–316.

cally what had been clear beyond his realm since Psammetichus I: that the Assyrians were no longer the great power, but rather Egypt. In contrast with the Assyrians, though, the pharaohs had no interest in the Judean heartland. Josiah's reform was thus no more anti-Assyrian than it was pro-Egyptian. Rather, it was the continuation of a development begun by Hezekiah and should be understood against the backdrop of the different functions of Jerusalem and Ramat Raḥel. Whereas the latter was an important economic center, Jerusalem had only religious importance. At the time of Josiah's reign, advocates for a YHWH cult stripped of elements of other religions became increasingly influential. This influence is attested to by a corresponding change in the iconography of the seventh century, which shows an increasing orientation to YHWH and a concomitant decrease in symbols of other deities.[55]

The de facto introduction of exclusive YHWH worship in the Jerusalem temple was an important step in Israel's religious history toward the worship of a single god to the exclusion of all other gods (monotheism) in the sixth to fifth century. It is yet another example of the effect of political circumstances on Israel's religious development. The Assyrian policy of controlling important Judean cities and their interest in the administrative center of Ramat Raḥel—and not Jerusalem—paved the way for the (new) role of Jerusalem as the site of YHWH worship. The fact that the city was significantly smaller than other cities of the period such as Ashkelon on the coast or Ekron on the Shephelah was not an issue, as Jerusalem's importance was neither political nor economic, but religious. Jerusalem had a temple and a scribal elite that, by the seventh century, had begun composing literature that exists today, in edited form, in the Hebrew Bible.[56]

4.5 Nebuchadnezzar II and the Two Conquests of Jerusalem (598/597 and 587/586)

Between the death of Josiah in 609 to the conquest of Jerusalem in 587/586, events moved quickly. After Josiah died in Megiddo, Pharaoh Necho II moved northward to support the Assyrians in their fight against the Neo-Babylonians, while in Judea the people of the land made Jehoahaz, Josiah's younger son, king (mentioned in Jer 22:11 as Shallum).[57] Three months later, however, he was summoned to Necho II's camp in Riblah on the Orontes, deposed as king, and

---

55. See Keel and Uehlinger, *Gods, Goddesses, and Images of God*, 354–62.

56. See Schmid, *Old Testament*, 67–69.

57. See Miller and Hayes, *History of Ancient Israel and Judah*, 461–62, and Schipper, "Egyptian Imperialism," 282.

deported to Egypt (2 Kgs 23:33–34). In his place, Necho installed as king one
of Josiah's older sons, Eliakim, though he had been passed over by the people
of the land and changed his name to Jehoiakim (608–598). The fact that the
Judean succession was being decided from an Egyptian camp in Syria, a good
500 km north of Jerusalem, shows that Necho II viewed the Kingdom of Judah
as politically insignificant. Whoever reigned there was ultimately unimportant,
so long as he was pro-Egyptian and paid his taxes. According to 2 Kgs 23:33,
35 Necho demanded a heavy tribute from King Jehoiakim before permitting him
to return to Jerusalem.

In 605 the Babylonian crown prince, Nebuchadnezzar, dealt a defeat to the
Egyptian army at Carchemish on the Euphrates (map 2). Following his succession to the throne after the death of his father, Nabopolassar, Nebuchadnezzar II
took over Hamat, in Northern Syria, and Syria-Palestine.[58] Along with other local
rulers, Jehoiakim of Judah became a Babylonian vassal (604).[59] Thus, after Neo-
Assyrian and the Egyptian rule, the Babylonians became the third hegemon in the
Southern Levant within three decades. The administrative system again remained
the same, with only the ruling elite replaced. As the Egyptians before them, the
Neo-Babylonians did not have the time to set up an entirely new administration
to control the area, but simply retained the still functioning Assyrian system.

Swift changes in ruling powers, along with the change in the Judean rulers
by Necho II, led to the politicization of Jerusalem. If one accepts the account in
Jeremiah, at the turn of the seventh to sixth centuries Jerusalem had both pro-
Egyptian and pro-Babylonian parties (Jer 38).[60] When the Neo-Babylonians
lost a decisive battle against the Egyptians at the Egyptian border in 601/600,[61]
Jehoiakim halted tribute payments. But while the Egyptians subsequently conquered Gaza, Syria-Palestine remained under Neo-Babylonian control. The letter from the ruler of Ekron to the Egyptian pharaoh (see above, 4.4) gives a sense
of the situation in the period. The ruler, king Adon, makes a vassal's appeals
for Egyptian military support against the advancing Babylonians (*COS* 3.54).[62]
He was without success, however, as neither Necho II nor his successors were
involved in political events of the following years. They did attempt to increase
their influence in Phoenician cities and sea trade, however, which is why Pharaoh Apries took advantage of the Neo-Babylonian siege of Jerusalem to attack
the Phoenician cities (see Jer 37:5, 7; 44:30; as well as Herodotus, *Hist.* 2.161).[63]

---

58. See Grayson, *Assyrian and Babylonian Chronicles*, 99–102.
59. See Lipschits, *Fall and Rise of Jerusalem*, 31–34.
60. See Görg, "Jeremia zwischen Ost und West," 190–207.
61. See Lipiński, "Egypto-Babylonian War," 236–39.
62. See above, note 48.
63. On this, see Schipper, *Israel and Egypt*, ch. 5.1.7, and for a contrary position see Kahn,
"Judean Auxiliaries," 507–16.

Nebuchadnezzar's punitive attack on Jerusalem took some time to prepare, but for that reason was that much worse. According to the Babylonian Chronicle, Nebuchadnezzar attacked Jerusalem in his seventh year (598/597; *COS* 1.137). It is unclear whether Jehoiakim was murdered by the pro-Babylonian party (Jer 22:18–19), killed by Nebuchadnezzar (Josephus, *Ant.* 10.97), deported to Babylon (2 Chr 36:6), or died a natural death (2 Kgs 24:12), though the latter is the most likely.[64] His son Jehoiachin surrendered a few months later, preventing the destruction of Jerusalem. He was exiled to Babylon and, according to information from Babylonian archives, lived there as a political prisoner in the vicinity of the king's court (see below, 5.1).

The Babylonian Chronicle reports that Nebuchadnezzar installed "a king of his choosing there" and "took heavy tribute" back to Babylon (*COS* 1.137). This included not only temple objects (2 Kgs 24:13; cf. Jer 27:18–22) but part of the Jerusalem elite. Alongside members of the royal family and specialist artisans, the prophet Ezekiel seems to have been taken as well (2 Kgs 24:15–16; Jer 29:2; Ezek 1:1–3).

Another of Josiah's sons, Mattaniah, became the next king of Jerusalem, under the name Zedekiah (597/596–587/586), ruling as a Babylonian vassal until 594/593, when Nebuchadnezzar appeared to be weakened in the aftermath of a rebellion in Babylon. At around the same time the Egyptian pharaoh Psammetichus II (595–589) intensified his connections with the Southern Levant; after a campaign in 591 against Nubia, he made a show of force in the Philistine region.[65] Zedekiah, believing himself to have Egyptian support (Jer 44:30), halted tribute payments to Babylonia. Among the Lachish Ostraca is a piece stating that "the comander-in-chief of the army, Konyahu, son of Elnatan" decended "to go to Egypt" (*COS* 3.42B). Whether this reflects an official plea for help or a high-ranking official fleeing a hopeless position is unclear,[66] but neither Psammetichus II or his successor Apries had any interest in Judah. Their focus was on the trade centers of the coastal plain.[67]

What followed was another punitive attack on Jerusalem by Nebuchadnezzar II, though the Babylonian king was not personally involved. Just as Necho II had done earlier, the king remained in Riblah on the Orontes. He sent his general, Nebusaradan, who laid siege to Jerusalem in 588 and (after a brief interruption) conquered the city in 587. Zedekiah attempted to flee, but he was caught at Jericho and taken to Nebuchadnezzar at Riblah, where he was forced to witness

---

64. See Lipschits, "'Jehoiakim Slept with His Father,'" 1–23.

65. It would be an exaggeration to call it a campaign; see Schipper, *Israel and Egypt*, ch. 5.1.8. Kahn, in contrast, does take it to have been a campaign; see his "Some Remarks on the Foreign Policy," 151–52.

66. See Frevel, *Geschichte Israels*, 274–75.

67. For a discussion of the literary evidence, see Vanderhooft, *Neo-Babylonian Empire*, 87–89.

the murder of his sons and was then blinded and exiled to Babylonia (2 Kgs 25:7; Jer 52:11).[68]

Presumably it was only after this that Nebuchadnezzar's order to destroy the city was fulfilled. It is unclear whether this included the destruction of the temple. Destruction of sanctuaries was not customary Babylonian practice in the period, though it is attested to in earlier sources (eighth century).[69] Either way, Jer 39:8 does not refer to the temple being destroyed. If it did occur, it was only a partial destruction, as Zech 7:3; 8:19; Ezek 33:25; and Jer 41:5 all attest to the continuation of worship at the temple after 587/586 (see below, 5.6).[70]

Archaeological evidence of destruction can be found in Jerusalem on the southeastern hill (House of Achiel, "Burnt House," "House of Bullae") as well as at the northern city wall.[71] In contrast to older scholarship, however, scholars no longer believe there to have been a wholesale destruction of Judah. Nebuchadnezzar's focus was primarily on Jerusalem and a few cities in the southwest, including Lachish/*Tell ed-Duwēr* II and perhaps ʿAzekah/*Tell Zakarīye* (see Jer 34:7). The Benjamin region in the north and the important city of Mispah remained essentially untouched. In the south, however, a few fortresses were destroyed in the sixth century (including Arad IV; Ḥorvat ʿUza, Ḥorvat Radum, *Tel ʿIra*, *Tell el Milḥ*), but it is not clear that these can be ascribed either to 587/586 or to the Neo-Babylonians. It is probable the Edomites took advantage of the situation in order to seize the trade route in the Arabah, though they might even have been helping the Neo-Babylonians conquer Jerusalem.[72] If one were after a historical basis for the negative image of Edom in the Hebrew Bible, it might be in connection with these events (see Jer 49:20–22; Joel 4:19; Obad 1:2, 8; Ps 137:7; Lam 4:21–22).

In the aftermath of the conquest the Neo-Babylonians installed one of their own administrators, Gedaliah, who resided in Mispah/*Tell en-Naṣbeh*, around 12 km north of Jerusalem and had not been destroyed. The city was converted into an important administrative center and continued to serve as such until the middle of the fifth century (Stratum II).[73] After Gedaliah's murder by anti-Babylonian forces a further deportation occurred, in 582 (Jer 52:30).

It is unclear how many people in total were ultimately deported by the Babylonians. Among the various figures offered in the Hebrew Bible—from the "ten

68. For an alternative interpretation, see Levin, "Empty Land," 204–09.
69. See Mayer, "Die Zerstörung des Jerusalemer Tempels," 20–21.
70. See Middlemas, *Trouble of the Templeless Judah*, 122–33, and Berlejung, "Notlösungen," 224–25.
71. Including arrowheads and stone bullets with a diameter of 5–6 cm, see Bieberstein, *Brief History of Jerusalem*, 83–92.
72. See Lemaire, "New Aramaic Ostraca," 413–52.
73. See Zorn, "Tell en-Naṣbeh," 413–47, and Lipschits, *Fall and Rise of Jerusalem*, 237–41.

thousand" mentioned in 2 Kgs 24:14 to the statement that everyone was deported (2 Kgs 25:11–12), a figure that gave rise to the myth of the "empty land,"[74]—Jer 52:28–30 offers more concrete numbers: 3023 Judeans in 598/597 BCE; 832 in 587/586 BCE and 745 in 582 BCE. However literally these numbers should be taken, they suggest that the deportation of 598/597 might have been more significant than in 587/586. Whatever the case, the second conquest of Jerusalem and the destruction of the city (and the temple) would become the central event in the cultural memory of Judaism.

4.6 Summary

The events of 587/586 marked a significant break in the history of ancient Israel. The Kingdom of Israel had lost its independence in 722/720; now it was Judah's turn. Technically speaking, the Northern Kingdom had only had genuine political independence for a brief period, under Omri in the ninth century, followed by a long period of formal dependence on Assyria.

The development of both kingdoms can be understood in the context of Neo-Assyrian expansion. This expansion served as an engine of cultural development, first in the Northern Kingdom, and thirty to fifty years later in the Southern Kingdom of Judah. The kings of Jerusalem had become Assyrian vassals at least as early as Ahaz (729), and they thrived only when they acquiesced to this vassalage. What Manasseh successfully accomplished in his long, fifty-five-year reign was of a wholly different order than his predecessor Hezekiah. Though Hezekiah is portrayed in the Hebrew Bible as an important king (see 2 Kgs 18–20; 2 Chr 29–32), from a historical perspective his foreign policy was disastrous, as he put his faith in Egypt and joined an anti-Assyrian coalition that fell apart as quickly as it had arisen. Assyria retaliated, and Hezekiah was forced to capitulate and free Padi, king of Ekron, whom he had imprisoned. The Neo-Assyrian king Sennacherib was content to accept tribute payments, which gives a sense of the insignificance of Jerusalem in that period.

Ultimately the kings of Judah remained in the shadow of larger political events in the ancient Near East. Manasseh paid what he had to, sent mercenaries for the Assyrian campaigns in Egypt, and otherwise spent his energy developing Judah. With his cultic reforms, King Josiah brought to fruition in the religious realm what Manasseh had begun in the sociopolitical level with his construction projects in and around Jerusalem. This religious focus can already be seen in Hezekiah, who sought to make Jerusalem the religious epicenter of Judah.

---

74. On this, see Barstad, *History and the Hebrew Bible*, 90–134, and the overview in Frevel, *Geschichte Israels*, 272–74.

It is possible that Jerusalem's significance as the center of religion and scribal culture comes from the fact that the Neo-Assyrians never used the city as an administrative center. That role was held by Ramat Raḥel, which controlled the grain production in the Beersheba valley and southern Judah that Manasseh had developed. Jerusalem, out of the limelight of political events, could gain importance as the religious center of Judah.

As before, the foreign policy of the Jerusalemite kings was unsuccessful. Josiah was killed by the Egyptians in Megiddo. Jehoahaz was deposed (also by the Egyptians) three months after having come to power. Jehoiakin and Zedekiah were besieged by the Babylonians, and the Egyptian help they counted on never materialized. Jerusalem was left to fend for itself and was ultimately conquered twice, the first time involving a more significant deportation than the second. But it was the latter conquest, of 587/586, and the partial destruction of the temple that the Hebrew Bible sees as the turning point in Israelite history: from kingdom to exile, and from exile back to Jerusalem and to the rebuilding of the temple.

CHAPTER 5

The Persian Period (550–333 BCE)

During the Persian era different social forms of the YHWH religion emerged that would evolve into the characteristic features of ancient Judaism.[1] These Persian period communities included the exiles living in the Babylonian *golah* (exile), the group that remained behind in the land (Jerusalem and environs), a new YHWH community in Egypt (Elephantine), and those who worshipped at the shrine to YHWH in the area of the former Northern Kingdom (Samaria). Each of these groups constituted a different form and dimension of "Yahwism" during the Persian period.[2] As such it would be misleading to see the Babylonian exile as having been simply a vale of tears and longing for Jerusalem, or the situation on Elephantine to have been nothing more than a syncretistic YHWH worship unrelated to a "genuine" Yahwism in the land of Israel. Quite the contrary. Given that early postexilic narratives from Ezra and Nehemiah are strongly theologically biased, and given that the priests of Elephantine were in correspondence with the high priest in Jerusalem, these other perspectives should be understood as historically no less legitimate or helpful for reconstructing the history of ancient Israel between the sixth and fourth centuries.

5.1 The Babylonian Exile

The famous verse from Psalm 137, "By the rivers of Babylon, there we sat down, and wept" has indelibly shaped the image of the Babylonian exile. One envisages the people of Israel in chains, mourning their forced exile by the Babylonians, and longing for the holy city of Jerusalem.[3] But this verse is only partly true. The lament should be taken as somewhat measured, given that the

---

1. In light of contemporary research, the term "ancient Judaism" should not be used before the Hellenistic period; see Cohen, *The Beginnings of Jewishness*, 84–93.

2. For the term "Yahwism," see Granerød, *Dimensions of Yahwism*, 325.

3. Bright, *History of Ancient Israel*, 348–50, and, more thoroughly, Noth, *History of Israel*, 295–96.

exiles were, in fact, thriving. They lived in their own settlements, could engage in trade, and some probably had slaves of their own.

There are two reasons for this sharp discrepancy between the biblical picture and the historical reality. First, Ps 137 is to be read as the product of a later scribe from the Persian period who intended to portray the Babylonian exile from a particular theological position, one in which Jerusalemite Yahwism was the only legitimate worship. Second, the Hebrew Bible notably offers almost no information on the exile. In the biblical tradition the exilic period is a historical black hole.[4] It recounts how it began (2 Kgs 24–25; Jer 39; 2 Chr 36) and how it ended (Ezra 1–2; cf. 2 Chr 36). Beyond that it refers only to a few individual events, such as the end of Gedaliah's reign and the aftermath (2 Kgs 25:22–26, cf. Jer 40:1–43:7) and Jehoiachin's release in the year 562 (Jer 52:31–34).

This latter episode sheds some interesting—and, for the Bible, rare—light on the situation in Babylon. As a political prisoner, Jehoiachin lived in the proximity of the Babylonian royal court and preserved his royal title. Babylonian texts do not give the impression of a prison, but of a large campus that housed many people.[5] Clay tablets from Nebuchadnezzar II's palace show a delivery of oil to Jehoiachin "the king of Judah" and his sons in 592 BCE (*ANET* 308).[6] The former Judean king also received twenty times more than the normal ration. If the account in 2 Kgs 25:22–26 is reliable, Jehoiachin was pardoned by Nebuchadnezzar's successor, King Amel Marduk (562–560). The account gives no further information about his subsequent fate, though he most likely remained in Babylonia.[7]

While the Judean royal family, as well as many craftspeople and other specialists resided around the royal court at least until the middle of the sixth century, the other exiles from Jerusalem had been settled in cities (map 2). The Hebrew Bible mentions Tel Abib on the Chebar River near Nippur (Ezek 3:15; see also Ezek 2:29; Neh 7:61), among others. Meanwhile the "city of the Judeans" (*Āl-Yāhūdāya*) near Nippur—attested to first in 572 (*DJE* 1) and called "city of Judah" (*Āl-Yāhūdu*) beginning in 498—[8]makes clear that the exiles had permanently established themselves in their new surroundings. Living in the "city of Judah" no longer required returning to the area of the former kingdom. For this reason some scholars dubbed *Āl-Yāhūdu* the "Jerusalem of Babylon."[9]

---

4. See Albertz, *Israel in Exile*, 3.
5. See Petersen, "Foreign Professionals in Babylon," 267–72.
6. See also Avishur and Heltzer, "Jehoiachin, King of Judah," 18–24.
7. See Vanderhooft, *Neo-Babylonian Empire*, 99–101.
8. *DJE*, 7.
9. See Joannès and Lemaire, "Trois tablettes cunéiformes," 26, and Lemaire, *Levantine Epigraphy and History*, 42.

Babylonian documents from the late sixth and early fifth century make clear that the exiles were neither prisoners of war nor slaves, and that their social status was no different from that of any other exiles.[10] Alongside the Murashu archives from Nippur, discovered in 1893, with their more than seven hundred clay tablets, another two hundred texts from *Āl-Yāḫūdu* and *Bīt Našar* (near Sippar), east and southeast of Babylon (map 2) have only recently been published, and are also significant for this period.[11] While the former texts originate from the second half of the Persian period (ca. 455–403), the latter come from the period between 572 and 477. Combined they offer extrabiblical source material for nearly the whole of the Babylonian exile and a large part of the Persian period.

These texts offer a glimpse into the form of the settlement of the people at the time, their legal status, and their religion.[12] Those who lived in the various settlements—including one southeast of Babylon called the "City of the House of Abra[ha]m" (*Bīt-Abīrâm*)—lived in social communities based on a principle of mutual solidarity (so-called "father-houses"). Up to four generations of particular clans can be reconstructed from the Neo-Babylonian texts.[13]

The Babylonians assigned the exiles land from the royal domain for them to be worked self-sufficiently ("land for service").[14] The "Judean fields" referred to in the texts (*DJE* 24+25) were irrigated with water from canals and were passed on to the next generation through hereditary lease.[15] Administration of the land parcels and the management of them was the responsibility of individual Judeans. The texts mention one Ahiqam of *Āl-Yāḫūdu* and a manager named Ahiqar who worked in the "city of Nashar" (*Ālu-ša-Našar*) and conducted business with Babylon (*DJE* 44+45). Individual Judeans rose to official positions: a source from 532 refers to a Judean called *Abdi-Yāḫûa* (= biblical: Obadiah, "servant of YHWH," see Obad 1:1), who had the position of tax collector.[16]

Other Judeans had to offer corvée labor as part of the "land for service" system and in a certain sense lived as dependents (Akk. *šušānu*).[17] But there is no evidence to support the biblical image of prisoners or slaves (Ps 137:3; Ezek 34:27; Bar 4:32).[18] One thing that is supported is the location of the Babylonian

10. See Pearce, "'Judean,'" 267–78.
11. For an overview of the material, see Pearce, "Cuneiform Sources," 230–43.
12. On the following, see the overview in Kratz, *Historical and Biblical Israel*, 148–53, and Lemaire, *Levantine Epigraphy and History*, 37–45.
13. See Lemaire, *Levantinte Epigraphy and History*, 41.
14. For the "land-for-service" system, see Jursa, *Aspects of the Economic History*, 246–51.
15. On this, see Wunsch, "Glimpses on the Lives of Deportees," 247–60.
16. See *DJE*, 33, and Pearce, "Continuity and Normality in Sources," 176.
17. Alstola, "Judeans in Babylonia," 224.
18. See Magdalene and Wunsch, "Slavery Between Judah and Babylon," 113–34.

exiles found in the book Ezekiel (Ezek 1:1, 3; 3:16).[19] The texts from *Āl-Yāhūdu* offer the geographic and economic background for the prophecies of Ezekiel, who had been deported to Babylonia in 598/597 (see above, 4.5).[20]

Another group of Judeans were traders who were fully integrated into the Babylonian economy, travelling the ancient Near Eastern world as far as Persia and presumably back to what had been Judah as well.[21] In sum there was a broad social and economic spectrum among the Judean exiles in Babylonia, from workers to wealthy Judeans with slaves of their own.[22]

The archive of the Murashu (455–403) bank and business offers evidence of both Judean continuity from the late sixth and early fifth century and at the same time their broad integration into Babylonian society.[23] The Babylonian documents and clay tablets from the sixth, fifth, and fourth centuries show unequivocally that a large segment of the Judeans deported to Babylon in 598/597, 587/586 and 562 remained there for generations. Babylonian onomastica from the fourth and third centuries include numerous names built on the theophoric *yah*, a shortened form of the biblical name of god, YHWH.[24] Names based on the particle "yah" (in Akkadian *yāhû–* or *–yāma*) indicate that the bearer of such a name is a worshipper of YHWH.

Texts from *Āl-Yāhūdu* and later source material attest to the coexistence of names referring to YHWH and Babylonian names. Thus one finds a man with one Babylonian and one Judean name: *Bēl-šar-uṣur* (*DJE* 2) points on the one hand to the chief Babylonian god, Bel-Marduk, while *Yāhû-šar-uṣur* (*DJE* 4) refers to the god YHWH. Another text (*DJE* 77) mentions two brothers, one of whom is named after the Babylonian god Nabu and the other after YHWH. There are also names that reference West Semitic gods, including Amurru and Bethel, as well as Egyptian, Iranian, and Arabic names.

In other words, the evidence does not show the exiles to have been separated from their Babylonian surroundings. Instead, one gets the sense of a multicultural community with a diverse mix of personal connections.[25] The exiles made contracts for inheritances and marriages, including marriages between YHWH worshippers and members of other ethnicities (exogamy). In one marriage contract from *Āl-Yāhūdu* Babylonian legal practice seems to be employed, as it involves Babylonian form and references to the gods Marduk, Zarpanitu, and

19. See Kratz, *Historical and Biblical Israel*, 152, and Pearce, "Continuity and Normality in Sources," 181–84.
20. See Nissinen, "(How) Does the Book of Ezekiel?," 85–98.
21. See Alstola, "Judean Merchants in Babylonia," 25–51.
22. See the case of a slave with a Yahwistic name in Alstola, "Judeans in Babylonia," 227.
23. On continuity, especially with the land-for-service model, see ibid., 179.
24. On this, see Zadok, *Earliest Diaspora*, 78.
25. See Kratz, *Historical and Biblical Israel*, 144.

Nabu.[26] Both the adoption of local legal practices and exogamy can be found in the Egyptian diaspora as well, and they might therefore be understood as a distinguishing characteristic of a certain form of Yahwism in the Persian period (see below, 5.4 and 5.5).

The exiles were well integrated in their societies both economically and socially, were in close contact with their neighbors and lived in Babylon for many generations. A biblical reference to this concept of identity in the Persian period might be found in the "Letter to the Exiles" in Jeremiah 29: "(5) Build houses and live in them; plant gardens and eat their fruits. (6) Take wives and have sons and daughters; take wives for your sons, and give your daughters in marriage, that they may bear sons and daughters. . . . (7a) And seek the welfare of the city . . . and pray to YHWH on its behalf."[27]

Given the situation depicted in the Babylonian texts, it is perhaps unsurprising that most likely only a small group of exiles returned to Judah. Even if the list of returnees in Ezra 2 does contain some historical truth, the number of returnees it gives, 42,360, is wholly unrealistic.[28] In the early Persian period the province of Yehud probably had only 12,000 inhabitants (Finkelstein), or perhaps at the most 30,000 (Lipschits).[29] At the same time, the archaeological record rules out the possibility of a mass return. Neither Jerusalem nor Yehud shows evidence of a spike in settlement growth in the early Persian period. A more realistic number of returnees would be around 4,000 people coming back to Yehud over several decades.[30]

Among the returnees were also scribes and elite artisans, probably including those who had been living alongside the royal family at the Babylonian court or those who had been a social elite from the exile settlements outside Babylon, in which literacy was also found.[31] Either way it seems reasonable to assume that this group of returnees represented a conservative circle that never felt at home in Babylonia. One thing that is clear, though, is that the group that decided to return were decisive for the biblical literature of the Second Temple period. The books of Ezra and Nehemiah show a version of religious identity that draws sharp boundaries but it must be seen among other forms of "Yahwism" in the Persian period.[32]

26. See Abraham, "Negotiating Marriage," 33–57.

27. See *DJE*, 5: "The present set of records relates to activities of those who remained in Babylonia, tilled the land, and built houses."

28. See, most recently, Bortz, *Identität und Kontinuität*, 146–49.

29. See Lipschits, "Demographic Changes," 364.

30. See Becking, "'We All Returned as One,'" 10.

31. On the phenomenon of literacy, see Hackl, "Babylonian Scribal Practices," 125–40.

32. For more details, see the different articles in Lipschits, Knoppers, and Oeming, *Judah and the Judeans*.

5.2 Persian Policy from 539 to 333

Neither the variety of forms of Yahwism in the fifth and fourth centuries nor the return of a group of exiles would have been possible, however, had there not been a sea change in the broader political situation. Beginning in 550, with Cyrus II, the Persian emperors built an empire worthy of the title. This empire, formed by Cambyses and Darius I through the incorporation of smaller states, stretched westward as far as the Aegean to the southern border of Egypt, and included the whole of Mesopotamia and the Iranian highlands in the east as far as the Indus valley (map 2).[33]

The beginning of the Persian period is generally dated to Cyrus II's conquest of Babylon (539), which was then ruled by the last Neo-Babylonian king, Nabonidus (556–539).[34] Shortly after coming to power Cyrus II (559–530) broke free of Median rule (550), and in 547–46 he extended his territory from Elam to Asia Minor. In 539 he moved on Babylon, taking advantage of the opposition of the priests of Marduk to Nabonidus, who had attempted to raise the status of Sîn (god of the moon) and Shamash (god of the sun) at the expense of the god of the city of Babylon. As Cyrus advanced, the priests of Marduk sided with him, and the city fell without a fight.

In the famous Cyrus Cylinder (*COS* 2.124) Cyrus celebrates the conquest of Babylon and presents himself as a loyal worshipper of the god Marduk.[35] From this royal ideological text and surprisingly similar statements in the book of Isaiah (Isa 44:28; 45:1–7), Hebrew Bible scholars have assumed that the great kings of Persia were religiously tolerant and supported local holy places.[36] But the religious policies of the Persians primarily served power politics and economic interests, which involved not only supporting local cults, but also containing them when necessary, which could include the destruction of their temples, as occurred in Didyma and Athens.[37]

The conquest of Babylon and the defeat of Nabonidus in 539 paved the way for further conquest. Though Cyrus II died in 530, in a campaign against the Massageteans in the east, his successors turned Persia into a world power. Cambyses (530–522) conquered Egypt, and Darius I (522–486) and Xerxes I (486–465) systematically organized the empire from the top down.

Shortly after Cambyses proclaimed himself pharaoh in Egypt (526, Twenty-seventh Dynasty) a rebellion broke out in Persepolis, under the leadership of

---

33. For the following, see Briant, *From Cyprus to Alexander*, 139–64.

34. See Grabbe, *History of the Jews and Judaism* 1:265–67.

35. See Kuhrt, "Cyrus Cylinder," 83–97.

36. See the objections of Donner, *Geschichte Israels* 2:426.

37. For the religious policy of the Achaemenids, see Kuhrt, "Problem of Achaemenid 'Religious Policy,'" 117–42.

a certain Gaumata, who claimed to be the lawful heir.[38] Cambyses died under unknown circumstances on his way home from Egypt, while Gaumata, who by then had taken the throne, was murdered by Persian tribal royalty.[39] It was in this turmoil that Darius I (522–486) became king.

A trilingual monumental inscription from Bisitun, on the ancient military road from Mesopotamia to Central Asia, gives an account of the turmoil around the throne and Darius I's seizure of power in Elamite, Babylonian, and ancient Persian.[40] Following the familiar pattern of chaos to order, the king's claim to power and its religious legitimations were grounded in the turbulence under Guamata and Darius's ascension to power is depicted as the return to orderly relations.[41] The Bisitun Inscription shows an effort to disseminate as broadly as possible the political claims of the Persian emperor. An Aramaic copy was also found on a papyrus from Elephantine, and it was presumably used in the Persian colony on the southern border of Egypt to train official scribes.[42]

The rapid succession of rulers in the subsequent history of the Persian Empire shows how the political circumstances changed between the conquest of Babylon in 539 to the Battle of Issos against Alexander the Great in 333. Beginning in the middle of the fifth century instability in the empire increased as a result of confrontations with the Greeks and the Egyptians. After the Ionian Revolt in Greece (500–494), the Battles of Marathon (490) and Salamis (480), and the defeat at Plataea (479), there was a a revolt in Egypt (464–454). With the help of the Delian League, the Libyan ruler Inaros took control of the Nile Delta, and the Persian administrative center of Memphis and made claims on the Levant as well.[43]

The Persian wars against the Greeks by Xerxes I (486–465) and Artaxerxes I (465–424/423) most likely did not end with what Herodotus (*Hist.* 7.151–152) portrayed as the "Peace of Callias" with the Greek cities (449). Rather, the clashes continued. Moreover, the uprising in the Western satraps of the same year (449) and in the satraps in Media and Asia Minor all added to the unrest in the empire.

For the Southern Levant the situation in Egypt was especially important. The Persians were able to put down the Inaros Rebellion in 454, but northern Egypt, with its various delta dynasts, continued to be a consistent source of

---

38. For this new dating, see Quack, "Zum Datum der persischen Eroberung Ägyptens," 226–46.

39. See Kuhrt, *Persian Empire*, 135–65, and Grabbe, *History of the Jews and Judaism* 1:268–69.

40. See Greenfield and Porten, *Bisitun Inscription*.

41. See Lincoln, "Bisitun and Persepolis," 107–26.

42. See Granerød, "'By the Favour of Ahuramazda,'" 455–80, and Kratz, *Historical and Biblical Israel*, 144–45.

43. For the following, see Briant, *From Cyprus to Alexander*, 515–692, and for Egypt see Ruzicka, *Troubles in the West*, 29–31.

unrest.[44] This ultimately led to Egypt freeing itself from Persian rule. Amyrtaios of Sais (404–398) founded a homegrown dynasty, and Egypt remained independent for sixty years. The pharaohs of the Twenty-eighth, Twenty-ninth, and Thirtieth Dynasties directed their attention to the Philistine and Phoenician cities of the Levant, effectively challenging the Persians—and leading to Persian countermeasures.[45]

Following the suppression of the satrap uprising in Phoenicia, Egypt was reintegrated into the Persian Empire under Artaxerxes III Ochos (359/358–338). This second iteration of Persian rule over Egypt lasted only a brief period (343–332), ending with Alexander the Great's defeat of Darius III Kodamannos (336–330) at the famous Battle of Issus and at the Battle of Gaugamela (331).

5.3 The Administrative System of the Persian Empire and the Province of Yehud Until the Fourth Century

Having conquered the Babylonian Empire, Cyrus adopted the administrative system already in place. The former Assyrian administrative center of Ramat Raḥel, near Jerusalem, had not been damaged and was expanded by the Persians.[46] Judah became the Province of Yehud (map 5) and was made part of the satrapy of Babylonia and Eber-Nari, a name reflected in the Hebrew *ebær hannāhār* [עבר הנהר], "beyond the river" (Neh 2:7–9; 3:7; Ezra 4:20; 8:36).

The Persian province of Yehud was very small, around 250 sq. km, with Jerusalem as its religious center and as administrative centers Ramat Raḥel and Mispah (the latter until around 450).[47] According to Neh 3, Yehud was divided into five districts: Jerusalem, Beth-Kerem, Mispah/*Tell en-Naṣbeh*, Beth-Zur, and Keilah. The archaeological record shows that Beth-Zur and Gibeon were sparsely settled, casting some doubt on the biblical account.[48] Yehud's borders can be pieced together through "Yehud stamp impressions," the majority of which come from Ramat Raḥel (307, or 53 percent of them) and significantly fewer from Jerusalem (163, or 28 percent).[49]

After the satrapy of Babylonia and Eber-Nari was founded, the Persian general Gubaru, who had participated in the conquest of Babylon, was named

44. See Ruzicka, *Troubles in the West*, 32–33.
45. See Betlyon, "Egypt and Phoenicia," 468–72.
46. See Lipschits et al., *What are the Stones Whispering?*, 98–104.
47. On the status of Mizpah/Tell en-Naṣbeh, see the summary in Grabbe, *History of the Jews and Judaism* 1:24, and Zorn, "Tell en-Naṣbeh," 443–45.
48. See Finkelstein, "Territorial Extent and Demography," 39–54.
49. See the overview in Lipschits and Vanderhooft, "Continuity and Change," 54, and in general Lipschits and Vanderhooft, *Yehud Stamp Impressions*

satrap. The reorganization of the empire might have begun as early as Darius I (522–486), but it was undeniably underway by the time of Artaxerxes I (465–424/423). According to Herodotus (*Hist.* 3.89–91) the province of Yehud was part of a smaller satrapy that included the territory of present-day Syria, Jordan, and Israel and was governed from Damascus.[50] Yehud was surrounded by the provinces of Idumea, Ashdod, Dor, Samaria, Gilead, Amon, and Moab (see map 5). The neighboring province of Samaria was especially significant, as it had a YHWH sanctuary of its own beginning in the middle of the fifth century (see below, 5.5).

Given the enormity of the Persian empire, the emperor's first priorities were to safeguard the borders from external invaders and to stabilize it internally with a tightly organized administrative system. This included an empire-wide postal system with messengers who guaranteed reliable communication of information,[51] a single language—so-called Imperial Aramaic—and a sophisticated tax system. There were local as well as centralized taxes generated by the provinces. Nehemiah 5:4 refers to a "king's tax/tribute," while Ezra 4:20 and 6:8 mention a "tribute of the province Beyond the River." Local contributions were also collected to finance the governor (Neh 5:14), local administrative tasks, and presumably the management of the temple as well (Neh 10:33–35; 13:12).[52]

The provinces were economically targeted toward international trade, and this period witnessed the beginning of the circulation of coinage as well. Silver Greek coins are attested in the Southern Levant as early as the sixth century.[53] From around 450 BCE coins were being minted in the Phoenician cities on the coast (Byblos, Sidon, Tyre), and from 440 BCE in the Philistine cities (Ashkelon, Ashdod, and Gaza). Originally based on the model of the Greek tetradrachma, Persian motifs began to appear as well, including the likenesses of Persian kings.[54] In Yehud the minting of coins began only in the early fourth century (see below, 5.6).[55]

Both the emergence of coins and the delay between their introduction on the coast and in Yehud occurred for political and economic reasons. After the Inaros revolt (464–454) and Egypt's separation from the empire in 404 BCE, the Persians needed to stabilize the Southern Levant, which had now de facto become more important for the empire. The coastal cities were given permission to mint their own coins, and Yehud became integrated into the economic area more fully

---

50. See Elayi, "Achemenid Persia and the Levant," 107–22.
51. See Kuhrt, "State Communication," 112–40.
52. For details, see Altmann, "Tithes for the Clergy," 215–29.
53. See note 99 below.
54. See Gitler and Tal, *Coinage of Philistia*, 63, 69.
55. This was the case for drachmas made in the minting cities of the Philistine coastal plain on behalf of Yehud and also for their own local minting; see ibid., 11–12, 63–64, 316–18.

than it had been before, as exemplified, for instance, by a rise in Greek imports.[56] The result was an economic upswing beginning in the second half of the fifth century, which was accompanied by a significant population growth.[57]

These political and economic changes suggest the value of distinguishing between a Persian Period I (539–450) and a Persian Period II (450–333) in the Southern Levant.[58] Though there is no significant typological change in the pottery,[59] the division corresponds to a change in political circumstances. In the first half of the Persian period Yehud sat on the sidelines of events, only coming to Persian attention with the new political environment of around 450. Most likely the structural arrangements found more broadly in the Persian Empire only took hold in Yehud beginning in this period: centralized monetary policy, unified administrative and governmental language (Imperial Aramaic), and the empire-wide system for disseminating information. It is still an open question whether Yehud only became its own province under Artaxerxes I (465–424/423)—before which it had belonged to the province of Samaria— or whether it had always the status of a province and its own governor.[60] Both the broader historical situation and the archaeological evidence seems to suggest the former, as the material culture of the early Persian period in Yehud shows significant continuities with the preceding period, with neither noteworthy demographic changes nor innovations in pottery. Large differences from the Babylonian period only begin to appear in the second half of the fifth century, and even more so in the fourth century.[61] These changes include the introduction of a new type of administrative seals, the so-called "Yehud stamp seals," which only include the name Yehud or an abbreviation of it (*yhd*; *yh*) from the beginning of the fourth century.[62] This leaves no doubt that Yehud—and thus Jerusalem as well—were less significant at the beginning of the Persian period, when the Persians were more interested in the Phoenician cities and Egypt.

5.4 Egypt and the "Judeans/Arameans" of Elephantine

Egypt offers a good example of Persian policies in the territories they controlled. After having been conquered by Cambyses in 526 the previous administrative

56. On this, see Ambar-Armon and Kloner, "Archaeological Evidence of Links," 1–22, n357.
57. See two contributions in Levin, *Time of Change*: Faust, "Settlement Dynamics and Demographic Fluctuation," and Edelman, "Settlement Patterns in Persian-Era Yehud."
58. See Carter, *Emergence of Yehud*, 115–17.
59. See Lipschits, *Fall and Rise of Jerusalem*, 193–94n34.
60. On this, see the overview in Frevel, *Geschichte Israels*, 300–301, and Grabbe, *History of the Jews and Judaism* 1:140–42.
61. See Lipschits, "Persian Period Judah," 194–96.
62. See Lipschits and Vanderhooft, "Continuity and Change," 59.

system was adopted, as it had been in Yehud, with top officials replaced by Persians.[63] Egyptian sources in Demotic language show that the scribes in the provinces were still Egyptian, while judicial offices were occupied by judges with Persian names (e.g., in Thebes). At the same time they continued to use local law, as in Babylonia. In Egypt this meant that it was probably only with the Persians that local legal tradition was first codified, in order to enable Persian officials to judge according to Egyptian law.[64]

To see what was actually entailed by the Persian policy of working with the circumstances they faced on the ground, we can look at the biography of the Egyptian official Udjahorresnet.[65] The son of a priest, Udjahorresnet served as the commander of the Egyptian fleet under the last two kings of the 26th Dynasty. When Cambyses captured Egypt (526), Udjahorresnet was taken to the royal court to serve as chief doctor and counselor.[66] While there he appealed to the king to allow for the restoration of the temple in the old capital of Sais (map 2). According to his account, from a naophorous statue from 519/518,[67] Udjahorresnet "taught" the king about the significance of the temple cult, requested that "all foreigners" be driven out of it, and asked Cambyses "to permit the temple all its privileges (again) as before." Cambyses thereupon went to Sais personally to sacrifice to the goddess Neith at the temple. According to the stela inscription, Udjahorresnet also served as a counselor to Darius I (522–486), who ordered the Egyptian to rebuild the scribal school—"the house of life" in Egyptian terminology—at the Temple of Sais. The scribes would be outfitted "with all good things . . . as it was written, just as it was earlier."[68]

The example of Udjahorresnet shows that in the early part of the period the Persians were interested in supporting important temples in their provinces in order to stabilize the empire (see below, 5.6).[69] Sais was the capital of the last native Egyptian kings and the seat of a powerful dynasty. It should be noted that Udjahorresnet's account shows Herodotus' account of Cambyses having destroyed the Egyptian temple to be false (*Hist.* 3.31–38).

The policy of the new Persian rulers of Egypt also affected a group of YHWH-worshippers who lived in a military colony in the south of Egypt in the fifth century. Information about this group, who referred to themselves as "Judeans/Arameans," comes from an archive of papyri discovered on the island

---

63. For the following, see Schütze, "Local Administration," 489–515.

64. For a critical evaluation, see Redford, "The So-Called 'Codification,'" 135–59.

65. See the overview in Kuhrt, *Persian Empire* 1:117–22.

66. On this, see Burkard, "Medizin und Politik," 35–57.

67. For the composition of the text and its religious dimension, see Baines, "On the Composition and Inscriptions," 83–92.

68. All quotes from Kuhrt, *Persian Empire* 1:117–19; see also Lichtheim, *Ancient Egyptian Literature* 3:36–41.

69. See Ruzicka, *Troubles in the West*, 22–23.

of Elephantine in the Nile at the beginning of the 20th century.[70] According to these texts, under the pharaohs of the 26th Dynasty—i.e., just before Cambyses—they had founded a temple for their God, whom they referred to as Yahu (*COS* 3.51). Part of this group might have come to Egypt after the conquest of Samaria (722/720),[71] while another part had arrived after the destruction of the Kingdom of Judah. According to Jer 41:16–17 (cf. also Jer 43:1–7 and 44:1) a group of Judeans had gone to Egypt after the murder of Gedaliah, including the prophet Jeremiah himself—if unwillingly.[72]

The Aramaic archive from Elephantine contained both private and official letters, contracts, onomastica, notes on ostraca, and literary texts. There were also numerous Egyptian texts in Demotic and Hieratic documenting the "Egyptian side" of Elephantine.[73] The texts and the archaeology of Elephantine show that the temple of the god Yahu and the temple of the Egyptian ram god Khnum were only one street apart. As the island was very small, people of a variety of backgrounds must have been living in very close proximity to one another. Elephantine was a "multicultural" community in Persian-era Egypt that included Persians, Egyptians, Syrians, Carians, Medes, and "Judeans/Arameans."[74] The quarter in which the Judeans lived was bordered in the south by the area of the temple of Khnum. Between them were the temple of Yahu and the street of the king. If the interpretation of the site's excavator, Cornelius von Pilgrim, is correct, the wall surrounding the Yahu temple extended as far as the Street of Kings. Perhaps this extension lies behind the destruction of the Jewish temple in 410 BCE, which according to the Aramaic papyri was ordered by the priests of the temple of Khnum (*COS* 3.51). The destruction might also have had religious motives, as the Judeans/Arameans sacrificed sheep, while for the Egyptians rams (male sheep) were holy. Notably, when the temple was rebuilt, burnt offerings were not further practiced (*COS* 3.52).[75]

A glimpse into the world of this multicultural community on Elephantine can be seen through the family archives of the Judean woman Mibtahiah.[76] Her name was built on the name YHWH ("[my] trust is YH[WH]"; cf. Pss. 40:5; 71:5), and she was the daughter of a "Judean" from Elephantine with land in the

---

70. For a good overview on the provenance of the Aramaic documents from Persian-period Egypt, see Siljanen, *Judeans of Egypt*, 67–93, with the map on page 68.

71. See Van der Toorn, "Anat-Yahu," 92–97.

72. See Ahituv, "Jeremiah in Egypt," 33–40.

73. On this, see Kratz, *Historical and Biblical Israel*, 137–47, and for the material Porten, *Elephantine Papyri*.

74. See *TAD* A6.7; B2.2; B2.3; B2.7; B2.8; B2.20; B3.6; D7.30 and Van der Toorn, "Ethnicity at Elephantine," 147–64, and Vittmann, "Arameans in Egypt," 239–40.

75. See the discussion in Vittmann, "Arameans in Egypt," 248, and Rohrmoser, *Götter, Tempel und Kult*, 214–18.

76. See Azzoni, *Private Lives of Women*, 134–35.

city of Elephantine. According to the texts she had first been married to a Judean by the name of Yezaiah, then to an Egyptian, the architect Pia, son of Pahi.[77] She was later divorced from him and, at the division of their assets, swore an oath on the Egyptian goddess Sati, the chief female deity of Elephantine. While Mibtahiah's third marriage was to an Egyptian, Eshor ("belonging to [the god] Horus"), their sons were nevertheless referred to as "Judeans of Elephantine" and "Aramean from Syene" (*TAD* B 2.6; 2.9; 2.11).

According to the archives of Mibtahiah and Ananiah, four Egyptian families had houses in the so-called Judean colony. One owner had the Egyptian name *Hwr bn pȝ-dj-ȝs.t*, Horus, son of Pediese (*pȝ dj ȝs.t* = "he whom [the Goddess] Isis has given"), referring to two of the most important Egyptian deities, Horus and Isis. He also bore the title "gardener of the god Khnum" (*gnn zy Ḥnwm 'lh'*),[78] meaning that Horus worked in the temple of the Khnum, the main deity of Elephantine.

Mibtahiah's archives also contain a number of contracts, including a certificate of the donation of her father's land, signed by eleven witnesses, the certificate of her marriage with Eshor, and the contract for the division of the estate among her sons (*TAD* B2.2–6 + 2.11; cf. *COS* 3.59–3.68). The names on the document give a sense of the cultural diversity in Elephantine. One witness has the biblical name Hoshea but was the son of one "Pete-Khnum," an Egyptian. Similar examples show that there was neither an undiluted YHWH cult nor a religious society in which marriages with people of other ethnoi and religions were impossible. Not only do the texts offer undeniable evidence of exogamy, they also contain numerous references to "other gods." Alongside Yahu/YHWH, the addressees of the letters and oaths also refer to Khnum, Sati, and the Babylonian gods Bel, Nabu, Shamash, and Nergal.[79] Syro-Palestinian deities are also mentioned, including Anat-Yahu, Anat-Bethel, Ashim-Bethel, and Herem-Bethel.[80] Meanwhile, a tax registry from the year 398 shows that alongside the god Yahu, Ashim-Bethel and Anat-Bethel were also worshipped by the cult community of Elephantine.

Monotheism—in the sense of an exclusive worship of one god, Yahu/YHWH, as demanded by the Ten Commandments—does not appear to have been important in the religion of the "Judeans/Arameans" of Elephantine,[81] nor do the texts give any evidence of the cultic rules and laws found in Deuteronomy. The Judeans celebrated the festival of Matzot and Passover—though

77. See Vittmann, "Arameans in Egypt," 241–47, with further examples.

78. *TAD* B3.10, l.10; pp. 90–93 (B3.11), l.6.

79. An overview on all deities represented in the theophoric names of the Aramaic documents can be found in Siljanen, *Judeans of Egypt*, 150.

80. See Becking, "Yehudite Identity," 403–19.

81. On this, see Knauf, "Elephantine und das vor-biblische Judentum," 179–88.

not in the manner prescribed in Deut 16—and had a Sabbath, but it was simply the name of a day of the week, not a rest day or holiday.[82] In nuce, the texts of Elephantine present a multicultural form of the YHWH religion not oriented around Deuteronomic prescriptions.

This divergence from the biblical tradition is especially notable given that Jerusalem and Elephantine were communicating with one another. When the Yahu temple was destroyed in 410/409 by a coalition of Egyptian troops and foreign mercenaries led by the commandant of Syene, Nāfina, the Judeans of Elephantine wrote to the governor of Yehud, the authorities in Samaria, and the high priest in Jerusalem. In these letters, the Judeans ask for permission to reconstruct the temple (*TAD* A4.5+4.7). The high priest and the authorities in Jerusalem did not respond (*TAD* A4.7: 19). Instead, according to a memorandum from 407, permission was granted by the governors of Yehud and Samaria, Bagawahya and Delaya (*TAD* A4.9). In other words, Elephantine was not cut off from the heartland of the YHWH religion, but maintained written correspondence with Yehud and Samaria, including the priests in Jerusalem, with the help of the Persian postal system and messengers (see below, 5.6).[1] This communication also points to a remarkable feature about the Judean community on Elephantine: given that around seven hundred Judeans and Arameans lived in Elephantine, and only five of the one hundred thirty witnesses in Aramaic documents did not personally sign their names, it seems that not only the religious elite but a significant part of the Judeans of Elephantine as a whole were literate.[83]

5.5 The YHWH-Sanctuary on Mount Gerizim and the Samaritans

Beyond the temple of Yahu at Elephantine, another YHWH temple is significant for reconstructing the religious history in Yehud. This one was on Mount Gerizim, near the city of Shechem (map 1). Both the archaeology and texts from the period suggest that the holy district was not only significantly larger than the one in Jerusalem—nearly 10,000 sq. m—but was probably also more important.[84] If one were looking for a preeminent YHWH community in Late Persian period Israel/Palestine, it would not be the cult in Jerusalem but the "Samaritans" at Gerizim. This is the group referred to in the New Testament and in other ancient

82. See Kratz, *Historical and Biblical Israel*, 140–42, and Becking, "Yehudite Identity," 406–15.
83. See Vittmann, "Arameans in Egypt," 241. On the calculation of the number of inhabitants, see Knauf, "Elephantine und das vor-biblische Judentum," 181–82, who argues for between 2,500 and 3,000 inhabitants; Rohrmoser, *Götter, Tempel und Kult*, 82, and Vittmann, "Arameans in Egypt," 239, agree with him. However, the archaeological evidence appears to rule out the possibility of such a high number of inhabitants (with thanks to Cornelius von Pilgrim).
84. So Frevel, *Geschichte Israels*, 324.

records as a syncretistic group (John 4:9; 8:48; Acts 8:25; and Josephus, *Ant.* 9.296). In historiography the term "Samaritan" designates a group of YHWH-worshippers on Mount Gerizim. In newer literature they are also referred to as "Samarian Yahwists."[85]

Until the excavations on Mount Gerizim in the 1980s scholars mostly relied on evidence from the Bible and other ancient works. All of these texts, whether from the Hebrew Bible (2 Kgs 17:24–41), the New Testament (Luke 9:51–56), or Josephus (*Ant.* 11.340–47; 12.257–64), portray the relationship between Samaria and Jerusalem as starkly opposing one another.[86] Historically the situation must have been different. No matter what position one takes on the relationship between the two temples, though, given the Gerizim sanctuary was built in the fifth century just 45 km north of Jerusalem, it is unlikely that the YHWH cult in Jerusalem was isolated from its neighbor to the north.

According to Yitzhak Magen, lead excavator of Mount Gerizim, the YHWH sanctuary was built around 480 BCE.[87] The site contained Persian-era coins and pottery, as well as bits of wood that offer a carbon dating for the first phase of the sanctuary between 480 and 332 BCE.[88] The complex was astonishingly large, between 98 and 96 meters on the sides, and had a massive wall.[89] At the north it had a six-room gate, similar to the Iron Age gates of Hazor, Gezer, and Megiddo (see above, 3.2). Inside the enormous sacred precinct was a main altar, whose exact position is unknown, and at least one peripheral altar. There was probably no temple in the first phase of the complex, only an open-air shrine that probably resembled the "high places" of the preexilic period (see, for example, 1 Sam 9:12–14).[90] It is possible, however, that a 6.5 × 18 m structure from the area was in fact a temple, a hypothesis strengthened by its three capitals with stylized palms.[91] Even if the actual "temple city" on Gerizim was only built in the third century, the archaeology attests to a monumental structure from the Persian period whose size greatly overshadows that of the Jerusalem temple and its sacred precinct.

Religious inscriptions from Mount Gerizim, as well as economic and administrative texts from Wadi ed-Daliyeh, located around 14 km north of Jericho,

---

85. See Dušek, *Aramaic and Hebrew Inscriptions*, 80–81 ("Samarian Yahwists"), and, for the classical distinction between "Samarians" and "Samaritans," see Kippenberg, *Garizim und Synagoge*, 34.

86. On this, see Hensel, *Juda und Samaria*, 13–14.

87. The earliest coin is a drachma from Cyprus dated ca. 480 BCE; see Magen, "Dating of the First Phase," 179–80.

88. For a slightly different position to Magen's, see Dušek, "Mt. Gerizim Sanctuary," 111–33.

89. See the overview in Magen, *Mount Gerizim Excavations* 2:98–103.

90. See Hensel, *Juda und Samaria*, 41.

91. Magen reconstructs it as an east-facing long-house temple, but this is too dependent on the model of the Jerusalem temple. See Magen, *Mount Gerizim Excavations* 2:141–44, and for a critique Hensel, *Juda und Samaria*, 44–46.

attest to a broad religious spectrum.[92] At one end, there was an almost classical YHWH cult on Mount Gerizim; on the other, a multicultural YHWH society rather similar to that of Elephantine and Babylonia, but located on the soil of the former Kingdom of Israel.

The Aramaic and Hebrew dedicatory inscriptions from the temple on Gerizim are predominantly from the Hellenistic period, but a few of the texts might date to the fifth and fourth centuries.[93] Most of the inscriptions were composed in Aramaic (Nos. 1–381) and refer to YHWH worshippers whose names differ little from those found in Yehud. Some of the names are based on YHWH, such as Delayahu or Yehonatan, others have "el" in them (a short form of Hebrew *ʾĕlohîm*), including Yishma-el or El-natan (Nos. 5 + 7). The tetragrammaton YHWH is found both in Paleo-Hebrew letters (No. 383, see also No. 389) and in Aramaic (No. 393). Pinchas and Eleazar, both names of priests in the Bible, are also attested to (Num 25:7, 11).[94]

In contrast to the dedicatory inscription from the temple on Mount Gerizim, the material from Wadi ed-Daliyeh is markedly more international.[95] The papyri, clay bullae, and coins from between 375 and 332 BCE most likely come from Samaria, the largest and most important city in Persian-era Palestine, and can therefore offer additional insights into the religious diversity of the Persian province of Samaria.[96] Alongside Israelite-Judean names, such as Yochanan, Hananiah, or Nehemiah, there are numerous Aramaic, Phoenician, Edomite, Akkadian, and Persian names.[97] For the most part the papyri are private contracts, such as deeds for slaves or property, loans, and security contracts, and possibly a transcript of a legal case. As in Elephantine, these texts give a picture of a local practice not organized around biblical guidelines—concerning the rights of slaves, for example—but influenced by other legal frameworks. For Elephantine it was Egyptian law; for the contracts of Wadi ed-Daliyeh, Babylonian law. Both the names and legal practices attested to in the Babylonian and Egyptian examples show the coexistence and interaction of various ethnoi to be a basic feature of life in the Persian empire.

The seals from Wadi ed-Daliyeh, meanwhile, as well as Samarian coins from the fourth century, show significant international influence as well. Alongside the Persian king (fig. 2) and the Phoenician demigod Bes and Baal of Tarsus one

---

92. For the following, see Kratz, *Historical and Biblical Israel*, 175–81.

93. See Magen et al., *Mount Gerizim Excavations* 1:14, 36–41, and Dušek, *Aramaic and Hebrew Inscriptions*, 5–7.

94. All numbers refer to Magen et al., *Mount Gerizim Excavations* 1.

95. See Dušek, *Manuscrits Araméens*, 487–89.

96. Zertal, "Pahwah of Samaria," 9–30.

97. See Dušek, *Manuscrits Araméens*, 486–95, and Lemaire, *Levantine Epigraphy and History*, 80–82.

FIGURE 2. Samaria coin with a Persian king seated on a throne, an Achaemenian fire altar, and the Greek inscription ΙΕΥΣ (fourth cent.). Drawing by Maria Bruske, after Meshorer and Qedar, *The Coinage of Samaria*, 51 (no. 38).

FIGURE 3. Yehud coin with the falcon and the inscription "Yehud" (fourth cent.). Drawing by Maria Bruske, after Keel, *Geschichte Jerusalems*, 2:981 (no. 608).

finds numerous Greek gods, including Zeus, Aphrodite, Heracles, Hermes, and Nike.[98] In contrast, the coins from Yehud of the same period also attest to Greek influence, but the breadth of motifs is markedly narrower than in Samaria and less international (fig. 3).[99]

5.6 Persian Religious Policy and the Second Temple in Jerusalem

To understand the religious and historical development of Yehud and Jerusalem as fully as possible—the construction of the Second Temple in particular—it must be studied in relation to the political events (see above, 5.2), administrative structures (5.3), and the YHWH communities of Elephantine, Babylon, and Samaria

---

98. See Meshorer and Qedar, *Coinage of Samaria*, 21–30.
99. See Wyssman, "Coinage Imagery of Samaria and Judah," 253–55.

(5.4; 5.5). This is especially important because the single vaguely reliable biblical source dates the construction of the temple to the reign of King Darius (Haggai 1:1*; 4:8; cf. Ezra 4:5, 24) [100]—but does not specify whether this was Darius I (522–486) or Darius II (423–404). If it is the latter, it would mean that the reconstruction of the temple and the religio-political developments that accompanied it occurred in the second half of the Persian era, when the YHWH temple on Mount Gerizim probably already existed.[101] Recent scholarship has offered a variety of scenarios for the reconstruction of the temple, from the thesis of a rivalry between Gerizim and Jerusalem to the argument that the small temple community in Jerusalem was something like a branch of the larger YHWH community at Gerizim.[102]

Scholarship has long gone along with the biblical account, from 2 Chr 36:22–23 and Ezra 1:1–4, in which the Persian king Cyrus officially decreed the rebuilding of the temple and the return of the cultic objects. The biblical texts on the "Edict of Cyrus" come from a significantly later period, however, and cannot support the thesis of a reconstruction of the temple under Cyrus II (559–530) on their own.[103] Given the history, moreover, it is also improbable that Cyrus II would have ordered actions to be taken in Jerusalem at the beginning of his rule (see above, 5.2).

With these issues in mind, there are two plausible scenarios for the construction of the temple. The first scenario begins with the idea that even after the conquest of Jerusalem in 587/586 a YHWH cult persisted in the area of the (only partly destroyed) temple (see above, 4.5), and that the Darius referred to in Haggai 1:1 was Darius II (423–404).[104] In this scenario the reconstruction of the temple and the religio-political developments would have occurred only when the Persian era province of Yehud began to attract the attention of the Persians (see above, 5.2) after the revolts in Egypt of 464–454 (Inaros) and in the satrapy of Eber-Nari (Megabyzos) in 449. Given the economic reorganization of around 450, it would seem reasonable to connect the religious developments in Jerusalem with the organization of Yehud in the second half of the fifth century. This thesis is strengthened by the fact that we know Darius II to have been involved with the religious life of a YHWH community elsewhere, as attested to by an Aramaic papyrus from Darius II officially establishing the date of a religious feast of the YHWH community of Elephantine (*TAD* A4.1).[105]

---

100. See Kratz, *Das Judentum im Zeitalter*, 89–92.

101. Edelman, *Origins of the Second Temple*, 332, connects the Second Temple either with Artaxerxes I or with the end of the rule of Xerxes.

102. See Hensel, *Juda und Samaria*, 413.

103. On the assessment of the (ahistorical) Edict of Cyrus in Ezra 6:3–5, see the overview in Grabbe, *History of the Jews and Judaism* 1:271–76.

104. Dequeker takes it to have been Darius II in "Darius the Persian," 88–89.

105. For a new interpretation of the wording in line 3 of *TAD* A4.1 see Dershowitz, "Darius II Delays the Festival."

While the first scenario dispenses with biblical accounts of Nehemiah and Ezra, the second scenario more closely resembles the classical model, with a few modifications.[106] It begins with the proposition that the Darius referred to in Haggai 1:1 is Darius I (522–486), and that the temple in Jerusalem was rededicated in the sixth year of his reign (515).[107] As in the case of Udjahorresnet (519/518), a member of the local elite—in this case from Jerusalem—acting as a special envoy for the Persian emperor had successfully lobbied for changes that benefited his religious community in the capital of his conquered kingdom.[108] Ezra 3:2 refers to a governor by the name of Zerubbabel who was a member of the house of David and who was involved in rebuilding the temple (see Hag 2:4; Zech 4:6–10). If something of the the cult at the Jerusalem temple did in fact remain, one might imagine Zerubbabel having undertaken a renovation project in Jerusalem similar to Udjahorresnet's in Sais.

The Hebrew Bible associates the real religious developments with Nehemiah and Ezra, though, both of whom are referred to in connection with a king called Artaxerxes. Traditionally Nehemiah (Neh 1:1) has been connected with Artaxerxes I (465–424/423), and Ezra's mission with Artaxerxes II (405/404–359/358; see Ezra 7:7),[109] for two reasons: first, Ezra's religio-political activities are presumed to have occurred only after the reconstruction of the Jerusalem city wall under Nehemiah. Second, a note in the book of Nehemiah has been read in connection with the famous Elephantine papyrus on the destruction of the Temple of Yaho (see above, 5.4). The letter, from 407, refers to the sons of Sinuballit of Samaria (*TAD* A4.7; *COS* 3.51). Sinuballit has been interpreted to be Sanballat, who is referred to in Neh 2:10, 19; 3:33. Hence Nehemiah is taken to have been active a generation before the sons referred to in the letter, i.e., between 445–433 (Artaxerxes I).[110]

According to Ezra 7:7–9, Ezra arose in the seventh year of a king Artaxerxes to announce the "law of the God of heaven" (Ezra 7:12) and to ensure the observance of the Torah. He is said to have supported cultic activities at the temple through financial contributions from the Persian court (Ezra 7:1–18; 8:26–27). Since the biblical account leads to historical contradictions—as it has Ezra and Nehemiah active at the same time—the "seventh year of King Artaxerxes" referred to in Ezra 7:7 is seen as referring to Artaxerxes II. This would

---

106. For the classical view, see Albertz, *Israel in Exile*, 119–32.

107. On this, see the overview in Frevel, *Geschichte Israels*, 306–10; Miller and Hayes, *History of Ancient Israel and Judah*, 518–20; for a classical position, Bright, *History of Ancient Israel*, 568–69.

108. See, for example, Blenkinsopp, who connects Udjahorresnet with Ezra and Nehemiah: "Mission of Udjahorresenet," 409–21.

109. See the overviews in Bright, *History of Israel*, 391–402, and Miller and Hayes, *History of Ancient Israel and Judah*, 528–30.

110. See Grabbe, *History of the Jews and Judaism* 1:295–97.

mean that Ezra would have appeared in Jerusalem around 398. According to the biblical account, at Artaxerxes's command Ezra proclaimed the Torah as divine law. This is often interpreted to mean that their local law was raised to the status of Persian Imperial law (Aram. *dāt*).[111] This would have been unparalleled in the Persian empire. And given that Ezra 7 was clearly written from a Jerusalemite perspective, and presumably originates from the Hellenistic period,[112] one ought to be cautious in drawing too many historical conclusions from this text.

The information from Nehemiah is historically implausible as well. While older scholarship attempted to reconstruct an authentic "Nehemiah memoir" out of Neh *1–7; *11–13, more recent scholarship sees this as unfeasible.[113] The biblical story, in which Nehemiah began as a cupbearer at the Persian court in Susa, but was sent to Jerusalem as a special envoy because he was so saddened by the destruction of Jerusalem, sounds as legendary as the idea that Jerusalem lay in ruins (Neh 2). Given all of the above, it is difficult to say what, if any historical information is to be found in the strongly theological accounts in Ezra and Nehemiah.

If one accepts the timing of the two special envoys, this history would resemble the first scenario: after 450, in the second half of the Persian period, political and economic developments lead to a growth in the importance of Yehud and its religious center in Jerusalem, enough that Jerusalem experienced religio-political development officially backed by Persia.

Whichever of the two scenarios one subscribes to, however, Jerusalem was a small temple city in this period.[114] The archaeological record shows that in the aftermath of the events of 587/586, the city had shrunk to encompass the old city of David on the southeastern hill (map 4). According to Israel Finkelstein, Jerusalem of the early Persian period was even smaller than that, and it had perhaps as few as between two hundred and five hundred inhabitants.[115] Only in the second half of the Persian period, after 450 BCE, did the population of Jerusalem rise to around one thousand people. As such only around three hundred more people were living in Jerusalem than in the YHWH community of Elephantine. Put another way, when the priests of Elephantine wrote to Jerusalem in 407, they were reaching out to a community barely larger than their own. This suggests that Jerusalem had a temple of transregional importance beginning in 407 at the

111. See Knoppers and Levinson, *Pentateuch as Torah.*
112. See Grätz, *Das Edikt des Artaxerxes,* 289.
113. See Gerstenberger, *Israel in the Persian Period,* 160–61.
114. For a "middle position," see Knauf and Guillaume, *History of Biblical Israel,* 159–60, who distinguish between a "first Second Temple" under Darius I and a "second Second Temple" after 450 BCE, but they connect the main religio-political activities with the latter.
115. See the overview in Geva, "Jerusalem's Population," 141–42, and for a contrary position Lipschits, "Demographic Changes," 365 (3,000 people at the end of the Persian period).

latest. The letter of the Yahu priests from Elephantine mentions "the high priest Yehochanan" and "the priests, who are in Jerusalem," as well as "the nobles of the Judeans" (*TAD* A4.7; *COS* 3.51).[116] This leads to the conclusion that at the end of the fifth century Jerusalem had a temple community with a priesthood, a high priest, and a Judean elite.

5.7 Summary

No era in the historiography of ancient Israel has undergone as radical revision over the last twenty years as the Persian period. While older scholarship took it for granted that one could broadly follow the biblical accounts from the books of Ezra and Nehemiah, there is no longer any doubt that the history played out rather differently, from the variety of forms of Yahwism in the period to the history and implications of the religious developments in Jerusalem.

To get the most reliable history of Israel in the Persian period one must rely on extrabiblical evidence. This begins with the fact that the largest and most important YHWH-sanctuary in the fifth and fourth century was not in Jersualem but on Gerizim, the holy mountain of the Samaritans. Even if one follows the traditional account, in which the Jerusalem temple was rededicated in 515, the temple should still be understood as being overshadowed in size and importance by the somewhat later temple on Gerizim.

Jerusalem only regained importance as a religious center when the Persian kings saw the value of organizing the Southern Levant more fully. This occurred after 450, when a new administrative structure was introduced and coins began to be minted, first in Phoenicia and Philistea and, starting with the fourth century, in Yehud (map 5). Over the course of this period important features of ancient Judaism developed: the weekly Sabbath, circumcision of male offspring, the centrality of Torah, and the belief in a single god (monotheism). [117]

A notable characteristic of the Persian period is the wide variety of forms of YHWH religion. At one end was the form of Yahwism practiced in Jerusalem and on Mount Gerizim, as described above. In contrast were the culturally open and flexible diaspora communities in Egypt and Babylonia. Both the Babylonian texts from *Āl-Yāḫūdu* and elsewhere, as well as the Aramaic texts from Elephantine, attest to a form of YHWH religion where people had a lively exchange with other ethnoi, practiced exogamy and, at least in the case of Elephantine, in which the Torah played no perceptible role.

---

116. See the copy of the letter with the wording "the nobles of Yehud" (*TAD* A4.8.18).
117. On this, see the contributions in Cohen and Frerichs, *Diasporas in Antiquity*.

Yet these two forms of the religion of YHWH in the Persian era were not entirely separate. The YHWH community in Elephantine was in epistolary contact with the temple community in Jerusalem and probably also with the one on Gerizim. Archaeological evidence also attests not only to a "Judean" settlement in Kition/Cyprus[118] and a Persian era YHWH temple in Idumea (*Hirbet el-Kōm*), but also to a YHWH sanctuary on the western border of Yehud (Lachish) itself.[119] This means that not only did a variety of forms of YHWH religion exist abroad but in the land itself, as well. This evidence suggests a further question: was the YHWH religion practiced in Jerusalem and Mount Gerizim the rule or the exception?[120]

However insoluble the question, the diversity of social forms of YHWH religion in the Persian era gives a sense of the sociohistorical environment in which the biblical literature of the period was composed. From the strict separation from all foreigners and a categorical rejection of exogamy in Ezra and Nehemiah on one extreme, to the advocacy of marriage with foreigners found in Ruth, which presents a religious identity based not on separation but integration, on the other—these, and the possibilities between them become comprehensible in the context of the variety of social forms of the YHWH religion that existed starting in the Persian era and continuing long into the Hellenistic era.

118. See Heltzer, "Epigraphic Evidence," 189–206.

119. See Lemaire, "New Aramaic Ostraca," 416–17, and, for Lachish, Stern, *Archaeology of the Land of the Bible* 2:479–80.

120. On this, see Levin, "Die Entstehung des Judentums," 2, who called Elephantine the "Normalfall."

CHAPTER 6

The Hellenistic Period (333–64/63 BCE)

Just as for the Persian period, the historical development of Jerusalem and Yehud in the Hellenistic age can only be understood in light of the changing political situation. The period can be divided into three phases: the relatively brief rule of Alexander the Great, the long period of the Ptolemies and Seleucids, and the Hasmonean Kingdom. To broadly summarize: in the third century the Southern Levant was controlled by the Ptolemies, in the second century by the Seleucids until the rise of the last "Jewish" kingdom under the Hasmoneans, after which Palestine was conquered by the Romans in 64/63 BCE.

6.1 Alexander the Great and the Rise of the Ptolemies

The book of Maccabees begins with the statement that Alexander, son of Philip of Macedon, defeated the Persian king while a young general, and died after a twelve-year reign as king of Macedonia (1:1–8). While the Macedonian kingdom lay at the edge of the Greek world, at the northwest of the Aegean Sea, it had become more influential under his father, Philip II (369–336).[1]

Through military development, access to new raw materials (wood and precious metal), and its reorientation to Greek ideals of eduction, the kingdom flourished. While the Persian King Artaxerxes III (359/358–338) had kept Philip II at bay at the siege of Perinthus (Thrace) in 340, Philip was nevertheless able to take control of the Greek Empire after his victory two years later, at the battle of Chaironeia (338). After Philip's death (336) his twenty-two-year-old son Alexander took over rule (334).

In a short time Alexander III—also called "the Great" (356–323)—had succeeded in creating a global empire. Following campaigns in Greece and the Balkans (335) he went on to conquer Persia. After defeating the Persian satraps in Asia Minor at the Battle of the Granicus River, near Troy (334), he came

---

1. For the following, see Briant, *Alexander the Great*, 7–22.

face-to-face with the Persian ruler himself, at the famous Battle of Issus (333). Alexander defeated the Persian king Darius III (336–330) and made himself emperor of Persia. As punishment for the Persian sacking of Athens in 480/479 Alexander had Persepolis burned to the ground ("panhellenic revenge"). In 332 he turned toward Egypt. The Phoenician city of Tyre fell after a seven-month siege, and Gaza after two months. Archaeological evidence of the destruction can be found all along the coastal plain, including in Tell Keisan (2b), Akko, Megiddo (II), and a Persian military post between Gaza and Ashkelon, excavated a few years ago (*Netiv HaAsarah*).[2]

According to Josephus, between the conquests of Tyre and Gaza, Alexander paid a courtesy visit to the high priest of Jerusalem. But this account, from "Antiquities of the Jews" (*Ant.* 11.304–345), is not historically reliable.[3] Alexander was focused on Egypt and, like Nebuchadnezzar II in 587/586, he left a general in charge of conquering the inland regions. Among these Samaria was of particular importance. The city resisted at first but fell in 332/331 and was converted into a Macedonian military colony. The cache of papyri, clay seals, coins, and jewelry found in a cave at Wadi ed-Daliyeh (see above, 5.5) was most likely the result of a flight of a group of Samaritans during these events. [4]

After the conquest of Egypt, Alexander made himself pharaoh, linking his reign with Egyptian royal ideology by taking the title "Son of Amun." He renovated the Amun-Temple of Thebes in Karnak, offered sacrifices to the Apis bull in Memphis, and made a pilgrimage to the oracle of the god Amun at the Siwa oasis, who was now worshipped as Zeus-Amon (map 2). In consequence the Egyptian priests accepted Alexander as the legitimate ruler. Notwithstanding his attempt to connect himself to the Egypt tradition, though, what Alexander did next would change the face of Egypt forever. In 331, he founded a city in the west of the Nile Delta that would become one of the most important metropoles of the Hellenistic age and ultimately marginalize the classical centers of Egypt: Alexandria.

While the city was only completed under Ptolemy II (285/283–246), even in Alexander's own lifetime it had become a major center for scholarship, literature, and philosophy. As a young man, Alexander had been tutored by Aristotle, a student of Plato's, who had already become a famous philosopher. Alexandria was a Greek city on Egyptian soil (*Alexandria ad Aegyptum*)[5] and, with members of many peoples choosing to settle there, it developed into a multicultural hub. Underwater discoveries from the 1990s has made it possible to get a sense

---

2. The site was excavated by Yael Abadi-Reiss from the Israel Antiquities Authority in 2014.
3. On the three versions of the legend, see Gruen, *Heritage and Hellenism*, 189–99.
4. See Dušek, *Manuscrits Araméens*, 606.
5. See McKenzie, *Architecture of Alexandria and Egypt*, 4.

of the importance of the city.[6] The construction of the lighthouse of Pharos, one of the seven wonders of the ancient world, had probably begun already with Alexander's successor Ptolemy I, as had the legendary Ptolemaic library, whose collection is estimated to have held forty thousand books.[7]

Judean and Samaritan Jews resided in Alexandria from its beginning. Further Jews came at the end of the fourth century as prisoners of war after the battle of Gaza, and in the third and second centuries as refugees.[8] According to the Greek historian Diodorus, late Hellenistic Alexandria had 300,000 inhabitants, including Egyptians, Greeks, Jews, Lycians, and Phrygians. According to the Letter of Aristeas, a pseudepigraphic epistolary novel from the late second century BCE, Jews were members of the larger community and were permitted a certain amount of self-governance, though not full political rights (*Politeuma*, see below, 6.4).[9]

It was in this Hellenistic, multicultural environment that the Septuagint, the Greek translation of the Hebrew Bible, was composed. According to the legend, Ptolemy II Philadelphos (285/283–246) is said to have requested, at the recommendation of his librarian Demetrius, a translation of the Jewish Torah to be composed by seventy-two translators—six translators from each of the twelve tribes of Israel. Contrary to the letter of Aristeas, however, it is clear that the Hebrew Bible was not translated all at once, but over a long period across the third and second centuries BCE.[10]

Shortly after the founding of Alexandria, Alexander went to Syria, to attack the heart of the Persian Empire. In 331, at the battle of Gaugamela on the upper Tigris River (present-day Armenia), he decisively defeated the Persians—one of his governors killing Darius III.

Alexander's empire reached its greatest proportions with the Indian campaign of 327–325. After his victory over the Indian rulers and the kings of the Punjab, he had Hellenistic cities built by the rivers of the Indus Valley. While preparing for further campaigns to the west and to Arabia, however, Alexander died in Babylon, at the age of only thirty-three (323).[11] As he had left no rightful heir—his half-brother Arrhidaios was considered mentally ill—his military elite clashed over the division of his great empire.[12] Alexander had preserved the Persian administrative system and installed some of his own people as satraps

---

6. For details, see Robinson and Wilson, *Alexandria and the North-Western Delta.*

7. See Nesselrath, "Das Museion und die Große Bibliothek," 65–90.

8. See Zangenberg, "Fragile Vielfalt," 96–99.

9. See Moore, *Jewish Ethnic Identity,* and Honigman, "Jewish Communities." See below note 50.

10. See the overview in Frevel, *Geschichte Israels,* 337–38, and see Grabbe, *History of the Jews and Judaism* 2:65–68.

11. See Briant, *Alexander the Great and His Empire,* 23.

12. See Hölbl, *History of the Ptolemaic Empire,* 11–14.

in the provinces. Ptolemy ruled in Egypt, Seleucus in Syria and the east of his empire. With these two centers of power, Alexander had essentially set the fault lines that would shape the breakup of his empire. This division put the Southern Levant, including "Judea" and Jerusalem, at the tense boundary between the two great powers—the Ptolemies in Alexandria, and Seleucids in Antiochia—where they would remain until the Romans finally conquered the region two centuries later.

The Wars of the Diadochi (from the Greek διάδοχοι, "successor"), which continued until 281, led to four subempires: Greece went to Cassander; Thrace and part of Asia Minor to Lysimachus; the rest of Asia Minor, Syria, and the eastern portions of the empire went to Seleucus; Egypt went to Ptolemy. While Palestine and the Phoenician coast were originally ruled by Ptolemy I Soter (323–283)—from 323–306 as the satrap of Egypt and from 306–283 as Ptolemaic king[13]—Antigonus I Monophthalmus and his son Demetrius Poliorcetes asserted a claim on the region as well. In the Battle of Gaza of 315, Ptolemy I received the support of Seleucus, then the satrap of Babylonia (321–305) and later the Seleucid king (305–281). Demetrius was defeated and the province of Babylon went to Ptolemy. In 302 Ptolemy occupied Jerusalem, leading to another migration to Egypt. At the Battle of Ipsos in Phrygia, in 301, Syria/Palestine was also taken by the Ptolemies. In 274 the "Six Syrian Wars" began, in which the Ptolemies and the Seleucids fought over control of the Southern Levant.[14] Only with the victory of Antiochus III (the "Great") against the Ptolemaic general Scopas at Paneas in 200/198 did the Seleucids finally achieve control over the entire region.

6.2 Judea Under Ptolemaic Rule (Third Cent.)

From around 320 until 200/198 the former Persian province of Yehud was controlled by the Ptolemies. The former province was part of Coele-Syria and, along with Libya, Cyprus, and Egypt, formed the heart of the Ptolemaic Empire. The empire was a single monetary zone, taxed by representatives of the king from Alexandria,[15] a practice that can be seen at play in Syria-Palestine in a decree by Ptolemy II from 260.[16]

The Ptolemies' economic interests also served as a catalyst for cultural development in the Southern Levant. They modified the Persian administrative

---

13. See ibid., 24–34, and Worthington, *Ptolemy I*, 147–65.
14. On this, see the overview in Frevel, *Geschichte Israels*, 330.
15. See Hölbl, *History of the Ptolemaic Empire*, 58–60.
16. See Grabbe, *History of the Jews and Judaism* 2, 55–56, and Huß, *Wirtschaft Ägyptens*, 49.

system, supported Greek influence, and their politics contributed to a greater importance of Jerusalem and the high priest.[17] All of these measures lead both to the political stabilization of the empire and its economic prosperity.

Egypt and the Southern Levant both experienced an economic upswing in the third century, a development that brought with it a widening of the separation between rich and poor. There were a few large property holders, but many farm laborers who had to struggle to earn their daily bread.[18]

As before, the former Persian province of Yehud—now referred to by the Greek "Judea" (Ἰουδαία)—encompassed only a small territory beyond the coastal plain. The settlement density in the hill country significantly increased, however, and it is estimated that around 40,000 people lived in Judea in the third century.[19] As in the Persian era, the colony of Samaria with the YHWH temple on Gerizim was at its northern end; in the west, Ashdod, with Yavneh as its main settlement; in the south, the western portion of Idumea, including Maresha/*Tell Sandaḥanna*; and in the east the Ammanites whose central town was Aduraim.

Coins and seals show that the Ptolemies were concentrated on the coastal plain. As their main interest from the provinces was economic, they were content simply to collect taxes from Judea and Jerusalem. In Egypt a complex tax system was introduced with more than 180 different taxes and duties known by name.[20] These taxes were connected with a political program that offered lower taxes to individuals and professional groups that contributed to the spread of Greek culture. As Egyptian texts show, these "Tax-Greeks" could also include Jews.[21]

As in Greece, the right to collect taxes was awarded to the highest bidder.[22] The Ptolemies thus made themselves economically useful to the local elites, as bids were based on the revenues they could expect to collect, giving locals a clear advantage over foreigners.[23]

The so-called "Zenon papyri" offer a window into Ptolemaic tax practices. This archive, from a Ptolemaic administrator named Zenon, contains around two thousand texts from between 261 and 239, around forty of which are concerned with Syria-Palestine.[24] One of the letters to Zenon informs him that certain farmers had done their work, but had not received their pay. As the workers

17. Grabbe, *History of the Jews and Judaism* 2:333–35.

18. On this, see the Zenon Papyri, note 24 below, and Adams, *Social and Economic Life*, 20–21, 82–90.

19. See Finkelstein, "Territorial Extent and Demography," 46–51.

20. See Huß, *Die Verwaltung des ptolemaiischen Reiches*, 244.

21. See Thompson, "Infrastructure of Splendour," 246–47.

22. On this, see Hölbl, *History of the Ptolemaic Empire*, 62–65.

23. See Knauf and Guillaume, *History of Biblical Israel*, 200, with reference to Josephus, *Ant.* 12.4.1–4 (Niese ed. §§154–77).

24. See the overview in Clarysse, "Zenon Papyri Thirty Years On," 31–43.

were generally paid in natural produce, they would need to borrow money in order to afford even the simplest necessities.[25] Such a situation often led to debts, prison, and slavery.

As part of his job as chief tax administrator for the Ptolemaic chief finance minister (Dioketes) Apollonius in Alexandria, Zenon travelled to the Southern Levant in 259. He began at Straton's Tower, which would later become Caesarea, went on to Jerusalem, and from there to the Transjordan, the main stop of his journey.[26] His numerous references to the abundance of wheat show that, as in the Persian period, Judea was primarily a grain producer. Ramat Raḥel remained an important administrative center, though Jerusalem was overtaking it in importance. Of the 312 stamp seals from the fourth and third centuries, 60 percent were from Ramat Raḥel, and 19 percent from Jerusalem. In the second century the reverse is true: of 142 pieces, 61 percent come from Jerusalem and 22 percent from Ramat Raḥel.[27]

In Judea, coins were now being minted with Ptolemaic motifs, such as the eagle, the head of Ptolemy II, or that of his sister-consort Arsinoe II, though they were still inscribed with the name "Yehud" (fig. 4).[28] Among the seal impressions, one group included a five-pointed star, the well-known pentagram, between whose points are engraved the five letters *jršlm* ("Yerushalaim" = Jerusalem).[29] It is possible that the two types—the coins with Ptolemaic motifs and the seals with the pentragram—pertained to two different tax systems: one for the Ptolemaic, another for the Jerusalem temple.[30] After all, the Ptolemies had a political interest in the temple as a guard against political instability, in order to keep profits flowing into Alexandria. The Ptolemy's focus on economic gain brought with it a certain flexibility when it came to established conditions.[31] Persian period arrangements were for the most part left in place—local *Yehud* coins, for example, continued to be minted long into the third century.

6.3 Jerusalem and the Ptolemies

In the third century, the religious community of Jerusalem was still organized as it had been described in the letter from the priest of Elephantine from 407:

---

25. See Reekmans, "Behaviour of Consumers," 120–24.
26. On this, see Keel, *Orte und Landschaften* 4/2:1137, and Grabbe, *History of the Jews and Judaism* 2:52–53.
27. See Lipschits and Vanderhooft, "Continuity and Change," 51, 54.
28. See Meshorer, *Treasury of Jewish Coins*, 19–20.
29. See Keel, *Orte und Landschaften* 4/2:1146.
30. This was suggested already by Lapp, "Observations on the Pottery of Thāj," 22–35.
31. On this, see Grabbe, "Hyparchs, *Oikonomi* and Mafiosi," 86–87.

a group of priests led by a high priest, as well as a council of elders, referred to in the Hellenistic period as the "Gerousia." While most of the archaeological remains of Jerusalem from the Hellenistic period come from the Hasmonean period, some have their origins in the Ptolemaic era.[32] On the southeastern hill—the old city of David—a rampart ("Macalister-Duncan wall") was constructed at the old "Stepped Stone Structure" (see above, 2.5; 3.4). According to the Letter of Aristeas (100–104 CE), the Acra, the first of what would eventually be three citadels, was built under Ptolemy II Philadelphus (283–246). Josephus writes that in 200 BCE the citadel served as the seat of the Ptolemaic garrison (*Ant.* 12.133–38), though, as with the letter, the reliability of this information is questionable. Recent excavations by the Hebrew University of Jerusalem in the so-called "Givati Parking Lot" northwest of the city of David (map 4) show that the Acra was not at the highest part of the city, as Josephus and the Letter of Aristeas have it, but far below the level of the Temple Mount.[33]

These various construction projects can be understood as arising partly in connection with the Ptolemaic conflicts with the Seleucids, partly with the Ptolemaic interest in promoting Greek culture in the region. One of the purposes of Hellenization for the Ptolemies was to have a Greek-educated local elite able to serve in official positions in the Ptolemaic empire. This increased Greek influence is also attested to in the archaeology of the third century. While Greek pottery was already to be found in Judah in the eighth century, the quantity increased significantly in the Ptolemaic period.[34] It was not an era of sudden "Hellenism" (from Ἑλλμνισμός in 2 Macc 4:13), as J.G. Droysen put it in 1836, but a continuation of a development that had already begun in the late period of the Judean monarchy, and which reached a temporary apex in the third to second century. The Yehud coins from the fourth and third centuries include more Greek motifs, such as the head of Athena, the Attic owl, the lily, or the falcon (fig. 4).[35] The repertoire of images is significantly smaller than Samarian coins from the same period (see above, 5.5). The coins are inscribed with the word Yehud, written as *yhd* or, on later coins, as *yhwd*. On one coin the Athenian owl is in the middle and to its left and right are the inscription "Yohanan the Priest" (see fig. 5),[36] while on another—again with the Athenian owl—are the words "Hezekiah the Governor" (*yḥzqyh hpḥh*). In other words, the coins attest to a Greek influence in Yehud that had achieved official status.

Greek influence is also visible in the more than fifteen-hundred jar and amphora handles from between 260–150 BCE found on the southeastern hill

---

32. For the following, see Bieberstein, *Brief History of Jerusalem*, 104–15.
33. See Ben-Ami and Tchekhanovets, "'. . . And They Also Were in the City'" 313–22.
34. See Wenning, "Griechischer Einfluss in Palästina?," 29–60.
35. See Wyssman, "Coinage Imagery of Samaria and Judah," 242–53.
36. See Meshorer, *Treasury of Jewish Coins*, 3/20.

FIGURE 4. Yehud coin, Ptolemy II, his sister-consort Arsinoe II, and the inscription "Yehud" (third cent.). Drawing by Maria Bruske, after Keel, *Geschichte Jerusalems*, 2:1136 (no. 665).

FIGURE 5. Yehud coin with the Athenian owl and the inscription "Jochanan, the priest" (fourth/third cent.). Drawing by Maria Bruske, after Keel, *Geschichte Jerusalems*, 2:988 (no. 620).

in Jerusalem. Alongside profane motifs, such as the Rose of Rhodes, there are also symbols of gods: the head of the sun god, Poseidon's trident, the staff of Hermes, and the *Thyrsus* of Dionysus.[37]

This might lend support to the argument that the adoption of the ideals of Greek education in Jerusalem, including a gymnasium and an *ephebeia*, did not begin with the high priest Jason (174–171 BCE, 2 Macc 4:9), but earlier, in the Ptolemaic period. At the gymnasium (γυμνάσιον) the Greek ideal of education (παιδεία) was passed on through a combination of literary and artistic education alongside athletic training. At the *ephebeia* (ἐφεβεῖον) young men (*ephephboi*) were trained to take on the responsibilities of full citizens.[38]

---

37. On this, see Ariel, *Excavations at the City of David*, 13–98, and Keel, *Orte und Landschaften* 4/2:1154–55, including figs. 669–74.

38. See Cambiano, "Becoming an Adult," 86–119.

Jerusalem had both a traditional temple school and Greek educational institutions. Since the city was still small in the third and second centuries—the great construction projects only occurred under the Hasmoneans—the Greek and Jewish schools were undoubtedly in close proximity to one another. This neighborhood might well have been significant to the literary production of the Hellenistic period, a setting in which the Jerusalemite scribes were encountering both questions of Jewish identity and relations with other *ethnoi*.

6.4 High Priests Between Ptolemies and Seleucids

As mentioned above, construction in Ptolemaic-era Jerusalem occurred against the backdrop of the political situation of the period. In the third and second centuries, the office of the high priest had begun to become politicized. Under the Ptolemies it became a hereditary position, passed down through a single family, perhaps imitating Egyptian practice.[39] This development led to feuds with other influential families. The rivalry between the Oniads, who controlled the office for multiple generations, and the Tobiads, a respected family of Jerusalem, was central to the politics of the temple city long into the second century. The Oniads leaned pro-Seleucid; the Tobiads pro-Ptolemaic. The Zenon papyri contain a reference to a landowner named Tobias, in 260, who was commander of a Ptolemaic cleruchy (military colony) in the district of Ammanites.[40] This broadly accords with Josephus's Tobiad novel (*Ant.* 12.1.154–236), which gives an account of a certain Joseph from the Tobiad family who won the bid for a Ptolemaic tax farming contract covering all of Coele-Syria and Phoenicia, which he held for twenty-one years.[41]

In what followed, the rival Oniad and Tobiad families allied themselves with the Ptolemies or the Seleucids depending on the political winds. In one example, the high priest Onias II halted tribute payments to the Ptolemies during the reign of Ptolemy III Euergetes (246–221), who responded by threatening to expropriate Jerusalem and convert it into a military colony.[42] Thereupon Onias handed leadership of the people (*prostasia*) over to his nephew, Joseph, of the Tobiad family, though he kept his position as high priest. The opposition between the high priest and the Tobiades escalated under Joseph's son, Hyrcanus. He oriented successfully to the Ptolemies and was given rule over Judea by Ptolemy IV Philopator (221–204). But he was unable to assert himself over

---

39. See Grabbe, "Were the Pre-Maccabean High Priests 'Zadokites'?," 205–15.
40. See, for example, Papyrus 59003, 59075, 59076, 59802; Edgar, *Zenon Papyri*.
41. See Hengel, *Judaica, Hellenistica et Christiana* 2:129.
42. See VanderKam, *From Joshua to Caiaphas*, 128–29.

the high priest Simon II (ca. 215–196), who had come into office in the interim. Hyrcanus fled to ʿIrāq al-Amīr in Transjordan, around 17 km west of present-day Amman (map 2). According to Josephus, Hyrcanus established a Jewish temple there, though excavations of the architecture from the third and second centuries resemble more a fortress than a temple.[43]

The changing political situation in Jerusalem is connected with the six Syrian wars fought between the Ptolemies and Seleucids over control of Syria-Palestine, from 274 to 168. In the conflicts of the third century the Ptolemies initially had the upper hand. This included the conflict with the Seleucid ruler Antiochus III Megas—also referred to as "the Great" (222–187)—in Antiochus's attempt to take over Phoenicia and Palestine at the end of the Fourth Syrian War (217), which he finally lost to Ptolemy IV Philopator (221–204) at the Battle of Raphia.[44] In the years that followed Antiochus III managed to extend his rule to Asia Minor and the eastern satrapies and collaborated with the Macedonian ruler Philip V (222–179). It was only in the Fifth Syrian War (201/200–198) that Antiochus III was able to inflict a crushing defeat to the Ptolemaic general Scopas in the Battle at Panium (Paneas) and bring "Syria and Phoenicia" into Seleucid hands.[45]

According to Josephus and the book of Sirach (Sir 50:1–4) the high priest Simon II (ca. 215–196) of the Tobiad family was able to negotiate a tax reduction for temple business. It is unclear how much historical fact is contained in the letter quoted by Josephus (*Ant.* 12.138–144), though one aspect that might speak for its historicity is that Antiochus III generally acts politically astutely, forging diplomatic contacts with the Ptolemies, culminating in a political marriage between his daughter Cleopatra I and Ptolemy V Epiphanes in 193. According to Josephus, Antiochus III granted a three-year tax holiday, reduced the tribute owed to the Ptolemies by a third, and granted officials from the temple and the council of elders (*gerousia*) exemptions from the personal tax and the head tax. Similar actions are attested to in Egypt, in which specific groups, such as priests or teachers, were exempted from particular taxes.[46]

At the same time the larger global political situation also demanded an easing of tensions in Palestine, Judea, and Jerusalem: Rome was becoming more powerful and was increasingly shaping Seleucid policy in Jerusalem.[47] At the same time, local privileges disappeared and sanctions increased. The evolving political situation led to conflicts in Jerusalem. Battles for power between the

---

43. On this, see Frevel, *Geschichte Israels*, 341.

44. An inscription from the Beth Shean region gives an account of the various phases of the conflict: Landau, "Greek Inscription Found," 54–70, and Berlin, "Between Large Forces," 13.

45. On this, see Bickermann, *Jews in the Greek Age*, 118–20.

46. See Huß, *Die Verwaltung des ptolemaiischen Reiches*, 248.

47. On the course of historical events, see Green, *Alexander to Actium*, 286–311.

pro-Ptolemaic and the pro-Seleucid parties led to the office of high priest being put up for sale. The last legitimate high priest was Onias III (196–175), the grandson of Onias II (220–215) and the son of Simon II (215–146), who took office during the reign of Seleucus IV Philopator (187–175), a period when Seleucid conflicts with the Romans were on the rise.[48]

What followed was a rapid change in the office of the high priest. Unrest began after the dismissal of Onias III, leading to a pro-Ptolemaic faction from Jerusalem (led perhaps by Onias IV?) to emigrate to Egypt. According to Josephus, Ptolemy VI (180–145) permitted the Jewish high priest to erect a temple to YHWH in what might already have been a Jewish settlement (*Ant.* 12.388; 13.65–71). It is not clear whether this temple in was in Leontopolis (*Tell el-Yehūdīye*) or Heliopolis (biblical On, Gen 41:45, map 2).[49] Alongside other Jewish communities in Memphis, Heracleopolis, Edfu, and Alexandria, Egypt exhibited a variety of forms of ancient Judaism.[50] Twenty papyri from Heracleopolis show that the Jews in the city were organized as a *politeuma*, which meant they had the right to limited self-rule, including the free exercise of religion and their own legal jurisdiction. Notably, the texts from Heracleopolis show no explicit connection with Jewish law found in the Torah.[51]

6.5 Antiochus IV and the Maccabean Revolt (Second Cent.)

The so-called Maccabean revolt is intimately related to wider political developments of the second century, when Seleucid politics were being decisively altered by their encounter with Rome. Philip V, king of Macedonia and an ally of Antiochus III, had provoked Rome by attacking Pergamon and Rhodes. This led to a war (200–197) ultimately won by Rome, that ended with the Battle of Cynoscephalae (197). Shortly after, Anitochus III, along with the Carthaginian general Hannibal, attempted to conquer Greece and failed, losing the famous Battle of Thermopylae (191) and the Battle of Magnesia (190). In the "Treaty of Apamea" (188/187) that followed, the Seleucid Empire was forced to cede all of its European territory as well as part of its territory in Asia Minor to Rome, Pergamon, and Rhodes.[52] Antiochus III was also obliged to pay vast reparations (15,000 talents of silver, i.e. over four hundred tons), which made it necessary

---

48. See VanderKam, *From Joshua to Caiaphas*, 181–92.
49. On this, see Frey, "Temple and Rival Temple," 186–94.
50. See Honigman, "Jewish Communities," 117–35.
51. On this, see Cowey and Maresch, *Urkunden des Politeuma*, 25–28, with a discussion of the position of Mélèze-Modrzejewski.
52. Green, *Alexander to Actium*, 421–24.

for the Seleucids to change their fiscal policy.[53] The tax privileges that had been granted to the pro-Seleucid high priest in Jerusalem, Simon II (215–196), were retracted, and temples across the empire were forced to pay higher taxes. While attempting to plunder the Baal temple near Susa in Persia in 187, Antiochus III was killed. As part of his family were being held captive in Rome, including the rightful heir, Antiochus IV, Seleucus IV Philopater (187–175) ascended to the throne. Seleucus attempted to skim off the profits from the temples to pay the high reparations demanded by the Romans. According to 2 Maccabees, he ordered his minister Heliodorus to take directly from the treasury of the Jerusalem temple. While the account in 2 Macc 3 has all the hallmarks of a legend, the core of the events are in fact attested to in two extrabiblical sources. A letter from the king to Heliodorus is mentioned on an unprovinanced stela, while three stela fragments from Maresha (Shephelah) attest to Seleucus giving his courtier Olympiodorus authority over the temples in Coele-Syria and Phoenicia.[54]

When Heliodorus had Seleucus IV murdered in Antiochia in 175, the political situation changed yet again. With Antiochus IV Epiphanes (175–164) came a ruler who is mentioned not only in biblical texts but also in Egyptian texts of the second century. In the book of Daniel he is referred to as the "small horn" (Dan 8:9); in the Egyptian prophecy of the Lamb of Bocchoris as "the Mede."[55]

The new leadership led to some significant changes in Jerusalem as well. Menelaus (171–162), presumably the son of the pro-Seleucid captain of the temple Simeon (2 Macc 4:23), offered Antiochus IV double the tribute that was given at the time, for which he was rewarded with the high priest's office. The previous high priest, Jason, fled to the Transjordan, probably to Hyrcanus's fortress at 'Irāq al-Amīr (see above, 6.3). But the offer of 660 talents of silver was unrealistic, and Menelaus began to take directly from the temple treasury. In the course of the Egyptian campaign of the Sixth Syrian war of 170/169 rumor had it that Antiochus IV had been killed, and the previous high priest, Jason, attacked Menelaus and brutally came back to power.[56] Antiochus IV viewed this as a rebellion and punished the city. In the process, he plundered the temple and took away the cultic objects. The crisis only deepened when Antiochus IV sent soldiers to Jerusalem, led by his general Apollonius, in the autumn of 168. Deadly clashes erupted in the city of David and in the southern temple area, at the end of which the Seleucids set up a military garrison on the Acra (2 Macc 5:24–25).

53. See Aperghis, *Seleukid Royal Economy*, 293–95.

54. See Cotton and Wörrle, "Seleukos IV to Heliodoros," 193, and Gera, "Olympiodoros, Heliodoros and the Temples," 131.

55. See Schipper, "Tradition und Innovation," 45–75.

56. See Bickermann, *Jews in the Greek Age*, 144 45.

Antiochus's actions were not primarily religio-political, as they are portrayed in the biblical account. In contrast to what is found in Daniel or Maccabees, his actions were not intended to inhibit the Jewish religion or abolish the YHWH cult, but to pacify a political trouble spot. The high priests had made Jerusalem into a political nuisance for the Seleucids that needed to be dealt with. Whether or not the high priest Menelaus had actively pursued hellenizing measures himself,[57] the political activities of the high priests in Jerusalem led the Seleucids to further hellenize Jerusalem, supporting powers that were culturally open and opposed to the priesthood and YHWH temple (see above, 5.5). Through various measures, including the introduction of Greek fashion (2 Macc 4:12) and a citizenship registry (2 Macc 4:9), the Seleucids sought to gradually transform Jerusalem into an Antiochene *polis*.[58]

The political attack on religious practices referred to in the biblical sources were at their heart of this attempted hellenization. According to Dan 7:25 and 2 Macc 6:6, 10–11, circumcision and the Sabbath were banned, and Jews were demanded to consume pork, in contravention of the biblical separation of pure and impure animals. According to 2 Macc 6:2 the YHWH temple was dedicated to Zeus Olympios. This should not be understood as a suppression of the Jewish god by the Greek, however, but as a Greek interpretation (*interpretatio graeca*) of the god YHWH.

In other words what was happening in Jerusalem was nothing more than what had occurred in the Philistine region in the late Persian era. On the obverse of a coin from 380 BCE is a man's head with a Corinthian helmet, and on the reverse a god on a winged wheel. The inscription can be read either as "Yehud" or "YHW" (Yahu; see fig. 6).[59] In one case a god is depicted who is in some way connected with "Yehud"; in another case it gives the name of the god, YHWH. Whichever way one reads it, the silver coin seems to attest to a hellenization (*interpretatio graeca*) of the god YHWH in the year 380—more than 200 years before Antiochus IV—in which YHWH is connected with a Greek god, probably Dionysus.[60] When read in their historical context, in other words, Antiochus IV's actions in 175 are not as radical as they might seem.[61]

And yet at one point Antiochus went beyond the earlier hellenization of Jerusalem: he ordered an offering of pig meat in the Jerusalem temple. This act,

---

57. See Haag, *Das hellenistische Zeitalter*, 69.

58. On the Hellenization and its limits, see Collins, *Jewish Cult and Hellenistic Culture*, 21–43.

59. On this, see Gitler and Tal, *Coinage of Philistia*, 230, who interpret the coin as a Philistian one. See also Grabbe, *History of the Jews and Judaism* 1:66–67, with a critical discusson of the question whether the god YHWH is meant.

60. See Keel, *Orte und Landschaften* 4/2:977–78, with figs. 603–5.

61. At its core, this is the same principle applied by Alexander the Great in Egypt when he began to worship Amun of the Siwa oasis as Amun-Zeus (see page 94).

FIGURE 6. Yehud coin with a god on a winged wheel and the inscription "Yehud" or "Yahu" (ca. 380 BCE). Drawing by Maria Bruske, after Keel, *Geschichte Jerusalems*, 2:978 (no. 603).

referred to as the "desolating sacrilege" (Dan 8:13; 1 Macc 1:57), led to a protest movement that helped precipitate the Maccabean Wars of 167–143/142.

The revolt was organized by Mattathias the Maccabee and his sons. The term "Maccabee" comes from the epithet for Judah, his third son, who was referred to in Hebrew as *maqqæbæt* and Aramaic *maqqaba'* ("hammer"). The Maccabees, in partnership with the traditionalists and the rural population, formed a revolutionary movement against the Hellenistic circle.[62] The Jerusalem elite, including some Hasidim, the "pious" (1 Macc 2:42; 7:12), may have had religio-political goals, but for the rural population the interest was economic. As in the Ptolemaic period, those living in the countryside were shouldering significant tax burdens.

At the beginning of the military conflicts with the Seleucids, the Maccabees gained the upper hand.[63] One reason for this was that Antiochus IV Epiphanes was facing a Parthian attack on the eastern front of his empire, and he must have seen events in Judea as being of secondary importance. In 164 Judas Maccabee entered Jerusalem and reconsecrated the temple on the 25th of Kislev. In doing so, he de facto returned the order to what it had been before the hellenizing measures of the Seleucids. This is not to say that he therefore purged it of all hellenizing tendencies, though. Even before Antiochus IV a coexistence had developed between the Hellenistic way of life and the Jewish focus on divine law (Torah observance). The conflict was depicted in sharp relief in the two Maccabee books, though, as it served Hasmonean political theology (see below, 6.6).[64] Judah Maccabee did not stop his revolution with the reinstatement of the

62. On this, see Sievers, *Hasmoneans and Their Supporters*, 34.

63. On Bar Kochba's and Judah Maccabee's military exploits, see Bar-Kochva, *Judas Maccabaeus*, 194–218.

64. According to Josephus (*Ant.* 12.265; *Jewish War* 1.36) the ancestor of Judah Maccabee's family was called Hasmon, hence the dynastic name Hasmonean. See Atkinson, "Historical Chronology," 7–27

YHWH cult. He built a fortress in the city of David and undertook wars of conquest in Gilead, the Galilee, Idumea, and the coastal plains—all geopolitically sensitive territory.[65]

After the Seleucids settled the fight over the throne following the death of Antiochus IV, the Seleucid governor Lysias turned his attention to the Maccabees.[66] Lysias, who was running the empire for the young Antiochus V Eupator (164–162), conquered Beth-Zur, and then Jerusalem, after a siege in 162. Only the outbreak of further conflicts over the Antiochian throne prevented the total annihilation of the Maccabees. With Roman support, Demetrius I Soter (162–151/150) ultimately became the new Seleucid ruler. Though the Maccabees were not wholly destroyed, they lost control of the office of the high priest. While the Maccabees achieved a few military victories against the Seleucids (against Nicanor at Cafar-Salama, and Adasa, 1 Macc 7:31–32, 39–49), Judas Maccabeus was killed at the Battle of Elasa in 161. The remainder of the insurgents retreated into the desert, led by his youngest brother, Jonathan Apphus.[67]

Political events in Antiochia allowed the Maccabees to achieve their goal, nonetheless. When Alexander Balas (150–145) disputed Demetrius I's position on the throne, Demetrius sent his strategist Bacchides to negotiate with the Maccabees. The fact that he was more intent on preserving his own rule than defeating the Maccabees gives a sense of the precarious balance of power in the Seleucid empire of this period. Jonathan was granted his own legal jurisdiction in Michmash, a town near Geba, northeast of Jerusalem. This meant that the Hasmoneans de facto had a parallel government to the Seleucids.[68] When Alexander Balas installed a government of his own in the coastal city of Acco in 152, Demetrius I withdrew his troops from Jerusalem and Beth Zur, effectively giving up the region. Alexander attempted to bring Jonathan over to his side, offering him the office of high priest in Jerusalem. Since Jonathan was not from the Zadokite Oniad dynasty, conservatives—the "pious" (Hasidim)—opposed such a move. This did not stop Jonathan, however, who wanted to use the opportunity, with Seleucid support, to take over the temple community in Jerusalem and extend his own power while the Seleucids were caught up in the events in Antiochia. Jonathan would become the first Maccabee to receive official Seleucid recognition. Having done so, he rearranged the Hasmonean kingship so that the office of the high priest would include temporal power as well.[69]

---

65. On this, see Sievers, *Hasmoneans and Their Supporters*, 49–57.
66. See Bar-Kochva, *Judas Maccabaeus*, 275–90.
67. See Haag, *Das hellenistische Zeitalter*, 89–91.
68. See also Rooke, *Zadok's Heir*, 298–99, with reference to 1 Macc 14:4–15 and Ps 72.
69. VanderKam, *From Joshua to Caiaphas*, 254.

6.6 The Hasmonean Kingdom: Judea in the Second and First Centuries

Given the dearth of extrabiblical sources, historical reconstruction of the Hasmonean period mostly comes from the books of Maccabees and Josephus. This can be problematic, of course. To give just one example, the books of Maccabees clearly stylize Simon Maccabee (Jonathan's brother and successor 143/142–134) along the lines of a *David* and *Solomon redivivus*, clearly betraying a theological agenda.[70] Nevertheless, these books offer basic information on the history of ancient Judaism from the Hasmoneans to the beginning of Roman rule.[71]

Jonathan's successors, including the founder of the Hasmonean Kingdom, John Hyrcanus I (135/134–104), were able to hold on to power for around one hundred years because they knew how to make the most of the changing power balance in the Seleucid kingdom. Under Alexander Balas, Jonathan was named general and meridarch ("part ruler") of the province of Coele-Syria. When he was caught, however, he was executed by a general of the Seleucid king Antiochus VI in 142. Simon Maccabee (142–134) was made leader of the Maccabees. This choice was confirmed by Demetrius II, and Simon was given wide-ranging rights. Simon conquered the Acra in Jerusalem from the Seleucids and expanded his power westward. In capturing Jaffa, the Hasmoneans gained control over a Mediterranean port, giving Judea direct access to international trade. Not long after, Judea was granted the right to mint its own coins by the Seleucid ruler Antiochus VII Sidetes (138–129), a right John Hyrcanus I (135/34–104), Simon's successor, would take significant advantage of.[72] While Simon did not refer to himself as king, over the course of his rule Judea gained political autonomy.

Simon was murdered in Jericho in 135, along with two of his sons. He was succeeded by another of his sons, John Hyrcanus I, who at the time was governor of the province of Gezer. With his ascension to the throne, Jerusalem had a king of native descent for the first time in the 450 years, since Zedekiah.[73] In 129 the Seleucid king Antiochus VII died fighting the Parthians, and Demetrius II again became the Seleucid ruler. John Hyrcanus used the opportunity to take over the most important northern and southern trade routes with his own army.

While the Hasmoneans were hellenized, they presented themselves as representatives of the Jewish people. This can be seen, for example, on coins that continued to use the Paleo-Hebrew alphabet rather than the "modern" Aramaic

---

70. Keel, *Orte und Landschaften* 4/2:1243, with reference to the work of Adrian Schenker and I Macc 14:4–15.

71. On this, see Sievers, *Hasmoneans and Their Supporters*, 105–54, and Haag, *Das hellenistische Zeitalter*, 91–95.

72. See Hübner, "Tradition und Innovation," 171–87.

73. On Hasmonean kingship, see Regev, *Hasmoneans*, 129–41.

square script.[74] The coins minted under John Hyrcanus I had an anchor on one side and a lily on the other. The first was a Seleucid symbol; the second, Hasmonean. Some coins were inscribed "*Yehoḥanan*/Johanan the high priest and chief of the *ḥeber*," i.e., "and chief of *ḥeber hayehudīm*," an expression can be understood to mean either the Jewish council or the Jewish people.[75] During the rule of John Hyrcanus I's the Samaritan temple on Mount Gerizim was destroyed (129/128). This point, at the latest, marked the schism between the YHWH-worshippers in Jerusalem and those on Gerizim.[76]

Alongside his conquest of the trade routes, Hyrcanus also annexed the Galilee and Idumea. He expanded Jerusalem, rebuilding the city walls, and built the Baris fortress as a residence for the Hasmoneans north of the temple area, in what today is the Old City. This was a continuation of construction from the early Hasmonean period, which included the city walls and towers, which ran near the current-day western border of the old city (based on excavations in the area of the modern-day "citadel"; coins from Alexander Janneus).[77] He also constructed a winter palace in the Hellenistic style in Jericho, which was expanded by Herod.[78] John Hyrcanus's successor, Aristobulus II, continued the construction of Jerusalem, including a new palace. Under the Hasmoneans, Jerusalem developed from a small temple city at the beginning of the Hellenistic period into a great city with a large city wall and three royal palaces: one in the south, one in the north, and one to the west of the temple platform. Over the same period, the population grew to eight thousand.[79]

John Hyrcanus I's son, Judah Aristobulus I (104–103), continued the northward expansion, leading to a large growth in settlement in the Galilee.[80] Under Alexander Jannaeus (103–76) Hasmonean territory grew further, ultimately including the whole of the Galilee, the Golan, the Transjordan to the southern end of the Dead Sea, and the whole of the West Bank, including the coast. These conquests also involved forced Jewish conversion, and anyone who refused circumcision was driven out.[81]

According to Josephus, opposition to the Hasmoneans quickly began to stir. The Pharisees—a group that may have evolved out of the "pious" (Hasidim)

74. See Meshorer, *Treasury of Jewish Coins*, 5–24, and Ostermann, *Die Münzen der Hasmonäer*, 55–56.

75. See the overview in Frevel, *Geschichte Israels*, 357, and Regev, *Hasmoneans*, 186–99.

76. For the dating of the destruction, see Hensel, *Juda und Samaria*, 233–35, with a discussion of the two possibilities: 129/128 or 108/107 BCE.

77. Bieberstein, *Brief History of Jerusalem*, 107–14.

78. Netzer, *Die Paläste der Hasmonäer*, 78–80.

79. See Bieberstein, *Brief History of Jerusalem*, 115. On the development of settlements, see Reich, "Note on the Population Size," 298–305, and Geva, "Jerusalem's Population," 144 (8,000 people in the Hasmonean period).

80. See Tal, "Hellenism in Transition," 59–61.

81. Frevel, *Geschichte Israels*, 358.

of the Second Temple period[82]—attempted, with the help of the Seleucid ruler Demetrius III Eukarios, to displace Alexander Jannaeus (95–87), though they ultimately failed. After Alexander's death, his successor, his wife Salome Alexandra (76–67), attempted to deescalate tensions. The Sadducees, however, followers of the Jerusalem elite and temple priests, sided with her younger son, the military leader Aristobulus II (67–63). A battle for dominance arose between him and her older son John Hyrcanus II (76–67; 63–40)—at the time high priest—which ended only with the intervention of the Roman general Pompeius.

The years between the death of Salome in 67 and the Roman takeover of power in 63 were marked by increasing destabilization. At the same time the period that ended with Roman rule also saw the development of the religious divisions central to understanding the New Testament: the Pharisees, the Sadducees, and the Essenes.[83] In this period, presumably around the end of the second or beginning of the first century, the Qumran community was formed. In contrast to the graecised Hasmoneans, this group offered an apolitical Judaism oriented toward Israel's holy scriptures.

6.7 Qumran

In 1947, when ancient scrolls were found in clay pots in the caves of _Ḥirbet Qumrān_ at the Dead Sea, scholars drew a connection between them and the Essenes, an ascetic Jewish community referred to by Josephus and other ancient historians (Pliny, _Natural History_ 5.73). The term "Qumran" is used in contemporary scholarship as a designation for a group that referred to themselves in the scrolls as "the Community" (_ha-Yahad_) and understood themselves to be the "true Israel."[84] They studied biblical and parabiblical texts and became important bearers of (ancient) biblical tradition.[85] This can be seen in the Community Rule (1QS V–VII), whose oldest version is connected to Ps 1:1–2: "Happy are those who do not follow the advice of the wicked, or take the path that sinners tread, or sit in the seat of scoffers; but their delight is in the law of the Lord, and on his law they meditate day and night." The Community Rule orders the Qumran community to "keep apart from the congregation of the men of injustice in order to constitute a community in law (Torah) and possessions" (1QS V, 1–2).[86]

---

82. See the overview in Schaper, "Pharisees," 402–27.

83. On the sociohistorical processes, see Baumgarten, _Flourishing of Jewish Sects_, 81–113; for a classical position, see Schaper, "Pharisees," 402–27; Stemberger, "Sadducees," 428–43; Betz, "Essenes," 444–70.

84. For the following see Kratz, _Historical and Biblical Israel_, 153–65.

85. See Segal, "Identifying Biblical Interpretation," 295–308.

86. See Martinez and Tigchelaar, _Dead Sea Scrolls_, 79.

As allusions from certain Qumranic texts make clear, this was an attempt to separate themselves from the Hasmonean rule.[87] A "Teacher of Righteousness" frequently mentioned in Qumranic literature is contrasted with a "Godless Priest" (1QpHab XI, 4–8); the Hasmonean Alexander Jannaeus is referred to as the "lion of fury" (4QpNah II, 2,8; 4QpHos[b] f2,1), and John Hyrcanus is mentioned in a list of false prophets (4Q339). Historical allusions such as descriptions of military actions (Isaiah Pesher, 4Q161 f5–6, 5–13) and other passages show that the Qumran community not only separated themselves from the Maccabees and the Hasmoneans, but also from the priests and Levites of the temple in Jerusalem.[88] They understood themselves as the true Israel, as the group referred to in biblical texts that would lead to God's "new covenant" with Israel (Jer 31:31; cf CD I–VIII; 1QS I–III).

The differing orders in the the Community Rule (QS) and in the Damascus Document (CD) show that the community lived in various places in Judea over time and altered the rules of communal life to fit a variety of circumstances.[89] To become a member of the group, one needed to adopt stringent rules that covered every aspect of life. The group was also organized in a strict hierarchy, with some in leadership roles, and a variety of classes of members. The orders (found in QS and CD) are organized around the biblical ideal of the people of Israel as an army encampment and a community led by priests (see Num 2). The Qumran community also developed their own particular interpretations of the biblical legal tradition and their own customs of prayer, and they understood life led according to Mosaic law and in personal prayer and praise of God as two parts needed to make a whole, righteous life.

Four types of texts were found at Qumran, if one includes all the Qumran scrolls not necessarily connected with the community:[90] (1) the oldest known manuscripts of the biblical books; (2) copies of texts not included in the biblical canon (so-called apocryphal texts) in both Aramaic and Hebrew, as well as pseudepigrapha (pseudonymous texts ascribed to famous authors); (3) literature that can be directly ascribed to the Qumran community, e.g., the Community Rule (1QS), the Damascus Document (CD) or the Hodayot (1QH[a]); and (4) other literature, such as economic or administrative texts or letters, most of which were found in nearby sites (e.g., Ketef Jericho, Masada), though some were found at Qumran as well.

87. For the following, see Xeravits and Porzig, *Einführung in die Qumran-Literatur*, 253–64, and Collins, "Reading for History," 295–315.

88. See Jassen, "Re-reading 4QPesher Isaiah A (4Q161)," 57–90.

89. For this, see the overview in Xeravits and Porzig, *Einführung in die Qumran-Literatur*, 142–63.

90. For the following, see Kratz, *Historical and Biblical Israel*, 154–56. See also the overview in Stökl Ben Ezra, *Qumran*, 173–88, 239–54.

Qumran is a good example of a conservative group from the Second Temple period that focused on biblical literature, especially legal texts, on the one hand, while at the same time having essential features that go far beyond the traditional biblical canon: the "Teacher of Righteousness," their strict purity rules, their perfect dualistic vision ("Sons of Darkness" vs. "Sons of Light"), as well as other characteristics such as their expectation of an apocalyptic war (1QM).

In other words, if one were looking for a form of Judaism in the second century grounded in the biblical tradition but eschewing both politics and Hellenistic influence, it would be found at the edge of the Dead Sea, not in Jerusalem or Alexandria.

6.8 Outlook: Palestine Under Roman Rule—From 63 BCE to the Destruction of the Second Temple in 70 CE

After conquering the Seleucid Empire (64) and Palestine (63) the Roman general Pompeius redefined the borders of Syria-Palestine.[91] The Roman governor Aulus Gabinius (58–54) was given charge of Palestine, but the conflict between Salome Alexandra's two sons continued unabated. John Hyrcanus II had originally been appointed high priest, and Aristobulus II as general. During the Roman civil war between Julius Caesar and Pompey beginning in 49 BCE, Hyrcanus II and Antipater, ruler of Idumea, aligned themselves with Caesar. After his victory Caesar rewarded them for their loyalty, naming Hyrcanus II a "friend of Rome" and promoting Antipater to Procurator. Herod, Antipater's son, was subsequently made Strategos (military leader) in the Galilee. After Caesar's murder in 44 BCE, the situation in Palestine became unstable and Herod fled to Rome as the new high priest, the Hasmonean Antigonus (40–37), drove out Hyrcanus II. In 40, however, the Roman senate named Herod *rex socius et amicus populi* and thus king of Judea. His reign, which began in 37 BCE, lasted thirty years.[92] This marked the end of Hasmonean rule, and the beginning of the Herodian Kingdom.

While the New Testament portrays Herod negatively (e.g., the legend of the murder of children in Matt. 2:16), his long rule (37 BCE–4 CE) over nearly all of Palestine (with the exception of the free cities of the "Decapolis") was a period of stability and economic prosperity. Herod built new fortifications and rebuilt destroyed ones—most famously Masada at the Dead Sea.[93] On the coast he built

---

91. On this, see Seeman, *Rome and Judea in Transition*, 132, and Gabba, "Social, Economic and Political History," 94–106.

92. See Marshak, *Many Faces of Herod the Great*, 139–41.

93. Netzer, *Architecture of Herod*, 202–17.

Caesarea Maritima, a large port city. A Hellenistic polis, it included two temples, one for Roma and one for Augustus. His greatest building project, however, was unquestionably the temple in Jerusalem. Between 30 and 9/8 BCE the temple precinct doubled in size and was encircled by huge stone blocks. These can still be seen at the Western Wall of the temple, which is referred to today as the Wailing Wall. The temple became the market and center of trade for the city. In the north of the temple precinct Herod also built the fortress of Antonia.[94]

Near the end of his reign tensions flared up between pro-Hasmonean and pro-Herodian/Roman parties.[95] Though Herod was married to the Hasmonean Mariamne, the daughter of Alexander, this proved no barrier to the rivalry, in which even Herod's sons took part. Because Jerusalem was a so-called "client kingdom" of Rome, the kingship was chosen on a personal basis. Herod's successor was chosen by Emperor Augustus (31 BCE–6 CE), who unceremoniously divided the rule among Herod's sons. Archelaus was given Judea, Samaria, and Idumea; Herod Antipas received the Galilee and Perea; and Philip inherited the Transjordanian region.[96] Archelaus drew the ire of the people and the elites in Jerusalem, and he was deposed and exiled to Gaul in 6 CE. The tetrarchy was brought under direct Roman rule, and jurisdiction over capital and tax rates was transferred from the synedrion/Sanhedrin in Jerusalem to the prefects in Caesarea Maritima.

In the New Testament the reorganization of Archelaus's territory by the special imperial envoy Quirinius is connected the year of Jesus's birth (Luke 2:1–4). In Jesus's time Herod Antipas ruled in the Galilee (4 BCE–39 CE), followed after the exile of Antipas by Herod Agrippa (39–44 CE). After having been given control of Judea, Samaria, and Idumea, Agrippa ruled nearly the whole of Herod the Great's kingdom.

Mass protests against Rome began during Agrippa I's rule, intensifying after his death in 44.[97] These protests were prompted not only by the imposition of the Roman imperial cult, but also by political and economic changes—especially the return of power over the region to the governor of Caesaria Maritima. The Zealots, a religious group whom their opponents called "bandits" or *Sicarii* (dagger-fighters) grew stronger, and they initiated a national revolutionary movement in the style of the Maccabees. The battles were referred to as the "Jewish War" and lasted from 66 to 70 CE, until the revolution was brutally ended by the Romans. Vespasian was given command over the Jewish war by Emperor Nero. When Vespasian himself became emperor in 69 CE, he handed

94. See Bieberstein, *Brief History of Jerusalem*, 119–24.
95. See Curran, "'Philorhomaioi,'" 493–522.
96. Schäfer, *History of the Jews in Antiquity*, 103–6.
97. For the following, see Popović, *Jewish Revolt Against Rome*.

the task of putting down the uprising in Judea to his son Titus. Jerusalem was besieged, and in 70 CE it finally fell. The temple was plundered, set ablaze, and completely destroyed. Jerusalem was resettled by non-Jewish inhabitants and converted into a pagan city and given the name Aelia Capitolina. The province of Judea was renamed Syria Palaestina, and the Jews were forbidden to enter the city of Jerusalem, under threat of death. This decisively marked the end of the Second Temple period.

6.9 Summary

The significance of the Hellenistic era for ancient Israel's history was long underestimated. All of this changed with the discovery of the Qumran scrolls and the later dating of parts of the Hebrew Bible. This has led to a significantly greater focus on the period between Alexander the Great (333) and the Romans (63).

As with previous centuries, for most of the Hellenistic period Jerusalem remained a relatively unimportant temple city in comparison with the great ancient Near Eastern kingdoms. This only changed under the Ptolemies, when the office of the high priest became hereditary and the temple in Jerusalem began to be financed through a tax of its own. Over the course of the clashes in the third and second centuries, the high priests were exposed to tensions in Jerusalem, and they positioned themselves in relation to the Ptolemies and Seleucids as the situation required. The opposition between the Oniads and Tobiads, meanwhile, determined the character of the conflict during the Ptolemaic and Seleucids periods. At the end of this nearly two-hundred-year process a Hasmonean kingdom arose, and a local king ruled in Jerusalem for the first time since 587/586. Despite all rhetoric to the contrary, this kingdom was not traditional in character, but had clearly Hellenistic traits.

Hellenistic influence can already be found in the second half of the Persian period in the iconography of the coins, but it increased significantly in the third and second centuries. The political aim of the Ptolemies to form a native bilingual elite who could handle administrative tasks in the Ptolemaic Empire probably lead to increasing hellenization in third century Judea. The Seleucids built on this with their religious policies. Biblical statements about "desolating sacrilege" (Dan 8:13; 1 Macc 1:57), which refer to the reinterpretation of the YHWH cult into a cult to Zeus Olympius under Antiochus IV Epiphanes (164), reflect the perspective of a conservative group at the Jerusalem temple. While this group represented a minority view, it was nevertheless highly influential in the development of ancient Judaism. The "Pious"—referred to in the Psalms as

"Hasidim" and in the Qumran texts as "Asidim"—became increasingly more significant.

Meanwhile, the politicization of the Jerusalem temple and the office of the high priest resulted in further differentiations in ancient Judaism. A new YHWH community emerged in Egypt following Onias IV's flight to Egypt in 170 with the foundation of the temple of Leontopolis/Heliopolis. At the same time, the settlement of a group of conservative scribes (*literati*) on the Dead Sea gave rise to yet another in Israel/Palestine.

On the eve of Roman rule there were many different forms of ancient Judaism. At one end were the Hellenized Jews of Alexandria, at the other the Qumran community, two profoundly different versions of "Jewish identity." Hellenistic diaspora Judaism was culturally open, with its own "holy scripture" in the Septuagint, the Greek translation of the Hebrew Bible, while the Judaism of Qumran followed the guidelines of law, prophets, and writings, but developed them in a unique direction. Between these poles were a variety of forms of "Jewish identity," including the YHWH community on Mount Gerizim, which strictly observed the Torah; the hellenized kingdom of the Hasmoneans in Jerusalem; and the Egyptian diaspora communities of Leontopolis/Heliopolis, and Heracleopolis, in which the Torah appears to have played no significant role.[98]

This variety left a strong imprint on the Second Temple period through its literary culture, both in its production of new texts and in its reworking of older literature. What is now contained in the Hebrew Bible is in large part the work of these scribes from the Persian and Hellenistic periods.

---

98. For this, see Levine, "Jewish Identities in Antiquity," 40; Honigman, "Jewish Communities of Hellenistic Egypt," 117–35; Geiger, "The Jew and the Other," 136–46.

ARCHAEOLOGICAL PERIODS

Middle Bronze I	2000–1550
Late Bronze I	1550–1400
Late Bronze IIA	1400–1300
Late Bronze IIB	1300–1150
Iron Age IA	1200–1140
Iron Age IB	1140–980
Iron Age IIA	980–840/830
(Iron Age IIA early)	980–925
(Iron Age IIA late)	925–830
Iron Age IIB	830–700
Iron Age IIC	700–587
Iron Age III	587–450
(Persian Period I)	539–450
(Persian Period II)	450–333
Hellenistic period	333–37
Roman period	37 BCE–324 CE

MAPS

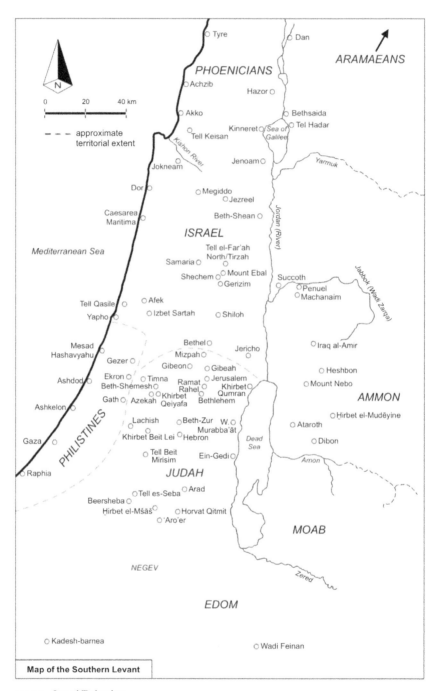

Map of the Southern Levant

MAP 1. Israel/Palestine

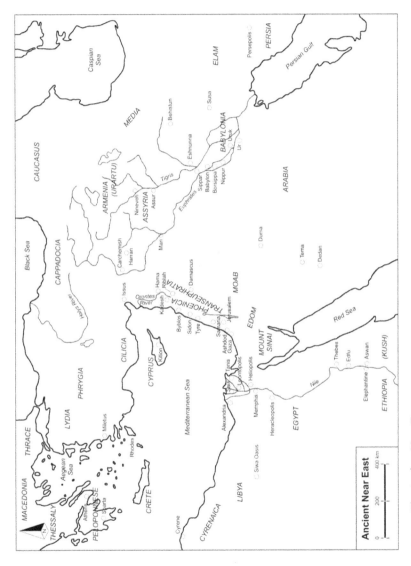

MAP 2. The Ancient Near East

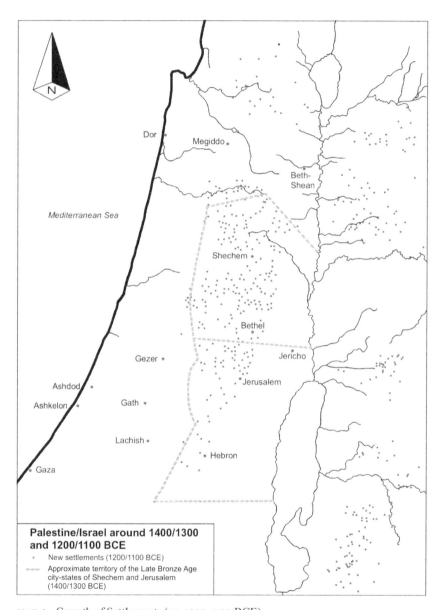

MAP 3. Growth of Settlements (ca. 1200–1100 BCE)

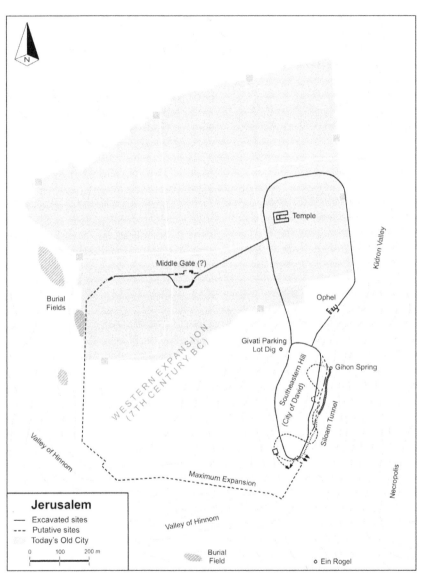

MAP 4. Jerusalem

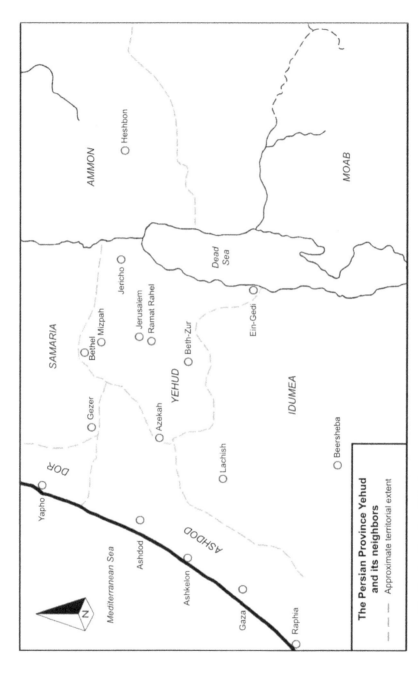

MAP 5. The Persian Province Yehud

BIBLIOGRAPHY

Abraham, Kathleen. "Negotiating Marriage in Multicultural Babylonia: An Example from the Judean Community in Āl-Yāḥūdu." Pages 33–57 in *Exile and Return: The Babylonian Context.* Edited by Jonathan Stökl, and Caroline Waerzeggers. BZAW 478. Berlin: de Gruyter, 2015.

Adams, Samuel L. *Social and Economic Life in Second Temple Judea.* Louisville: Westminster John Knox, 2014.

Aharoni, Yohanan. *The Land of the Bible.* 2nd ed. London: Burns & Oates, 1979.

Ahituv, Shmuel. "Jeremiah in Egypt." *Eretz-Israel: Archaeological, Historical and Geographical Studies* 27 (2003): 33–40.

Albertz, Rainer. *Israel in Exile: The History and Literature of the Sixth Century B.C.E.* Translated by David Green. Studies in Biblical Literature 3. Atlanta: SBL, 2003.

Alstola, Tero. "Judean Merchants in Babylonia and Their Participation in Long-Distance Trade." *WO* 47 (2017): 25–51.

———. "Judeans in Babylonia: A Study of Deportees in the Sixth and Fifth Centuries BCE." PhD diss., Leiden University, 2017.

Alt, Albrecht. "Syrien und Palästia im Onomastikon des Amenope (1950)." Pages 231–45 in *Kleine Schriften zur Geschichte des Volkes Israel.* Vol. 1. 2nd ed. Edited by Albrecht Alt. München: C. Kaiser, 1959.

Altmann, Peter. "Tithes for the Clergy and Taxes for the King: State and Temple Contributions in Nehemiah." *Catholic Biblical Quarterly* 76 (2014): 215–29.

Ambar-Armon, Einat, and Amos Kloner. "Archaeological Evidence of Links Between the Aegean World and the Land of Israel in the Persian Period." Pages 1–22 in Levin, *Time of Change.*

Amit, Yairah. "When Did Jerusalem Become a Subject of Polemic?" Pages 365–74 in *Jerusalem in Bible and Archaeology: The First Temple Period.* Edited by Andrew G. Vaughn and Ann E. Killebrew. SBL Symposium Series 18. Atlanta: SBL, 2003.

Aperghis, Gerassimos G. *The Seleukid Royal Economy: The Finances and Financial Administration of the Seleukid Empire.* Cambridge: Cambridge University Press, 2004.

Arie, Eran. "Reconstructing the Iron Age II Strata at Tel Dan: Archaeological and His-torical Implications." *TA* 35 (2008): 6–64.

Ariel, Donald T. *Excavations at the City of David 1978–1982: Directed by Yigal Shiloh. Vol II.* Qedem 30. Jerusalem: The Institute of Archaeology and The Hebrew University of Jerusalem, 1990.

Assmann, Jan. *The Mind of Egypt.* Translated by Andrew Jenkins. New York: Metropolitan, 2002.

Atkinson, Kenneth. "The Historical Chronology of the Hasmonean Period in the War and Antiquities of Flavius Josephus: Separating Fact from Fiction." Pages 7–27 in *Flavius Josephus: Interpretation and History.* Edited by Jack Pastor, Pnina Stern, and Menahem Mor. JSJSup 146. Leiden: Brill, 2011.

Avishur, Yitzak, and Michael Heltzer. "Jehoiachin, King of Judah in Light of Biblical and Extra Biblical Sources: His Exile and Release According to Events in the Neo-Babylonian Kingdom and the Babylonian Diaspora." *Transeu* 34 (2007): 17–36.

Azzoni, Annalisa. *The Private Lives of Women in Persian Egypt.* Winona Lake, IN: Eisenbrauns, 2013.

Bagg, Ariel M. *Die Assyrer und das Westland.* OLA 216. Leuven: Peeters, 2011.

Baines, John. "On the Composition and Inscriptions on the Vatican Statue of Udjahorresne." Pages 83–92 in *Studies in Honor of William Kelly Simpson.* Vol. 1. Edited by Peter der Manuelian. Boston: Museum of Fine Arts, 1996.

Banks, Diane. *Writing the History of Israel.* LHBOTS 438. New York: T & T Clark, 2006.

Barkay, Gabriel. "Royal Palace, Royal Portrait? The Tantalizing Possibilities of Ramat Raḥel." *Biblical Archaeology Review* 32 (2006): 34–44.

Bar-Kochva, Bezalel. *Judas Maccabaeus: The Jewish Struggles Against the Seleucids.* Cambridge: Cambridge University Press, 1989.

Barrick, W. Boyd. "Another Shaking of Jehoshaphat's Family Tree." *VT* 51 (2001): 9–25.

Barstad, Hans M. *History and the Hebrew Bible.* FAT I/61. Tübingen: Mohr Siebeck, 2008.

Baumgarten, Joseph A. *The Flourishing of Jewish Sects in the Maccabean Era: An Interpretation.* JSJSup 55. Leiden: Brill, 1997.

Becking, Bob. *The Fall of Samaria: A Historical and Geographical Study.* Studies in the History of the Ancient Near East 2. Leiden: Brill, 1992.

———. "The Two Neo-Assyrian Documents from Gezer in their Historical Context." *Jaarbericht Ex Oriente Lux* 27 (1983): 76–89.

———. "'We All Returned as One': Critical Notes on the Myth of Mass Return." Pages 3–18 in Lipschits and Oeming, *Judah and the Judeans in the Persian Period.*

———. "Yehudite Identity in Elephantine." Pages 403–19 in *Judah and the Judaeans in the Achaemenid Period: Negotiating Identities in an International Context.* Edited by Oded Lipschits, Gary N. Knoppers, and Manfred Oeming. Winona Lake, IN: Eisenbrauns, 2011.

Begrich, Joachim. "Der syrisch-ephraimitische Krieg und seine weltpolitischen Zusammenhänge (1929)." Pages 99–131 in *Gesammelte Studien zum Alten Testament.* Edited by Joachim Begrich. Theologische Bücherei 21. München: Chr. Kaiser, 1964.

Ben-Ami, Doron, and Yana Tchekhanovets. ". . . And They Also Were in the City of David in Jerusalem, Who Had Made Themselves a Tower' (1 Macc. 14.36): The Seleucid Fortification System at the Givati Parking Lot, City of David." Pages 313–22 in vol. 9 of *New Studies in the Archaeology of Jerusalem and Its Region: Collected Papers.* Edited by Guy D. Stiebel, Orit Peleg-Barkat, and Doron Ben-Ami, and Yuval Gadot. Jerusalem : Israel Antiquities Authority, 2015.

Ben-Dor Evian, Shirly. "The Battles Between Ramesses III and the 'Sea-Peoples.'" *ZAW* 143 (2016): 151–68.

———. "Egypt and the Levant in the Iron Age I–IIA: The Ceramic Evidence." *TA* 38 (2011): 94–119.

Ben-Tor, Daphna. "A Scarab of the Mass-Production Groups: The Origin and Date of Early Iron Age Scarabs in the Southern Levant." Pages 319–22 in *Yadin's Expedition to Megiddo*. Edited by Anabel Zarzecki-Peleg. Qedem 56. Jerusalem: The Institute of Archaeology. The Hebrew University of Jerusalem, 2016.

Berlejung, Angelika, ed. *Disaster and Relief Management: Katastrophen und ihre Bewältigung*. FAT I/81. Tübingen: Mohr Siebeck, 2012.

———. "Notlösungen: Altorientalische Nachrichten über den Tempelkult in Nachkriegszeiten." Pages 224–25 in *Kein Land für sich allein: Studien zum Kulturkontakt in Kanaan, Israel/Palästina und Ebirnari für Manfred Weippert zum 65. Geburtstag*. Edited by Ulrich Hübner and Ernst A. Knauf. OBO 186. Fribourg: Universitätsverlag; Göttingen: Vandenhoeck und Ruprecht, 2002.

Berlejung, Angelika, Aren M. Maeir, and Andreas Schüle, eds. *Wandering Arameans: Arameans Outside Syria: Textual and Archaeological Perspectives*. Leipziger Altorientalische Studien 5. Wiesbaden: Harrassowitz, 2017.

Berlejung, Angelika, and Michael P. Streck, eds. *Arameans, Chaldeans, and Arabs in Babylonia and Palestine in the First Millennium B.C.* Leipziger Altorientalische Studien 3. Wiesbaden: Harrassowitz, 2013.

Berlin, Andrea M. "Between Large Forces: Palestine in the Hellenistic Period." *Biblical Archaeologist* 60.1 (1997): 3–51.

Betlyon, John W. "Egypt and Phoenicia in the Persian Period: Partners in Trade and Rebellion." Pages 455–77 in *Egypt, Israel, and the Ancient Mediterranean World: Studies in Honor of Donald B. Redford*. Edited by Gary N. Knoppers and Antoine Hirsch. Probleme der Ägyptologie 20. Leiden: Brill, 2004.

Betz, Otto. "The Essenes." Pages 444–70 in vol 3 of Horbury et al., *Cambridge History of Judaism*.

Bickermann, Elias J. *The Jews in the Greek Age*. Cambridge: Harvard University Press, 1988.

Bieberstein, Klaus. *A Brief History of Jerusalem*. ADPV 47. Wiesbaden: Harrassowitz, 2017.

Bishop Moore, Megan. *Philosophy and Practice in Writing a History of Ancient Israel*. LHBOTS 435. New York: T & T Clark, 2006.

Blenkinsopp, Joseph. "The Mission of Udjahorresenet and Those of Ezra and Nehemia." *Journal of Biblical Literature* 106 (1987): 409–21.

Bornstein, Arye. "Shechem." Pages 348–56 in vol. 2 of Master, *Oxford Encyclopedia of the Bible and Archaeology*.

Bortz, Anna Maria. *Identität und Kontinuität: Form und Funktion der Rückkehrerliste Esr 2*. BZAW 521. Berlin: de Gruyter, 2018.

Briant, Pierre. *Alexander the Great and His Empire: A Short Introduction*. Translated by Amélie Kuhrt. Princeton: Princeton University Press, 2010.

———. *From Cyrus to Alexander: A History of the Persian Empire*. Winona Lake, IN: Eisenbrauns, 2002.

Bright, John. *History of Israel*. 4th ed. Louisville: Westminster John Knox, 2000.

Bruneau, Philippe. "Les Israelites de Délos et la juiverie délienne." *Bulletin de Correspondence Hellénique* 106 (1982): 466–504.

Burkard, Günter. "Medizin und Politik: Altägyptische Heilkunst am persischen Königshof." *Studien zur altägyptischen Kultur* 21 (1994): 35–57.

Cambiano, Guiseppe. "Becoming an Adult." Pages 86–119 in *The Greeks*. Edited by Jean-Pierre Vernant. Translated by Charles Lambert and Teresa Lavender Fagan. Chicago: University of Chicago Press, 1995.

Carter, Charles E. *The Emergence of Yehud in the Persian Period: A Social and Demographic Study*. JSOTSup 294. Sheffield: Sheffield Academic Press, 1999.

Chadwick, Jeffrey R. "Discovering Hebron: The City of the Patriarchs Slowly Yields Its Secrets." *Biblical Archaeology Review* 31.5 (2005): 24–33, 70–71.

Clark, Elizabeth A. *History, Theory, Text. Historians and the Linguistic Turn*. Cambridge: Harvard University Press, 2004.

Clarysse, Willy. "The Zenon Papyri Thirty Years On." Pages 31–43 in *100 Anni di Istituzioni Fiorentine per la Papirologia*. Edited by Guido Bastianini and Angelo Casanova. Studi e Testi di Papirologia N.S. 11. Florence: Istituto Papirologico G. Vitelli, 2009.

Cohen, Shaye J. D. *The Beginnings of Jewishness: Boundaries, Varieties, Uncertainties*. Hellenistic Culture and Society 31. Berkeley: University of California Press, 1999.

Cohen, Shaye J. D. and Ernest S. Frerichs, eds. *Diasporas in Antiquity*. Brown Judaic Studies 288. Atlanta: Scholars Press, 1993.

Cohen-Weinberger, Anat. "Petrographic Analysis of the Egyptian Forms from Stratum VI at Tel Beth Shean." Pages 406–12 in *Mediterranean Peoples in Transition: Thirteenth to Early Tenth Centuries BCE; In Honor of Trude Dothan*. Edited by Seymour Gitin and Amihai Mazar. Jerusalem: Israel Exploration Society, 1998.

Cohn, Dorrit. *The Distinction of Fiction*. Baltimore: Johns Hopkins University Press, 1999.

Collins, John J. *Jewish Cult and Hellenistic Culture*. JSJSup 100. Leiden: Brill, 2005.

———. "Reading for History in the Dead Sea Scrolls." *Dead Sea Discoveries* 18 (2011): 295–315.

Confino, Alon. "History and Memory." Pages 36–51 in *The Oxford History of Historical Writing. Vol 5*. Edited by Axel Schneider and Daniel Woolf. Oxford: Oxford University Press, 2011.

Cotton, Hannah. and Michael Wörrle. "Seleukos IV to Heliodoros: A New Dossier of Royal Correspondence from Israel." *Zeitschrift für Papyrologie und Epigraphik* 159 (2007): 191–205.

Cowey, James M. S., and Klaus Maresch. *Urkunden des Politeuma der Juden von Herakleopolis (144/3–133/2)*. Papyrologica Coloniensia 39. Cologne: Westdeutscher Verlag, 2001.

Curran, John. "'Philorhomaioi': The Herods between Rome and Jerusalem." *Journal for the Study of Judaism in the Persian, Hellenistic, and Roman Period* 45 (2014): 493–522.

Davies, Graham. "Was There an Exodus?" Pages 23–40 in Day, *In Search of Pre-exilic Israel*.

Davies, Philipp R. *In Search of "Ancient Israel."* 2nd ed. JSOTSup 148. Sheffield: JSOT Press, 1995.

Day, John, ed. *In Search of Pre-exilic Israel*. JSOTSup 406. London: T & T Clark, 2004.

————. *Yahweh and the Gods and Goddesses of Canaan*. JSOTSupp 265. Sheffield: Sheffield Academic Press, 2000.

De Groot, Alon, and Hannah Bernick-Greenberg. *Excavations at the City of David 1978–1985. Vol VIIA*. Qedem 53. Jerusalem: The Hebrew University, 2012.

Demsky, Aaron. "The 'Izbet Sarṭah Ostracon Ten Years Later." Pages 186–97 in *'Izbet Ṣarṭah*. Edited by Israel Finkelstein. BAR International Series 299. Oxford: BAR, 1986.

Dequeker, Luc. "Darius the Persian and the Reconstruction of the Jewish Temple in Jerusalem (Ezra 4,24)." Pages 67–92 in *Ritual and Sacrifice in the Ancient Near East*. Edited by Jan Quaegebeur. OLA 55. Leuven: Peeters, 1993.

Dershowitz, Idan. 2018. "Darius II Delays the Festival of Matzot in 418 BCE." *The Torah*. Viewed 6 December 2018. https://thetorah.com/darius-ii-delays-the -festival-of-matzot-in-418-bce/.

Dever, William G. *Beyond the Texts: An Archaeological Portrait of Ancient Israel and Judah*. Atlanta: SBL, 2017.

Dietrich, Manfried, Oswald Loretz, and Joaquín Sanmartín, *Die keilalphabetischen Texte aus Ugarit*. Münster: Ugarit-Verlag, 2013.

Donner, Herbert. *Geschichte des Volkes Israel und seiner Nachbarn in Grundzügen*. 4th ed. Grundrisse zum Alten Testament 4. 2 vols. Göttingen: Vandenhoeck & Ruprecht, 2008.

Dorsey, David A. *The Roads and Highways of Ancient Israel*. Baltimore: Johns Hopkins University Press, 1992.

Dothan, Trude, and David Ben-Shlomo. "Mycenaean IIIC:1 Pottery in Philistia. Four Decades of Research." Pages 29–35 in Killebrew and Lehmann, *Philistines and Other "Sea People."*

Dušek, Jan. *Aramaic and Hebrew Inscriptions from Mt. Gerizim and Samaria between Antiochus III and Antiochus IV Epiphanes*. CHANE 54. Leiden: Brill, 2012.

————. *Les Manuscripts Araméens du Wadi Daliyeh et la Samarie vers 450–332 av. J.C.* CHANE 30. Leiden: Brill, 2007.

————. "Mt. Gerizim Sanctuary, Its History and Enigma of Origin." *HeBAI* 3 (2014): 111–33.

Edelman, Diana. *The Origins of the Second Temple: Persian Imperial Policy and the Rebuilding of Jerusalem*. London: Equinox, 2005.

————. "Settlement Patterns in Persian-Era *Yehud*." Pages 52–64 in Levin, *Time of Change*.

Edgar, Campbell C. *Zenon Papyri*. Vol. 1. Cairo: Service de Antiquites de l'Égypte, 1925.

Elat, Moshe. "The Campaigns of Shalmaneser III Against Aram and Israel." *IEJ* 25 (1975): 25–35.

Elayi, Josette. "Achemenid Persia and the Levant." Pages 107–22 in *The Oxford Handbook of the Archaeology of the Levant: c. 8000–332 BCE*. Edited by Margreet L. Steiner and Ann E. Killebrew. Oxford: Oxford University Press, 2014.

————. *Sargon II, King of Assyria*. Archaeology and Biblical Studies 22. Atlanta: SBL, 2017.

Fantalkin, Alexander. "Mezad Ḥashavyahu: Its Material Culture and Historical Background." *TA* 28 (2001): 3–165.

————. Was There a 'Greek Renaissance' in 7th Century BCE Philistia?" Pages 83–99 in *Alphabets, Texts, and Artifacts in the Near East: Studies Presented to Benjamin*

Sass. Edited by Israel Finkelstein, Christian Robin, and Thomas Römer. Paris: Van Dieren, 2016.

Faust, Avraham. "The Emergence of Iron Age Israel: On Origins and Habitus." Pages 467–82 in Levy et al., *Israel's Exodus in Transdisciplinary Perspective*.

———. *Israel's Ethnogenesis: Settlement, Interaction, Expansion and Resistance*. Approaches to Anthropological Archaeology. London: Routledge, 2014.

———. "On Jerusalem's Expansion During the Iron Age II." Pages 256–85 in *Exploring the Narrative: Jerusalem and Jordan in the Bronze and Iron Ages*. Edited by Eveline van der Stehen, Jeannette Boertien, and Noor Mulder-Hymans. London: Bloomsbury, 2014.

———. "Settlement Dynamics and Demographic Fluctuation." Pages 23–51 in Levin, *Time of Change*.

Faust, Avraham, and Ehud Weiss. "Judah, Philistia, and the Mediterranean World: Reconstructing the Economic System of the Seventh Century B.C.E." *BASOR* 338 (2005): 71–92.

Finkelstein, Israel. *The Archaeology of the Israelite Settlement*. Jerusalem: Israel Exporation Society, 1988.

———. "Comments on the Date of Late-Monarchic Judahite Seal Impressions." *TA* 39 (2012): 203–11.

———. *The Forgotten Kingdom*. Ancient Near East Monographs 5. Atlanta: SBL, 2013.

———. "The Great Wall in Tell en-Naṣbeh (Mizpah), the First Fortifications in Judah, and 1 Kings 15,16–22." *VT* 62 (2012): 14–28.

———. "Observations on the Layout of Iron Age Samaria." *TA* 38 (2011): 194–207.

———. "Pots and People Revisited: Ethnic Boundaries in the Iron Age I." Pages 216–37 in *The Archaeology of Israel: Constructing the Past, Interpreting the Present*. Edited by Neil A. Silberman and David B. Small. JSOTSup 237. Sheffield: Sheffield Academic Press, 1997.

———. "Shechem in the Late Bronze and Iron I." Pages 349–56 in *Timelines: Studies in Honour of Manfred Bietak*. Edited by Ernst Czerny et al. OLA 149. Leuven: Peeters, 2006.

———. "The Territorial Extent and Demography of Yehud/Judea in the Persian and Early Hellenistic Period." *RB* 117 (2010): 39–54.

———. "The Territorial-Political System of Canaan in the Late Bronze Age." *UF* 28 (1996): 221–55.

Finkelstein, Israel, Eran Arie, Mario A. S. Martin, and Eli Piasetzky. "New Evidence on the Late Bronze/Iron I Transition at Megiddo: Implications for the End of the Egyptian Rule and the Appearance of Philistine Pottery." *Ägypten und Levante* 27 (2017): 261–80.

Finkelstein, Israel, and Alexander Fantalkin. "Khirbeit Qeiyafa: An Unsensational Archaeological and Historical Interpretation." *TA* 39 (2012): 38–62.

Finkelstein, Israel, Ido Koch, and Oded Lipschits. "The Mound on the Mount: A Solution of the 'Problem with Jerusalem.'" *JHS* 11 (2011): 2–24.

Finkelstein, Israel, and Oded Lipschits. "Omride Architecture in Moab, Jahaz and Atharoth." *ZDPV* 126 (2010): 29–42.

Finkelstein, Israel, and Nadav Na'aman. "Shechem of the Amarna Period and the Rise of the Northern Kingdom of Israel." *IEJ* 55 (2005): 172–93.

Fitzmyer, Joseph. "The Aramaic Letter of King Adon to the Egyptian Pharaoh (1965)." Pages 231–41 in *A Wandering Aramean: Collected Aramaic Essays*. Edited by

Joseph Fitzmyer. Society of Biblical Literature. Monograph Series 25. Missoula, MO: Scholars Press, 1979.

Fleming, David E. *The Legacy of Israel in Judah's Bible: History, Politics, and the Reinscribing of Tradition.* Cambridge: Cambridge University Press, 2012.

Frahm, Eckart. "The Neo-Assyrian Period (ca. 1000–629 BCE)." Pages 161–208 in *A Companion to Assyria.* Edited by Eckart Frahm. Hoboken, NJ: John Wiley & Sons, 2017.

———. "Revolts in the Neo-Assyrian Empire: A Preliminary Discourse Analysis." Pages 76–89 in *Revolt and Resistance in the Ancient Classical World and the Near East: In the Crucible of Empire.* Edited by John J. Collins and Joe G. Manning. CHANE 85. Leiden: Brill, 2016.

Frame, Grant. "The Inscription of Sargon II at Tang-I Var." *Orientalia* (Nova Series) 68 (1999): 31–57.

Frevel, Christian. *Geschichte Israels.* Studienbücher Theologie 2. Stuttgart: Kohlhammer, 2016.

Frevel, Christian, Katharina Pyschny, and Izak Cornelius, eds. *A "Religious Revolution" in Yehûd? The Material Culture of the Persian Period as a Test Case.* OBO 267. Fribourg: Academic Press; Göttingen: Vandenhoeck & Ruprecht, 2014.

Frey, Jörg. "Temple and Rival Temple: The Cases of Elephantine, Mt. Gerizim, and Leontopolis." Pages 171–203 in *Gemeinde ohne Tempel.* Edited by Beate Ego, Armin Lange, and Peter Pilhofer. WUNT 118. Tübingen: Mohr Siebeck: 1999.

Gabba, Emilio. "The Social, Economic and Political History of Palestine 63 BCE–CE 70." Pages 94–167 in vol. 3 of Horbury et al., *Cambridge History of Judaism.*

Gadot, Yuval. "The Iron I in the Samaria Highlands: A Normal Settlement Wave or Urban Expansion?" Pages 103–14 in Lipschits et al., *Rethinking Israel.*

Gadot, Yuval, and Joe Uziel. "The Monumentality of Iron Age Jerusalem Prior to the 8th Century BCE." *TA* 44 (2017): 123–40.

Gardiner, Alan H. *Ancient Egyptian Onomastica.* Vol. 3. Oxford: Oxford University Press, 1947.

Garfinkel, Yosef. "Khirbet Qeiyafa in the Shephelah: Data and Interpretations." Pages 5–60 in Schroer and Münger, *Khirbet Qeiyafa in the Shephelah.*

Gaß, Erasmus. *Die Moabiter, Geschichte und Kultur eines ostjordanischen Volkes im 1. Jahrtausend.* ADPV 38. Wiesbaden: Harrassowitz, 2009.

———. "Schoschenq and Jerusalem: Probleme einer historischen Rekonstruktion." *UF* 46 (2015): 115–59.

Geiger, Joseph. "The Jew and the Other: Doubtful and Multiple Identities in the Roman Empire." Pages 136–46 in Levine and Schwartz, *Jewish Identities in Antiquity.*

Gera, Dov. "Olympiodoros, Heliodoros and the Temples of Koilē Syria and Phoinikē." *Zeitschrift für Papyrologie und Epigraphik* 169 (2009): 125–55.

Gershon, Galil. "Shalmaneser and the West." *RB* 109 (2002): 40–56.

Gerstenberger, Erhard S. *Israel in the Persian Period: The Fifth and Fourth Centuries B.C.E.* Translated by Siegfried S. Schatzmann. Biblical Encyclopedia SBL 8. Atlanta: SBL, 2011.

Gertz, Jan C. "Konstruierte Erinnerung: Alttestamentliche Historiographie im Spiegel von Archäologie und literarhistorischer Kritik am Fallbeispiel des salomonischen Königtums." *Berliner Theologische Zeitschrift* 21 (2004): 3–29.

Gertz, Jan C., Angelika Berlejung, Konrad Schmid, and Markus Witte. *T & T Clark Handbook to the Old Testament: An Introduction to the Literature, Religion and History of the Old Testament.* London: T & T Clark, 2012.

Geva, Hillel. "Jerusalem's Population in Antiquity: A Minimalistic View." *TA* 41 (2014): 131–60.

Gilboa, Ayelet. "Dor and Egypt in the Early Iron Age: An Archaeological Perspective of (Part of) the Wenamun Report." *Aegypten und Levante* 25 (2015): 247–74.

Gilboa, Ayelet, Ilan Sharon, and Elizabeth Bloch-Smith. "Capital of Solomon's Fourth District? Israelite Dor." *Levant* 47 (2015): 209–44.

Gilboa, Ayelet, Paula Waiman-Barak, and Han Sharon. "Dor, the Carmel Coast and Early Iron Age Mediterranean Exchanges." Pages 85–109 in *The Mediterranean Mirror: Cultural Contacts in the Mediterranean Sea Between 1200 and 750 B.C.* Edited by Andrea Babbi, Friederike Bubenheimer-Erhart, Beatriz Marín-Aguilera, and Simone Mühl. RGZM-Tagungen 20. Mainz: Römisches-Germanisches Zentralmuseum, 2015.

Gitin, Seymour. "Neo-Assyrian and Egyptian Hegemony over Ekron in the Seventh Century BCE: A Response to Lawrence E. Stager." *Eretz-Israel: Archaeological, Historical and Geographical Studies* 27 (2003): 55*–61*.

———. "Tel Miqne-Ekron in the 7th Century B.C. City Plan Development and the Olive Oil Industry." Pages 219–42 in *Olive Oil in Antiquity*. Edited by David Eitam and Michael Heltzer. History of Ancient Near East Studies VII. Padova: Sargon, 1996.

Gitler, Haim, and Oren Tal. *The Coinage of Philistia of the Fifth and Fourth Centuries BC: A Study of the Earliest Coins of Palestine.* Collezioni numismatiche 6. Milano: Edizioni Ennerre, 2006.

Goedicke, Hans, ed. *Perspectives on the Battle of Kadesh.* Baltimore: Halgo, 1985.

Goedicke, Hans, and Edward F. Wente. *Ostraka Michaelides.* Wiesbaden: Harrassowitz, 1962.

Gogel, Sandra L. *A Grammar of Epigraphic Hebrew.* SBL Resources for Biblical Study 23. Atlanta: Scholars Press, 1998.

Goren, Yuval, Shlomo Bunimovitz, Israel Finkelstein, and Nadav Na'aman, eds. *Inscribed in Clay.* Monograph Series of the Institute of Archaeology, Tel Aviv University 23. Tel Aviv: Emery and Claire Yass Publications in Archaeology, 2004.

Görg, Manfred. "Jeremia zwischen Ost und West (Jer 38,1–6): Zur Krisensituation in Jerusalem am Vorabend des Babylonischen Exils (1982)." Pages 190–207 in *Studien zur biblisch-ägyptischen Religionsgeschichte.* Edited by Manfred Görg. Stuttgarter biblische Aufsatzbände 14. Stuttgart: Katholisches Bibelwerk, 1992.

Götze, Albrecht. "Zur Schlacht von Qades." *Orientalistische Literaturzeitung* 32 (1929): 832–38.

Grabbe, Lester L. *Ancient Israel: What Do We Know and How Do We Know It?* Revised Edition. London: T & T Clark, 2017.

———. *Can a 'History of Israel' Be Written?* JSOTSup 245. Sheffield: Sheffield Academic Press, 1997.

———, ed. *Good Kings and Bad Kings.* JSOTSup 393. London: T & T Clark, 2007.

———. *A History of the Jews and Judaism in the Second Temple Period.* Vol 1: *Yehud: A History of the Persian Province of Judah.* LSTS 47. London: T & T Clark, 2004.

———. *A History of the Jews and Judaism in the Second Temple Period.* Vol 2: *The Coming of the Greeks, The Early Hellenistic Period (335–175 BCE).* LSTS 68. London: T & T Clark, 2008.

———. "Hyparchs, *Oikonomi* and Mafiosi: The Governance of Judah in the Ptolemaic Period." Pages 70–90 in *Judah Between East and West: The Transition from*

Persian to Greek Rule (ca. 400–200 BCE). Edited by Lester L. Grabbe and Oded Lipschits. LSTS 75. London: T & T Clark, 2011.

———. "The Kingdom of Israel from Omri to the Fall of Samaria: If We Only Had The Bible. . . ." Pages 54–99 in *Ahab Agonistes: The Rise and Fall of the Omri Dynasty*. Edited by Lester L. Grabbe. LHBOTS 421. London: T & T Clark, 2007.

———. "Late Bronze Age Canaan: If We Had Only The Bible. . . ." Pages 11–56 in *The Land of Canaan in the Late Bronze Age*. Edited by Lester L. Grabbe. LHBOTS 636. London: Bloosmbury, 2016.

———, ed. *"Like a Bird in a Cage": The Invasion of Sennacherib in 701 BCE*. JSOTSup 363. Sheffield: Sheffield Academic Press, 2003.

———. "Were the Pre-Maccabean High Priests 'Zadokites'?" Pages 205–15 in *Reading from Right to Left: Essays on the Hebrew Bible in Honour of David J. A. Clines*. Edited by J. Cheryl Exum and Hugh G. M. Williamson. JSOTSup 373. Sheffield: Sheffield Academic Press, 2003.

Granerød, Gard. "'By the Favour of Ahuramazda I am King': On the Promulgation of a Persian Propaganda Text among Babylonians and Judaeans." *Journal for the Study of Judaism in the Persian, Hellenistic, and Roman Period* 44 (2013): 455–80.

———. *Dimensions of Yahwism in the Persian Period: Studies in the Religion and Society of the Judean Community at Elephantine*. BZAW 488. Berlin: de Gryuter, 2016.

Grätz, Sebastian. *Das Edikt des Artaxerxes*. BZAW 337. Berlin: de Gruyter, 2004.

Grayson, Albert Kirk. *Assyrian and Babylonian Chronicles: Texts from Cuneiform Sources V*. Locust Valley, NY: Augustin, 1975.

Green, Peter. *Alexander to Actium: The Hellenistic Age*. London: Thames and Hudson, 1990.

Greenfield, Jonas, and Bezalel Porten. *The Bisitun Inscription of Darius the Great: Aramaic Version*. Corpus Inscriptionum Iranicarum 1. London: Humphries, 1982.

Gruen, Erich S. *Heritage and Hellenism: The Reinvention of Jewish Tradition*. Berkeley: University of California Press, 1998.

Guil, Shlomo. "A New Perspective on the Various Components of the Siloam Water System in Jerusalem." *ZDPV* 133 (2017): 145–71.

Guillaume, Philipp. "Jerusalem 720–705: No Flood of Israelite Refugees." *Scandinavian Journal of the Old Testament* 22 (2008): 195–211.

Haag, Ernst. *Das hellenistische Zeitalter: Israel und die Bibel im 4. bis 1. Jahrhundert v. Chr*. Biblische Enzyklopädie 9. Stuttgart: Kohlhammer, 2003.

Hackl, Johannes. "Babylonian Scribal Practices in Rural Contexts: A Linguistic Survey of the Documents of Judean Exiles and West Semites in Babylonia (CUSAS 28 and BaAr 6)." Pages 125–40 in Berlejung et al., *Wandering Arameans*.

Hagedorn, Anselm C. "Historiography in the Hebrew Bible." In *The Biblical World*. 2nd ed. Edited by Katharine J. Dell. London: Routledge, forthcoming.

Hallo, William W. and K. Lawson Younger, eds. *The Context of Scripture*. 4 vols. Leiden: Brill, 1997–2016.

Hasel, Michael G. *Domination & Resistance*. Probleme der Ägyptologie 11. Leiden: Brill, 1998.

Heltzer, Michael. "Epigraphic Evidence Concerning a Jewish Settlement in Kition (Larnaca, Cyprus) in the Achaemenid Period (IV cent. B.C.E.)." *Aula Orientalis* 7 (1989): 189–206.

Hengel, Martin. *Judaica, Hellenistica et Christiana: Kleine Schriften II*. WUNT 109. Tübingen: Mohr Siebeck, 1999.

Hensel, Benedikt. *Juda und Samaria: Zum Verhältnis zweier nachexilischer Jahwismen.* FAT I/110. Tübingen: Mohr Siebeck, 2016.

Herzog, Ze'ev. "The Fortress Mound at Tel Arad: An Interim Report." *TA* 29 (2002): 3–109.

Higginbotham, Carolyn R. *Egyptianization and Elite Emulation in Ramesside Palestine.* CHANE 2. Leiden: Brill, 2000.

Hoch, James E. *Semitic Words in Egyptian Texts of the New Kingdom and Third Intermediate Period.* Princeton: Princeton University Press, 1994.

Høgenhaven, Jesper. "The Prophet Isaiah and Judaean Foreign Policy Under Ahaz and Hezekiah." *Journal of Near Eastern Studies* 49 (1990): 351–54.

Hölbl, Günther. *A History of the Ptolemaic Empire.* Translated by Tina Saavedra. London: Routledge, 2000.

Hölscher, Lucian. *Die Entdeckung der Zukunft.* Göttingen: Wallstein, 2016.

Honigman, Sylvie. "Jewish Communities of Hellenistic Egypt: Diverging Responses to a Varying Socio-Cultural Environment." Pages 117–35 in Levine and Schwartz, *Jewish Identities in Antiquity.*

Horbury, William, William D. Davies, and John J. Sturdy, eds. *The Cambridge History of Judaism.* Vol. 3: *The Early Roman Period.* Cambridge: Cambridge University Press, 1999.

Houston, Walter. "Was There a Social Crisis of the 8th Century?" Pages 130–49 in Day, *In Search of Pre-exilic Israel.*

Hübner, Ulrich. "Tradition und Innovation: Die Münzprägungen der Hasmonäer des 2. und 1. Jahrhunderts als Massenmedien." Pages 171–87 in *Medien im antiken Palästina.* Edited by Christian Frevel. FAT II/10. Tübingen: Mohr Siebeck, 2005.

Huß, Werner. *Die Verwaltung des ptolemaiischen Reiches.* München: C. H. Beck, 2011.

———. *Die Wirtschaft Ägyptens in hellenistischer Zeit.* München: C. H. Beck, 2012.

Jansen-Winkeln, Karl. "Zur historischen Authentizität ägyptischer und biblischer Quellen: Der Palästinafeldzug Schoschenks I." *Orientalistische Literaturzeitung* 103 (2008): 165–76.

Jassen, Alex. "Re-reading 4QPesher Isaiah A (4Q161): Forty Years After DJD V." Pages 57–90 in *The Mermaid and the Partridge.* Edited by George J. Brooke and Jesper Høgenhaven. Studies on the Texts of the Desert of Judah 96. Leiden: Brill, 2011.

Jenkins, Keith. *On "What Is History?" From Carr and Elton to Rorty and White.* London: Routledge, 1995.

———. *Re-thinking History.* London: Routledge, 1991.

Joannès, Francis, and André Lemaire. "Trois tablettes cunéiformes à onomastique ouest-sémitique." *Transeu* 17 (1999): 17–34.

Jursa, Michael. *Aspects of the Economic History of Babylonia in the First Millennium BC: Economic Geography, Economic Mentalities, Agriculture, the Use of Money and the Problem of Economic Growth.* AOAT 377. Münster: Ugarit-Verlag, 2010.

Kahn, Dan'el. "The Assyrian Invasions of Egypt (673–663 B.C.) and the Final Expulsion of the Kushites." *Studien zur altägyptischen Kultur* 34 (2006): 251–67.

———. "The Inscription of Sargon II at Tang-i Var and the Chronology of Dynasty 25." *Orientalia* (Nova Series) 70 (2001): 1–18.

———. "Judean Auxiliaries in Egypt's War Against Kush." *Journal of the American Oriental Society* 127 (2007): 507–16.

———. "Some Remarks on the Foreign Policy of Psammetichus II in the Levant (595–589 B.C.)." *Journal of Egyptian History* 1 (2008): 139–57.

———. "Why Did Necho II Kill Josiah?" Pages 511–28 in *There and Back Again— The Crossroads II.* Edited by Jana Mynářová, Pavel Onderka, and Peter Pavúk. Prague: Charles University. Faculty of Arts, 2015.

Kamlah, Jens. "Das Ostjordanland im Zeitalter der Entstehung Israels." *Theologische Quartalschrift* 186 (2006): 118–33.

———. "Temples of the Levant: Comparative Aspects." Pages 507–34 in *Temple Building and Temple Cult.* Edited by Jens Kamlah. ADPV 41. Wiesbaden: Harrassowitz, 2012.

Keel, Othmar. *Corpus der Stempelsiegelamulette aus Palästina/Israel.* Vol 3. OBO Series Archaeologica 29. Fribourg: Academic Press; Göttingen: Vandenhoeck & Ruprecht, 2010.

———. *Orte und Landschaften der Bibel.* Vol. 4: *Die Geschichte Jerusalems und die Entstehung des Monotheismus.* 2 vols. Göttingen: Vandenhoeck & Ruprecht, 2007.

Keel, Othmar, Max Küchler, and Christoph Uehlinger. *Orte und Landschaften der Bibel,* Vol 1. *Geographische Landeskunde.* Göttingen: Vandenhoeck & Ruprecht, 1984.

Keel, Othmar, and Christoph Uehlinger. *Gods, Goddesses, and Images of God in Ancient Israel.* Translated by Thomas H. Trapp. London: T & T Clark, 1998.

Kessler, Rainer. *The Social History of Ancient Israel: An Introduction.* Translated by Linda Maloney. Minneapolis: Fortress, 2008.

Kiderlen, Moritz, Michael Bode, Andreas Hauptmann, and Yannis Bassiakos. "Tripod Cauldrons Produced at Olympia Give Evidence for Trade with Copper from Faynan (Jordan) to South West Greece: c. 950–750 BCE." *Journal of Archaeological Science Reports* 8 (2016): 303–13.

Killebrew, Ann E. *Biblical Peoples and Ethnicity.* Atlanta: SBL, 2005.

Killebrew, Ann E., and Gunnar Lehmann, eds. *The Philistines and Other "Sea People" in Text and Archaeology.* Archaeological and Biblical Studies 15. Atlanta: SBL, 2013.

Kippenberg, Hans G. *Garizim und Synagoge: Traditionsgeschichtliche Untersuchungen zur samaritanischen Religion der aramäischen Periode.* Religionsgeschichtliche Versuche und Vorarbeiten 30. Berlin: de Gruyter, 1971.

Kisilevitz, Shua. "The Iron IIA Judahite Temple at Moza." *TA* 42 (2015): 147–64.

Kistenfeger, Jens. *Historische Erkenntnis zwischen Objektivität und Perspektivität.* Frankfurt: Ontos Verlag, 2011.

Kitchen, Kenneth A. *The Third Intermediate Period in Egypt (1100–650 B.C.).* Rev. ed. Warminster: Aris & Phillips, 1986; Liverpool: Liverpool University Press, 1996.

Klengel, Horst. *Syria: 3000 to 300 B.C. A Handbook of Political History.* Berlin: Akademie Verlag, 1992.

Kletter, Raz. *Economic Keystones: The Weight System of the Kingdom of Judah.* JSOTSup 276. Sheffield: Sheffield Academic Press, 1998.

———. "Pots and Polities: Material Remains of Late Iron Age Judah in Relation to its Political Borders." *BASOR* 314 (1999): 19–54.

Knauf, Ernst Axel. "Elephantine und das vor-biblische Judentum." Pages 179–88 in *Religion und Religionskontakte im Zeitalter der Achämeniden.* Edited by Reinhard G. Kratz. Veröffentlichungen der Wissenschaftlichen Gesellschaft für Theologie 22. Gütersloh: Gütersloher Verlagshaus, 2002.

———. "From History to Interpretation." Pages 26–64 in *The Fabric of History.* Edited by Diana V. Edelman. JSOTSup 127. Sheffield: JSOT Press, 1991.

———. "The Glorious Days of Manasseh." Pages 164–88 in Grabbe, *Good Kings and Bad Kings.*

———. *Die Umwelt des Alten Testaments*. Neuer Stuttgarter Kommentar, Altes Testament 29. Stuttgart: Katholisches Bibelwerk, 1994.

Knauf, Ernst Axel, and Philipp Guillaume. *A History of Biblical Israel: The Fate of the Tribes and Kingdoms from Merenptah to Bar Kochba*. Worlds of the Ancient Near East and Mediterranean. London: Equinox, 2016.

Knoppers, Gary N. *Jews and Samarians: The Origins and History of Their Early Relations*. Oxford: Oxford University Press, 2013.

Knoppers, Gary N., and Bernard M. Levinson, eds. *The Pentateuch as Torah*. Winona Lake, IN: Eisenbrauns, 2007.

Koch, Ido, and Oded Lipschits. "The Rosette Stamped Jar Handle System and the Kingdom of Judah at the End of the First Temple Period." *ZDPV* 129 (2012): 55–78.

Kratz, Reinhard G. *The Composition of the Narrative Books of the Old Testament*. Translated by John Bowden. London: T & T Clark, 2005.

———. *Historical and Biblical Israel: The History, Tradition, and Archives of Israel and Judah*. Translated by Paul Michael Kurtz. Oxford: Oxford University Press, 2015

———. *Das Judentum im Zeitalter des Zweiten Tempels*. FAT I/42. Tübingen: Mohr Siebeck, 2004.

Kuhrt, Amélie. "The Cyrus Cylinder and Achaemenid Imperial Policy." *Journal for the Study of the Old Testament* 25 (1983): 83–97.

———. *The Persian Empire*. 2 vols. London: Routledge, 2007.

———. "The Problem of Achaemenid 'Religious Policy.'" Pages 117–42 in *Die Welt der Götterbilder*. Edited by Brigitte Groneberg and Hermann Spieckermann. BZAW 376. Berlin: de Gruyter, 2007.

———. "State Communication in the Persian Empire." Pages 112–40 in *State Correspondence in the Ancient World*. Edited by Karen Radner. Oxford: Oxford University Press, 2014.

Lamprichs, Roland. *Die Westexpansion des neuassyrischen Reiches: Eine Strukturanalyse*. AOAT 239. Neukirchen-Vluyn: Butzon & Bercker, 1995.

Landau, Yohanan A. "A Greek Inscription Found Near Hefzibah." *IEJ* 16 (1966): 54–70.

Lapp, Paul W. "Observations on the Pottery of Thāj." *BASOR* 172 (1963): 22–35.

Lehmann, Gunnar. "The Northern Coast Plain During the Early Iron Age (Iron I–Early Iron IIA)." Forthcoming.

———. "Reconstructing the Social Landscape of Early Israel: Rural Marriage Alliances in the Central Hill Country." *TA* 31 (2004): 141–75.

———. "Survival and Reconstruction of Judah in the Time of Manasseh." Pages 289–309 in Berlejung, *Disaster and Relief Management*.

Lehmann, Gunnar, and Hermann Michael Niemann. "When Did the Shephela become Judahite?" *TA* 41 (2014): 77–94.

Lehmann, Gunnar, Steven A. Rosen, Angelika Berlejung, Bat-Ami Neumeier, and Hermann Michael Niemann. "Excavations at Qubur al-Walaydah, 2007–2009." *WO* 40 (2010): 137–59.

Lemaire, André. *Levantine Epigraphy and History in the Achaemenid Period (539–332 BCE)*. The Schweich Lectures of the British Academy 2013. Oxford: Oxford University Press, 2015.

———. "Levantine Literacy ca. 1000–750 BCE." Pages 11–54 in *Contextualizing Israel's Sacred Writings: Ancient Literacy, Orality, and Literary Production*. Edited by Brian B. Schmidt. Ancient Israel and Its Literature 22. Atlanta: SBL, 2015.

———. "New Aramaic Ostraca from Idumea and Their Historical Interpretation." Pages 413–56 in Lipschits and Oeming, *Judah and the Judeans in the Persian Period*.

———. "Prières en temps de crise: Les inscriptions de Khirbet Beit Lei." *RB* 83 (1976): 558–68.

———. "Solomon et la fille de Pharaon: Un problème d'interprétation historique." Pages 699–710 in *"I Will Speak in the Riddles of Ancient Times": Archaeological and Historical Studies in Honor of Amihai Mazar on the Occasion of His Sixtieth Birthday*. Edited by Aren M. Maeir and Pierre de Miroschedji. 2 vols. Winona Lake, IN: Eisenbrauns, 2006.

Leuchter, Mark. "The Sociolinguistics and Rhetorical Implications of the Source Citations in Kings." Pages 119–34 in *Soundings in Kings*. Edited by Klaus-Peter Adam and Mark Leuchter. Minneapolis: Fortress, 2010.

Levin, Christoph. "The Empty Land in Kings." Pages 195–220 in *Re-Reading the Scriptures: Essays on the Literary History of the Old Testament*. FAT I/87. Tübingen: Mohr Siebeck, 2013.

———. "Die Entstehung des Judentums als Gegenstand der alttestamentlichen Wissenschaft." Pages 1–17 in *Congress Volume Munich 2013*. Edited by Christl Maier. VTSup 163. Leiden: Brill, 2014.

———. *The Old Testament*. Translated by Margaret Kohl. Princeton: Princeton University Press, 2005.

———. "The Synchronistic Excerpt from the Annals of the Kings of Israel and Judah." Pages 183–93 in *Re-Reading the Scriptures: Essays on the Literary History of the Old Testament*. FAT I/87. Tübingen: Mohr Siebeck, 2013.

Levin, Yigal, ed. *A Time of Change: Judah and Its Neighbours in the Persian and Early Hellenistic Periods*. LSTS 65. London: T & T Clark, 2007.

Levine, Lee I., and Daniel R. Schwartz, eds. *Jewish Identities in Antiquity: Studies in Memory of Menahem Stern*. TSAJ 130. Tübingen: Mohr Siebeck, 2009.

Levy, Thomas E., Thomas Schneider, and William H. C. Propp, eds. *Israel's Exodus in Transdisciplinary Perspective*. Heidelberg: Springer, 2015.

Lichtheim, Miriam. *Ancient Egyptian Literature*. Vol. 3: *The Late Period*. Berkeley: University of California Press, 1980.

Lincoln, Bruce. "Bisitun and Persepolis." Pages 107–26 in *"Happiness for Mankind": Achaemenian Religion and the Imperial Project*. Edited by Bruce Lincoln. Acta Iranica 53. Leuven: Peeters, 2012.

Lipiński, Edward. "The Arameans in the West (13th–8th Centuries)." Pages 123–43 in Berlejung and Streck, *Arameans, Chaldeans, and Arabs*.

———. *The Arameans: Their Ancient History, Culture, Religion*. OLA 100. Leuven: Peeters, 2000.

———. "The Egypto-Babylonian War of the Winter 601–600 B.C." *Annali dell'Istituto Orientale di Napoli* 32 (1972): 235–41.

———. "Hiram of Tyre and Solomon." Pages 251–72 in *The Book of Kings*. Edited by André Lemaire and Baruch Halpern. VTSup 129. Leiden: Brill, 2010.

Lipschits, Oded. "Archaeological Facts, Historical Speculations and the Date of the LMLK Storage Jars: A Rejoinder to David Ussishkin." *JHS* 12 (2012): 1–15.

———. "Bethel Revisited." Pages 233–46 in Lipschits et al., *Rethinking Israel*.

———. "Demographic Changes in Judah between the Seventh and the Fifth Centuries B.C.E." Pages 326–343 in Lipschits and Blenkinsopp, *Judah and the Judeans in the Neo-Babylonian Period*.

———. *The Fall and Rise of Jerusalem*. Winona Lake, IN: Eisenbrauns, 2005.

———. "'Jehoiakim Slept with His Father ...' (II Kings 24:6): Did He?" *JHS* 4 (2002): 1–23.

———. "Persian Period Judah: A New Perspective." Pages 187–212 in *Text, Contexts and Readings in Postexilic Literature*. Edited by Louis Jonker. FAT II/53. Tübingen: Mohr Siebeck, 2011.

Lipschits, Oded, and Joseph Blenkinsopp, eds. *Judah and the Judeans in the Neo-Babylonian Period*. Winona Lake, IN: Eisenbrauns 2003.

Lipschits, Oded, Yuval Gadot, and Matthew J. Adams, eds. *Rethinking Israel: Studies in the History and Archaeology of Ancient Israel in Honor of Israel Finkelstein*. Winona Lake, IN: Eisenbrauns, 2017.

Lipschits, Oded, Yuval Gadot, Benjamin Arubas, and Manfred Oeming, eds. *What Are the Stones Whispering?* Winona Lake, IN: Eisenbrauns, 2017.

Lipschits, Oded, Gary N. Knoppers, and Mandred Oeming, eds. *Judah and the Judeans in the Achaemenid Period: Negotiating Identity in an International Context*. Winona Lake, IN: Eisenbrauns, 2011.

Lipschits, Oded, and Manfred Oeming, eds. *Judah and the Judeans in the Persian Period*. Winona Lake, IN: Eisenbrauns 2006.

Lipschits, Oded, Omer Sergi, and Ido Koch. "Judahite Stamped and Incised Jar Handles: A Tool for the Study of the History of Late Monarchic Judah." *TA* 38 (2011): 5–41.

Lipschits, Oded, and David S. Vanderhooft. "Continuity and Change in the Persian Period Judahite Stamped Jar Administration." Pages 43–66 in Frevel et al., *"Religious Revolution" in Yehûd?*

———. *The Yehud Stamp Impressions*. Winona Lake, IN: Eisenbrauns, 2011.

Liverani, Mario. *Israel's History and the History of Israel*. London: Routledge, 2005.

Macalister, Robert A. S. "Sixteenth Quarterly Report on the Excavation at Gezer." *PEQ* 40 (1908): 13–25.

Maeir, Aren M. "Gaza." Pages 451–53 in vol. 1 of Master, *Oxford Encyclopedia of the Bible and Archaeology*.

———. "Khirbet Qeiyafa in its Regional Context: A View from Philistine Gath." Pages 61–67 in Schroer and Münger, *Khirbet Qeiyafa in the Shephelah*.

———. "Philistia and the Judean Shephelah After Hazael." Pages 41–62 in Berlejung, *Disaster and Relief Management*.

———. "Philistine Gath after 20 Years: Regional Perspectives on the Iron Age." Pages 133–54 in *The Shephelah During the Iron Age*. Edited by Oded Lipschits and Aren M. Maeir. Winona Lake, IN: Eisenbrauns, 2017.

Maeir, Aren M., Brent Davis, and Louise A. Hitchcock. "Philistine Names and Terms Once Again: A Recent Perspective." *Journal of Eastern Mediterranean Archaeology and Heritage* 4 (2016): 321–40.

Magdalene, F. Rahel, and Cornelia Wunsch. "Slavery Between Juda And Babylon: The Exilic Experience." Pages 113–34 in *Slaves and Household in the Near East*. Edited by Laura Culbertson. Chicago: The Oriental Institute, 2011.

Magen, Yitzhak. "The Dating of the First Phase of the Samaritan Temple on Mount Gerizim in Light of the Archaeological Evidence." Pages 157–211 in *Judah and the Judeans in the Fourth Century B.C.E.* Edited by Oded Lipschits, Gary N. Knoppers, and Rainer Albertz. Winona Lake, IN: Eisenbrauns, 2007.

———. *Mount Gerizim Excavations*. Vol. 2: *A Temple City*. Judea and Samaria Publications 8. Jerusalem: Israel Antiquities Authority, 2008.

Magen, Yitzhak, Haggai Misgav, and Levana Tsfania. *Mount Gerizim Excavations.* Vol. 1: *The Aramaic, Hebrew and Samaritan Inscriptions.* Judea and Samaria Publications 2. Jerusalem: Israel Antiquities Authority, 2004.

Malamat, Abraham. "The Kingdom of Judah between Egypt and Babylonia: A Small State Within a Great Power Confrontation." Pages 322–37 in *History of Biblical Israel: Major Problems and Minor Issues.* Edited by Abraham Malamat. CHANE 7. Leiden: Brill, 2001.

Marshak, Adam Kolman. *The Many Faces of Herod the Great.* Grand Rapids, MI: Eerdmans, 2015.

Martin, Mario A. S., and Israel Finkelstein. "Iron IIA Pottery from the Negev Highlands: Petrographic Investigations and Historical Implications." *TA* 40 (2013): 6–45.

Martinez, Florentino G., and Eibert J. Tigchelaar, eds. *The Dead Sea Scrolls Study Edition.* 2 vols. Leiden: Brill, 1999.

Master, Daniel M., ed. *The Oxford Encyclopedia of the Bible and Archaeology.* 2 vols. Oxford: Oxford University Press, 2013.

Matthieu, Bernard. "Mais qui est donc Osiris? Ou la politique sous le linceul de la religion." *Egypte Nilotique et Méditerranéenne* 3 (2012): 77–107.

Mayer, Walter. *Politik und Kriegskunst der Assyrer.* Abhandlungen zur Literatur Alt-Syrien-Palästinas und Mesopotamiens 9. Münster: Ugarit Verlag, 1995.

———. "Sennacherib's Campaign of 701 BCE: The Assyrian View." Pages 168–200 in Grabbe, *"Like a Bird in a Cage."*

———. "Die Zerstörung des Jerusalemer Tempels 587 v. Chr. im Kontext der Praxis von Heiligtumszerstörungen im antiken Vorderen Orient." Pages 1–22 in *Zerstörungen des Jerusalemer Tempels: Geschehen—Wahrnehmung—Bewältigung.* Edited by Johannes Hahn. WUNT 147. Tübingen: Mohr Siebeck, 2002.

Mayes, Andrew D. H. "The Palestinian Campaign of Pharaoh Shishak." Pages 55–68 in *On Stone and Scroll: Essays in Honour of Graham Ivor Davies.* Edited by James K. Aitken, Katharine J. Dell, and Brian A. Mastin. BZAW 420. Berlin: de Gruyter, 2011.

Mazar, Amihai. *Archaeology of the Land of the Bible 10,000–586 B.C.E.* Anchor Yale Bible Reference Library. 1992. Repr., New Haven: Yale University Press, 2009.

———. "Culture, Identity and Politics Relating to Tel Reḥov in the 10th–9th Centuries BCE." Pages 89–119 in Sergi et al., *In Search for Aram and Israel.*

———. "The Egyptian Garrison Town at Beth-Shean." Pages 155–89 in *Egypt, Canaan and Israel: History, Imperialism, Ideology, and Literature.* Edited by Shay Bar, Dan'el Kahn, and J. J. Shirley. CHANE 52. Leiden: Brill, 2011.

———. "Jerusalem in the 10th Century: The Glass Half Full." Pages 255–72 in *Essays on Ancient Israel in Its Near Eastern Context.* Edited by Yairah Amit. Winona Lake, IN: Eisenbrauns, 2006.

McKenzie, Judith. *The Architecture of Alexandria and Egypt: 300 BC–AD 700.* New Haven: Yale University Press, 2007.

Meshorer, Ya'akov. *A Treasury of Jewish Coins: From the Persian Period to Bar Kohkba.* Jerusalem: Amphora, 2001.

Meshorer, Ya'akov, and Shraga Qedar. *The Coinage of Samaria in the Fourth Century BCE.* Jerusalem: Numismatic Fine Arts International, 1991.

Middlemas, Jill. *The Trouble of the Templeless Judah.* Oxford Theological Monographs. Oxford: Oxford University Press, 2005.

Middleton, Guy. "Telling Stories: The Mycenaean Origins of the Philistines." *Oxford Journal of Archaeology* 34 (2015): 45–65.

Miller, J. Maxwell, and John H. Hayes. *A History of Ancient Israel and Judah.* 2nd ed. Louisville: Westminster John Knox, 2006.

Moore, Stewart Alden. *Jewish Ethnic Identity and Relations in Hellenistic Egypt: With Walls of Iron?* JSJSup 171. Leiden: Brill, 2015.

Morenz, Ludwig. "Wortwitz—Ideologie—Geschichte: 'Israel' im Horizont Mer-en-ptahs." *ZAW* 120 (2008): 1–13.

Morkot, Robert. *A Short History of New Kingdom Egypt.* London: I. B. Tauris, 2018.

Moyal, Yigal, and Avraham Faust. "Jerusalem's Hinterland in the Eighth-Seventh Centuries BCE: Towns, Villages, Farmsteads, and Royal Estates." *PEQ* 147 (2015): 283–98.

Münger, Stefan. "Early Iron Age Kinneret—Early Aramaean or Just Late Canaanite? Remarks on the Material Culture of a Border Site in Northern Palestine at the Turn of an Era." Pages 149–82 in Berlejung and Streck, *Arameans, Chaldeans, and Arabs.*

———. "References to the Pharaoh in the Local Glyptic Assemblage of the Southern Levant During the 1st Part of the 1st Millennium BC." *Journal of Ancient Egyptian Interconnections* 18 (2018): 40–62.

———. "Stamp-Seal Amulets and Early Iron Age Chronology—An Update." Pages 381–404 in *The Bible and Radiocarbon Dating.* Edited by Thomas E. Levy and Thomas Higham. London: Equinox, 2005.

Münger, Stefan, and Thomas E. Levy. "The Iron Age Egyptian Amulet Assemblage." Pages 741–65 in *New Insights into the Iron Age Archaeology of Edom, Southern Jordan.* Edited by Thomas E. Levy. Monumenta Archaeologica 35. 2 vols. Los Angeles: Cotsen Institute of Archaeology Press, 2014.

Na'aman, Nadav. "An Assyrian Residence at Ramat Raḥel?" *TA* 28 (2001): 260–81.

———. "Dismissing the Myth of a Flood of Israelite Refugees in the Late Eighth Century." *ZAW* 126 (2014): 1–14.

———. "Esarhaddon's Treaty with Baal and Assyrian Provinces Along the Phoenician Coast." *Rivista di studi fenici* 22 (1994): 3–8.

———. "The Exodus Story: Between Historical Memory and Historiographical Composition." *Journal of Ancient Near Eastern Religions* 11 (2011): 39–69.

———. "The Historical Background of the Conquest of Samaria (720 BC)." *Biblica* 71 (1990): 206–55.

———. "Khirbet Qeiyafa in Context." *UF* (2010): 497–526.

———. "The Kingdom of Judah in the 9th Century BCE." *TA* 40 (2013): 247–76.

———. "The Kingdom of Judah Under Josia." *TA* 18 (1991): 3–71.

———. "King Mesha and the Foundation of the Moabite Monarchy." *IEJ* 47 (1997): 83–92.

———. "Out of Egypt or Out of Canaan? The Exodus Story Between Memory and Historical Reality." Pages 527–33 in Levy et al., *Israel's Exodus in Transdisciplinary Perspective.*

———. "The Royal Dynasties of Judah and Israel." *Zeitschrift für altorientalische und biblische Rechtsgeschichte* 22 (2016): 59–73.

———. "Sources and Composition in the History of Solomon." Pages 57–80 in *The Age of Solomon.* Edited by Lowell K. Handy. Studies in the History and Culture of the Ancient Near East 9. Leiden: Brill, 1997.

———. "Tel Dor and Iron Age IIA Chronology." *BASOR* 376 (2016): 1–5.

———. "The Temple Library of Jerusalem and the Composition of the Book of Kings." Pages 129–52 in *Congress Volume Leiden 2004*. Edited by André Lemaire. VTSup 109. Leiden: Brill, 2006.

———. "Yenoʿam." *TA* 4 (1977): 168–77.

Nam, Roger S. "Power Relations in the Samaria Ostraka." *PEQ* 144 (2012): 155–63.

Nesselrath, Heinz-Günther. "Das Museion und die Große Bibliothek von Alexandria." Pages 65–90 in *Alexandria*. Edited by Tobias Georges, Felix Albrecht, and Reinhard Feldmeier. Civitatum Orbis Mediterranei Studia 1. Tübingen: Mohr Siebeck, 2013.

Netzer, Ehud. *The Architecture of Herod, the Great Builder*. Grand Rapids, MI: Baker Academics, 2006.

———. "Observations on the Layout of Iron Age Samaria: A Reply to Israel Finkelstein." *UF* 43 (2011): 325–34.

———. *Die Paläste der Hasmonäer und Herodes' des Großen*. Zaberns Bildbände zur Archäologie 40. Mainz: Philipp von Zabern, 1990.

Niemann, Hermann Michael. "Comments and Questions About the Interpretation of Khirbet Qeiyafa." *Zeitschrift für altorientalische und biblische Rechtsgeschichte* 23 (2017): 245–62.

———. "Juda und Jerusalem: Überlegungen zum Verhältnis von Stamm und Staat und zur Rolle Jerusalems in Juda." *UF* 47 (2016): 178–90.

———. "Observations on the Layout of Iron Age Samaria: A Reply to Israel Finkelstein." *UF* 43 (2011): 325–34.

Nissinen, Martti. "(How) Does the Book of Ezekiel Reveal Its Babylonian Context?" *WO* 45 (2015): 85–98.

Noth, Martin. *The History of Israel*. 2nd ed. Translated by P. R. Ackroyd. London: Black, 1960.

Oded, Bustenay. *Mass Deportations and Deportees in the Neo-Assyrian Empire*. Wiesbaden: Reichert, 1979.

Ofer, Avi. "ʿAll the Hill Country of Judah': From a Settlement Fringe to a Prosperous Monarchy." Pages 92–121 in *From Nomadism to Monarchy*. Edited by Israel Finkelstein and Nadav Naʾaman. Jerusalem: Yad Izha Ben-Zvi, 1994.

Onasch, Hans Ulrich. *Die Assyrischen Eroberungen Ägyptens*. Vol. 1. Ägypten und Altes Testament 27/1. Wiesbaden: Harrassowitz 1998.

Oren, Eliezer D. "Governor's Residences' in Canaan Under the New Kingdom: A Case Study of Egyptian Administration." *Journal of the Society for the Study of Egyptian Antiquities* 14 (1984): 37–56.

Ostermann, Siegfried. *Die Münzen der Hasmonäer*. Novum Testamentum et Orbis Antiquus 55. Fribourg: Academic Press; Göttingen: Vandenhoeck & Ruprecht, 2005.

Pearce, Laurie E. "Continuity and Normality in Sources Relating to the Judean Exile." *HeBAI* 3 (2014): 163–84.

———. "Cuneiform Sources for Judeans in Babylonia in the Neo-Babylonian and Achaemenid Periods: An Overview." *Religion Compass* 10.9 (2016): 230–43.

———. "ʿJudean': A Special Status in Neo-Babylonian and Achemenid Babylonia?" Pages 267–78 in Lipschits et al., *Judah and the Judeans in the Achaemenid Period*.

Pearce, Laurie E., and Cornelia Wunsch. *Documents of Judean Exiles and West Semites in Babylonia in the Collection of David Sofer*. Cornell University Studies in Assyriology and Sumerology 28. Bethesda, MD: CDL Press, 2014.

Petersen, Olof. "Foreign Professionals in Babylon: Evidence from the Archive in the Palace of Nebuchadnezzar II." Pages 267–72 in *Ethnicity in Ancient Mesopotamia*. Edited by Wilfred H. van Soldt. Leiden: Nederlands Instituut voor het Nabije Oosten, 2005.

Pfeiffer, Henrik. "The Origins of YHWH and its Attestation." Pages 115–44 in *The Origins of Yahwism*. Edited by Jürgen van Oorschot and Markus Witte. BZAW 484. Berlin: de Gruyter, 2017.

Pioske, Daniel. "Memory and Its Materiality: The Case of Early Iron Age Khirbet Qeiyafa and Jerusalem." *ZAW* 127 (2015): 78–95.

Popović, Mladen, ed. *The Jewish Revolt Against Rome: Interdisciplinary Perspectives.* JSJSup 154. Leiden: Brill, 2011.

Porten, Bezalel. *The Elephantine Papyri in English: Three Millennia of Cross-Cultural Continuity and Change*. Documenta et Monumenta Orientis Antiqui: Studies in Near Eastern Archaeology and Civilisation 22. Atlanta: SBL, 2011.

Porten, Bezalel, and Ada Yardeni, eds. *Textbook of Aramaic Documents from Ancient Egypt*. 4 vols. Winona Lake, IN: Eisenbrauns, 1989–1993.

Pratico, Gary D. *Nelson Glueck's 1938–1940 Excavations at Tell el-Kheleifeh: A Reappraisal.* American Schools of Oriental Research Archaeological Reports 3. Atlanta: Scholars Press, 1993.

Pritchard, James B., ed. *Ancient Near Eastern Texts Relating to the Old Testament.* 3rd ed. Princeton: Princeton University Press, 1969.

Pulak, Cemal. "The Uluburun Shipwreck: An Overview." *The International Journal of Nautical Archaeology* 27 (1988): 188–224.

Quack, Joachim Friedrich. "Zum Datum der persischen Eroberung Ägyptens unter Kambyses." *Journal of Egyptian History* 4 (2011): 226–46.

Rainey, Anson F. "The World of Sinuhe." *Israel Oriental Studies* 2 (1972): 369–408.

Rainey, Anson F., William Schniedewind, and Zipora Cochavi-Rainey, eds. *The El-Amarna Correspondence*. Handbuch der Orientalistik I/110. Leiden: Brill, 2015.

Redford, Donald B. *Egypt, Canaan, and Israel in Ancient Times*. Princeton: Princeton University Press, 1992.

———. *The Medinet Habu Records of the Foreign Wars of Ramesses III*. CHANE 91. Leiden: Brill, 2018.

———. "The So-Called 'Codification' of Egyptian Law Under Darius I." Pages 135–59 in *Persia and Torah: The Theory of Imperial Authorization of the Pentateuch*. Edited by James W. Watts. SBL Symposium Series 17. Atlanta: SBL, 2001

Reekmans, Tony. "The Behaviour of Consumers in the Zenon Papyri." *Ancient Society* 25 (1994): 119–40.

Regev, Eyal. *The Hasmoneans: Ideology, Archaeology, Identity*. Journal of Ancient Judaism Supplements 10. Göttingen: Vandenhoeck & Ruprecht, 2013.

Reich, Ronny. "A Note on the Population Size of Jerusalem in the Second Temple Period." *RB* 121 (2014): 298–305.

Reich, Ronny, and Eli Shukron. "The Date of the Siloam Tunnel Resonsidered." *TA* 38 (2011): 147–57.

Reich, Ronny, Eli Shukron, and Noa Landau. "Recent Discoveries in the City of David, Jerusalem." *IEJ* 57 (2007): 153–69.

Ritner, Robert K. *The Libyan Anarchy: Inscriptions from Egypt's Third Intermediate Period*. Edited by Edward Wente. Writings from the Ancient World 21. Atlanta: SBL, 2009.

Robinson, Damian, and Andrew Wilson. *Alexandria and the North-Western Delta.* Oxford Centre of Maritime Archaeology 5. Oxford: School of Archaeology, University of Oxford, 2010.

Robker, Jonathan. *The Jehu Revolution: A Royal Tradition from the Northern Kingdom and Its Ramifications.* BZAW 435. Berlin: de Gruyter, 2012.

Rohrmoser, Angelika. *Götter, Tempel und Kult der Judäo-Aramäer von Elephantine: Archäologische und schriftliche Zeugnisse aus dem perserzeitlichen Ägypten.* AOAT 396. Münster: Ugarit-Verlag, 2014.

Römer, Thomas. *The So-Called Deuteronomistic History.* London: T & T Clark, 2005.

———. "How Jeroboam II became Jeroboam I." *HeBAI* 6 (2017): 372–82.

Rooke, Deborah W. *Zadok's Heir: The Role and Development of the High Priesthood in Ancient Israel.* Oxford Theological Monographs. Oxford: Oxford University Press, 2000.

Rosen, Steven A., and Gunnar Lehmann. "Hat das biblische Israel einen nomadischen Ursprung? Kritische Beobachtungen aus der Perspektive der Archäologie und Kulturanthropologie." *WO* 40 (2010): 160–83.

Routledge, Bruce. *Moab in the Iron Age: Hegemony, Polity, Archaeology.* Philadelphia: University of Pennsylvania Press, 2004.

Rüsen, Jörn. *Zeit und Sinn: Strategien historischen Denkens.* Frankfurt: Fischer Taschenbuch Verlag, 1990.

Ruzicka, Stephen. *Troubles in the West: Egypt and the Persian Empire, 525–332 BC.* Oxford: Oxford University Press, 2012.

Sagona, Claudia. "Phoenician Settlement: How It Unfolded in Malta." Pages 351–72 in *Phéniciens d'Orient et d'Occident: Mélanges Josette Elayi.* Edited by André Lemaire. Paris: J. Maisonneuve, 2014.

———. "The Phoenicians in Spain from a Central Mediterranean Perspective." *Ancient Near Eastern Studies* 41 (2004): 240–66.

Sapir-Hen, Lidar, Guy Bar-Oz, Yuval Gadot, and Israel Finkelstein. "Pig Husbandry in Iron Age Israel and Judah." *ZDPV* 129 (2013): 1–20.

Schäfer, Peter. *History of the Jews in Antiquity: The Jews of Palestine from Alexander the Great to the Arab Conquest.* Luxembourg: Harwood, 1995.

Schaper, Joachim. "The Pharisees." Pages 402–27 in vol. 3 of Horbury et al., *Cambridge History of Judaism.*

Schipper, Bernd U. "Egypt and the Kingdom of Judah Under Josiah and Jehoiakim." *TA* 37 (2010): 200–26.

———. "Egyptian Imperialism After the New Kingdom: The 26th Dynasty and the Southern Levant." Pages 268–90 in *Egypt, Canaan and Israel: History, Imperialism, Ideology and Literature.* Edited by Shay Bar, Dan'el Kahn, and J. J. Shirley. CHANE 52. Leiden: Brill, 2011.

———. "Die 'eherne Schlange': Zur Religionsgeschichte und Theologie von Num 21,4–9." *ZAW* 121 (2009): 369–87.

———. *Die Erzählung des Wenamun: Ein Literaturwerk im Spannungsfeld von Politik, Geschichte und Religion.* OBO 206. Fribourg: Academic Press; Göttingen: Vandenhoeck & Ruprecht, 2005.

———. *Israel and Egypt During the Monarchic Period: Cultural Contacts from the 10th to the 6th Century BCE.* Translated by Stephen Germany. Ancient Near East Monographs. Atlanta: SBL, 2020.

———. "Raamses, Pithom, and the Exodus: A Critical Evaluation of Ex 1:11." *VT* 65 (2015): 265–88.

———. "Tradition und Innovation: Eine religions- und traditionsgeschichtliche Lektüre von Daniel 7." Pages 45–75 in *Apokalyptik in Antike und Aufklärung*. Edited by Jürgen Brokoff and Bernd U. Schipper. Studien zu Judentum und Christentum. Paderborn: Schöningh, 2004.

———. "Wer war 'So,' König von Ägypten' (2 Kön 17,4)?" *Biblische Notizen* 92 (1998): 71–84.

Schmid, Konrad. "Genesis and the Exodus as Two Formerly Independent Traditions of Origins for Ancient Israel." *Biblica* 93 (2012): 187–208.

———. *Genesis and the Moses Story*. Translated by James D. Nogalski. Siphrut 3. Winona Lake, IN: Eisenbrauns, 2010.

———. *The Old Testament. A Literary History*. Translated by Linda M. Maloney. Minneapolis: Fortress, 2012.

Schoors, Antoon. *The Kingdoms of Israel and Judah in the Eighth and Seventh Century*. Translated by Michael Lesley. Biblical Encyclopedia 5. Atlanta: SBL, 2013.

Schroer, Silvia, and Stefan Münger, eds. *Khirbet Qeiyafa in the Shephelah*. OBO 282. Fribourg: Academic Press; Göttingen: Vandenhoeck & Ruprecht, 2017.

Schütze, Alexander. "Local Administration in Persian Period Egypt According to Aramaic and Demotic Sources." Pages 489–515 in *Administration in Achaemenid Empire*. Edited by Bruno Jacobs, Wouter F. M. Henkelman, and Manfred W. Stolper. Classica et Orientalia 17. Wiesbaden: Harrassowitz, 2017.

Seeman, Chris. *Rome and Judea in Transition*. New York: Lang, 2013.

Segal, Michael. "Identifying Biblical Interpretation in Parabiblical Texts." Pages 295–308 in *The Dead Sea Scrolls in Context: Integrating the Dead Sea Scrolls in the Study of Ancient Texts, Languages, and Cultures*. Vol 1. Edited by Armin Lange, Emmanuel Tov, and Mathias Weigold. Leiden: Brill, 2011.

Sergi, Omer. "The Emergence of Judah as Political Entity Between Jerusalem and Benjamin." *ZDPV* 133 (2017): 1–23.

———. "Judah's Expansion in Historical Context." *TA* 40 (2013): 226–46.

———. "Rethinking Israel and the Kingdom of Saul." Pages 371–88 in Lipschits et al., *Rethinking Israel*.

Sergi, Omer, and Yuval Gadot. "Omride Palatial Architecture in as Symbol in Action: Between State Formation, Obliteration, and Heritage." *Journal of Near Eastern Studies* 76 (2017): 103–111.

Sergi, Omer, and Assaf Kleiman. "The Kingdom of Geshur and the Expansion of Aram-Damascus into the Northern Jordan Valley: Archaeological and Historical Perspectives." *BASOR* 379 (2018): 1–18.

Sergi, Omer, Manfred Oeming, and Izaak J. de Hulster, eds. *In Search for Aram and Israel*. Orientalische Religionen in der Antike 20. Tübingen: Mohr Siebeck, 2016.

Shea, William H. "Adad-Nirari III and Jehoash of Israel." *Journal of Cuneiform Studies* 30 (1978): 101–13.

Siddal, Luis Robert. *The Reign of Adad-Nīrārī III: An Historical and Ideological Analysis of an Assyrian King and His Times*. Cuneiform Monographs 45. Leiden: Brill, 2013.

———. "Tiglath-pileser III's Aid to Ahaz: A New Look at the Problems of the Biblical Accounts in Light of the Assyrian Sources." *Ancient Near Eastern Studies* 46 (2009): 93–116.

Sievers, Joseph. *The Hasmoneans and Their Supporters. From Mattathias to the Death of John Hyrcanus I.* South Florida Studies in the History of Judaism 6. Atlanta: Scholars, 1990.

Siljanen, Esko. *Judeans of Egypt in the Persian Period (539–332 BCE) in Light of the Aramaic Documents*. Helsinki: University of Helsinki, Department of Biblical Studies, 2017.

Spalinger, Anthony. "Psammetichus, King of Egypt." *Journal of the American Research Center in Egypt* 13 (1976): 133–47.

Steindorff, Georg. "The Statuette of an Egyptian Commissioner in Syria." *Journal of Egyptian Archaeology* 25 (1939): 30–33.

Stemberger, Günter. "The Sadducees—Their History and Doctrines." Pages 428–43 in vol. 3 of Horbury et al., *Cambridge History of Judaism*.

Stern, Ephraim. *Archaeology of the Land of the Bible 2: The Assyrian, Babylonian and Persian Periods 732–332 B.C.E.* Anchor Yale Bible Reference Library. New Haven: Yale University Press, 2014.

Stökl Ben Ezra, Daniel. *Qumran: Die Texte vom Toten Meer und das Antike Judentum*. Jüdische Studien 3. Tübingen: Mohr Siebeck, 2016.

Suter, Claudia. "Images, Tradition and Meaning: The Samaria and Other Levantine Ivories of the Iron Age." Pages 219–41 in *A Common Cultural Heritage: Studies on Mesopotamia and the Biblical World in Honor of Barry L. Eichler*. Edited by Grant Frame. Bethesda, MD: CDL Press, 2011.

Tadmor, Hayim. *The Inscriptions of Tiglath-pileser III, King of Assyria*. Jerusalem: Israel Academy of Sciences and Humanities, 1994.

Takahashi, Yuko. "Reconsiderung Meẓad Ḥashavyahu." *Annual of the Japanese Biblical Institute* 39 (2013): 5–19.

Tal, Oren. "Hellenism in Transition from Empire to Kingdom: Changes in the Material Culture of Hellenistic Palestine." Pages 55–73 in *Jewish Identities in Anqiquity*. Edited by Lee I. Levine and Daniel R. Schwartz. TSAJ 130. Tübingen: Mohr Siebeck, 2009.

Tebes, Juan M., ed. *Unearthing the Wilderness: Studies on the History and Archaeology of the Nevev and Edom in the Iron Age*. Ancient Near Eastern Studies Supplement Series 45. Leuven: Peeters, 2014.

Tetley, M. Christine. "The Date of Samaria's Fall as a Reason for Rejecting the Hypothesis of Two Conquests." *Catholic Biblical Quarterly* 42 (2002): 59–77.

Thareani, Yifat. "Enemy at the Gates? Archaeological Visibility of the Arameans at Dan." Pages 169–97 in Sergi et al., *In Search for Aram and Israel*.

Thompson, Dorothey J. "The Infrastructure of Splendour: Census and Taxes in Ptolemaic Egypt." Pages 242–57 in *Hellenistic Constructs: Essays in Culture, History, and Historiography*. Edited by Paul Cartledge, Peter Garnsey, and Erich Gruen. Berkeley: University of California Press, 1997.

Török, Laszlo. *The Kingdom of Kush: Handbook of the Napatan-Meriotici Civilization*. Handbuch der Orientalistik 1/31. Leiden: Brill, 1997.

Torrey, Charles C. *The Composition and Historical Value of Ezra-Nehemiah*. BZAW 2. Gießen: Ricker'sche Verlagsbuchhandlung, 1896.

Uehlinger, Christoph. "Der Amun-Tempel Ramses' III. in pȝ-Knʿn, seine südpalästinischen Tempelgüter und der Übergang der Ägypter- zur Philisterherrschaft: Ein Hinweis auf einige wenig beachtete Skarabäen (1988)." Pages 3–26 in *Studien zu den Stempelsiegeln aus Palästina/Israel III*. Edited by Othmar Keel, Hildi Keel-Leu, and Sivlia Schroer. OBO 100. Fribourg: Universitätsverlag; Göttingen: Vandenhoeck & Ruprecht, 1990.

———. "Clio in a World of Pictures: Another Look at the Lachish Reliefs from Sennacherib's Southwest Palace at Ninive." Pages 221–305 in Grabbe, *"Like a Bird in a Cage."*

———. "Was There a Cult Reform Under King Josiah?" Pages 297–316 in Grabbe, *Good Kings and Bad Kings*.

Ussishkin, David. "Sennacherib's Campaign in Judah: The Conquest of Lachish." *Journal of Semitics* 24 (2015): 719–58.

———. "Sennacherib's Campaign to Judah: The Archaeological Perspective with an Emphasis on Lachish and Jerusalem." Pages 75–103 in *Sennacherib at the Gates of Jerusalem: Story, History, Geography*. Edited by Isaac Kalimi and Seth Richardson. CHANE 71. Leiden: Brill, 2014.

———. "Was Jerusalem a Fortified Stronghold in the Middle Bronze Age? An Alternative View." *Levant* 48 (2016): 135–51.

Uziel, Joe, and Nahshon Szanton. "New Evidence of Jerusalem's Urban Development in the 9th Century BCE." Pages 429–39 in Lipschits et al., *Rethinking Israel*.

Vanderhooft, David S. *The Neo-Babylonian Empire and Babylon in the Latter Prophets*. Harvard Semitic Museum Monographs 59. Atlanta: Scholars Press, 1999.

VanderKam, James C. *From Joshua to Caiaphas: High Priests After the Exile*. Minneapolis: Fortress, 2004.

Van der Toorn, Karel. "Anat-Yahu, Some Other Deities, and the Jews of Elephantine." *Numen* 39 (1992): 80–101.

———. "Ethnicity at Elephantine: Jews, Arameans, Caspians." *TA* 43 (2016): 147–64.

Vittmann, Günter. "Arameans in Egypt." Pages 229–79 in Berlejung et al., *Wandering Arameans*.

Weingart, Kristin. *Stämmevolk—Staatsvolk—Gottesvolk? Studien zur Verwendung des Israel-Namens im Alten Testament*. FAT II/68. Tübingen: Mohr Siebeck, 2014.

Weippert, Manfred. *Historisches Textbuch zum Alten Testament*. Grundrisse zum Alten Testament 10. Göttingen: Vandenhoeck & Ruprecht, 2010.

Wenning, Robert. "Griechischer Einfluss in Palästina in vorhellenistischer Zeit?" Pages 29–60 in *Die Griechen und das antike Israel*. Edited by Stefan Alkier and Markus Witte. OBO 201. Fribourg: Academic Press; Göttingen: Vandenhoeck & Ruprecht, 2004.

White, Hayden. *Tropics of Discourse*. Baltimore: Johns Hopkins University Press, 1985.

Worthington, Ian. *Ptolemy I: King and Pharaoh of Egypt*. Oxford: Oxford University Press, 2016.

Wunsch, Cornelia. "Glimpses on the Lives of Deportees in Rural Babylonia." Pages 247–60 in Berlejung and Streck, *Arameans, Chaldeans, and Arabs*.

Wyssman, Patrick. "The Coinage Imagery of Samaria and Judah in the Late Persian Period." Pages 221–66 in Frevel et al., *"Religious Revolution" in Yehûd?*

Xeravits, Géza G., and Peter Porzig. *Einführung in die Qumran-Literatur*. Berlin: de Gruyter, 2015.

Yasur-Landau, Assaf. *The Philistines and Aegean Migration at the End of the Late Bronze Age*. Cambridge: Cambridge University Press, 2010.

Yoffe, Norman. *Myths of the Archaic State*. Cambridge: Cambridge University Press, 2007.

Younger, Lawson K., Jr. *A Political History of the Arameans: From their Origins to the End of their Polities*. Archaeology and Biblical Studies 13. Atlanta: SBL, 2016.

———. "Shalmaneser III and Israel." Pages 225–56 in *Israel: Ancient Kingdom or Late Invention?* Edited by Daniel I. Block. Nashville: Broadman & Holman, 2008.

Young, Robb A. *Hezekiah in History and Tradition*. VTSup 155. Leiden: Brill, 2012.

Yurco, Frank J. "Merenptah's Canaanite Campaign and Israel's Origin." Pages 27–55 in *Exodus: The Egyptian Evidence.* Edited by Ernest S. Frerichs and Leonard H. Lesko. Winona Lake, IN: Eisenbrauns, 1997.

Zadok, Ran. *The Earliest Diaspora: Israelites and Judeans in Pre-Hellenistic Mesopotamia.* Publications of the Diaspora Research Institute 151. Tel Aviv: Diaspora Research Institute, Tel Aviv University, 2002.

Zangani, Frederico. "Amarna and Uluburun: Reconsidering Patterns of Exchange in the Late Bronze Age." *PEQ* 148 (2016): 230–44.

Zangenberg, Jürgen. "Fragile Vielfalt: Beobachtungen zur Sozialgeschichte Alexandrias in hellenistisch-römischer Zeit." Pages 91–107 in *Alexandria.* Edited by Tobias Georges, Felix Albrecht, and Reinhard Feldmeier. Civitatum Orbis Mediterranei Studia 1. Tübingen: Mohr Siebeck, 2013.

Zertal, Adam. "The Pahwah of Samaria (Northern Israel) During the Persian Period: Types of Settlement, Economy, History and New Discoveries." *Transeu* 3 (1990): 9–30.

Zorn, Jeffrey R. "Tell en-Naṣbeh and the Problem of the Material Culture of the Sixth Century." Pages 413–47 in Lipschits and Blenkinsopp, *Judah and the Judeans in the Neo-Babylonian Period.*

Zwingenberger, Ute. *Dorfkultur der frühen Eisenzeit in Mittelpalästina.* OBO 180. Fribourg: Universitätsverlag; Göttingen: Vandenhoeck & Ruprecht, 2001.

INDEX OF AUTHORS

INDEX OF PLACE AND PERSONAL NAMES

INDEX OF SCRIPTURE

INDEX OF OTHER ANCIENT SOURCES

CPSIA information can be obtained
at www.ICGtesting.com
Printed in the USA
FSHW011006261219
65466FS